Practical Interventions for Young People at Risk

Edited by
Kathryn Geldard

SAGE

Los Angeles | London | New Delhi
Singapore | Washington DC

First published 2009

Reprinted 2010

SAGE Publications Ltd
1 Oliver's Yard
55 City Road
London EC1Y 1SP

SAGE Publications Inc.
2455 Teller Road
Thousand Oaks, California 91320

SAGE Publications India Pvt Ltd
B 1/I 1 Mohan Cooperative Industrial Area
Mathura Road
New Delhi 110 044

SAGE Publications Asia-Pacific Pte Ltd
33 Pekin Street #02-01
Far East Square
Singapore 048763

Library of Congress Control Number: 2009925552

British Library Cataloguing in Publication data

A catalogue record for this book is available from the British Library.

ISBN 978-1-84787-561-7
ISBN 978-1-84787-562-4 (pbk)

Typeset by C&M Digitals (P) Ltd, Chennai, India
Printed and bound in Great Britain by
TJ International Ltd, Padstow, Cornwall
Printed on paper from sustainable resources.

Mixed Sources
Product group from well-managed
forests and other controlled sources
www.fsc.org Cert no. TT-COC-2082
© 1996 Forest Stewardship Council
FSC

Practical Interventions
for Young People at Risk

This book is dedicated to my two sons Matthew and Tomos Newkirk, from whom I learned about uniqueness and difference and the notion that one solution doesn't fit all.

Contents

About the Contributors

SusanW. Blaakman, MS, RN, NPP, is Assistant Professor of Clinical Nursing at the University of Rochester School of Nursing, teaching in the Child/Adolescent and Adult/Family Psychiatric–Mental Health Nurse Practitioner programmes. She has been a consultant to Fireproof Children Inc. since 2004 and has trained diverse groups across the United States to address the multifaceted problem of juvenile fire-setting.
Contact details: University of Rochester School of Nursing, Box SON, 601 Elmwood Avenue, Rochester, NY 14610, USA. *E-mail*: Susan_Blaakman@ URMC.Rochester.edu

Alan Carr, PhD, is Professor and Director of Clinical Psychology at University College Dublin, Ireland. He also has a clinical practice at the Clanwilliam Institute, Dublin, where he works with young people and families facing a wide range of challenges. He has been involved in clinical psychology for 30 years in Ireland, Canada and the UK and produced over 20 volumes and 200 academic papers and presentations.
Contact details: Professor Alan Carr, School of Psychology, University College Dublin, Belfield, Dublin 4, Ireland. *E-mail*: alan.carr@ucd.ie

Rocío Chang, PsyD, received her doctorate in clinical psychology from the University of Hartford. She is a research associate in the Department of Psychiatry at the University of Connecticut School of Medicine. Dr Chang has been working in school settings with adolescent girls who have experienced multiple traumatic events. Dr Chang is a certified Wellness Recovery Action Plan (WRAP) Facilitator and has participated in peer support trainings.
Contact details: Department of Psychiatry, University of Connecticut Health Center, Farmington, CT06030, USA. *E-mail*: chang@psychiatry. uchc.edu

Robert E. Cole, PhD, is Associate Professor of Clinical Nursing at the University of Rochester and also President of Fireproof Children/Prevention First, a fire safety education and training company. Dr Cole's research interest has focused on juvenile fire-setting, fire play and unintentional injuries to young children. He works extensively with fire departments and early childhood professionals to promote a better understanding of children's interest in fire and the adoption of systematic fire prevention education.
Contact details: University of Rochester School of Nursing, Box SON, 601 Elmwood Avenue, Rochester, NY 14610, USA. *E-mail*: Robert_Cole@ URMC.Rochester.edu

Jan Foster, PhD, is Head of the Social Work Unit at the University of the Sunshine Coast in Australia. She has been involved in direct practice and policy development for young people at risk, the development of locally based services for children and community-based family support programmes. Her current research centres on developing frameworks for collaborative models of care for young people with complex needs and analysis of protective behaviour programmes.
Contact details: Senior Lecturer and Program Leader, Social Work Coordinator, Learning and Teaching Faculty of Arts and Social Sciences, University of the Sunshine Coast, Maroochydore DC Qld 4558, Australia. *E-mail*: jfoster @usc.edu.au

David Geldard is a psychologist who has specialized in working with young people in mental health, community health and private practice settings. He is the co-author of a number of internationally published textbooks on counselling.
Contact details: *E-mail*: david@geldard.com.au

Kathryn Geldard, PhD, is senior lecturer in counselling in the Faculty of Arts and Social Sciences at the University of the Sunshine Coast, Australia. Her research interests include adolescent peer counselling and counselling effectiveness as perceived by the client and counsellor training and assessment. Kathryn has conducted research with Australian Aboriginal adolescents with regard to developing a culturally sensitive peer support programme in a regional community. She is the author of a number of textbooks on counselling and has several years' experience in supervising and training counsellors.
Contact details: School of Social Sciences, University of the Sunshine Coast, Maroochydore DC Qld. 4558, Australia. *E-mail*: kgeldard@usc.edu.au

Scott W. Henggeler, PhD, is Professor of Psychiatry and Behavioral Sciences at the Medical University of South Carolina and Director of the Family Services Research Center (FSRC). FSRC projects have included numerous community-based randomized trials with challenging clinical populations (violent and chronic juvenile offenders, youths presenting psychiatric emergencies, substance-abusing juvenile offenders and maltreating families, for example) and dissemination studies for multisystemic therapy and other evidence-based treatments are being conducted in multiple states and nations.
Contact details: MUSC/Family Services Research Center, Department of Psychiatry and Behavioral Sciences, 67 President Street, Suite MC406 MSC 861, Charleston, SC 29425, USA. *E-mail*: henggesw@musc.edu

Simon Hallsworth, PhD, is a professor at the London Metropolitan University, London, England. He is Director of the CSER and holds the Chair in Social Research in the Department of Applied Social Science. He is a sociologist by background, educated at the London School for Economics and Leicester University. He has advised many statutory and governmental bodies on issues relating to violent crime. Simon has written extensively on punishment in modern society, the local politics of crime and community safety and, more recently, violent street worlds. His research interests include street violence, weapon use and the development of the security state.

Contact details: *E-mail*: s.hallsworth@londonmet.ac.uk

Rebecca Hoge is a researcher at the School of Psychology and Counselling, Queensland University of Technology, Australia. She has a special interest in the promotion of resilience and has been involved with the Resourceful Adolescent Programme since its development in 1997. Rebecca is currently working on the Resourceful Adolescent Programme for Teachers (RAP-T) Project, which aims to assist teachers in promoting school connectedness in their students.

Contact details: School of Psychology and Counselling, Queensland University of Technology, Victoria Road, Kelvin Grove, Brisbane, Australia. *E-mail*: r.hoge@qut.edu.au

Renee Rienecke Hoste, PhD, is an Instructor of Psychiatry at the University of Chicago's Eating Disorders Programme. After earning her Bachelor's degree at the University of Michigan, Dr Hoste received her PhD from Northwestern University and completed her clinical psychology internship at the University of Chicago. Her research interests include the impact of the family on treatment outcome for adolescent eating disorders, the role of expressed emotion in treatment outcome and cross-cultural differences in expressed emotion.

Contact details: Eating Disorders Program, University of Chicago, 5841 South Maryland Avenue, MC 3077, Chicago, IL 60637, USA. *E-mail*: rhoste@yoda. bsd.uchicago.edu

Richard Ives is Director of *educari*, which is an independent consultancy concerned with children and young people, drugs, education and health. The work of educari includes research, evaluation and policy analysis, consultancy and training, publications, website design and development and international work. Educari offers expertise in the area of drug policy analysis and policy development. The company has experience of working with education departments to develop drug policies for schools and other educational establishments (such as youth projects).

Contact details: Director educari, Manor Farm, Kettlestone, Norfolk NR21 OAU, UK. *E-mail*: richard@educari.com

Carolyn E. Kourofsky, President of Excelsior Editorial Consulting, has fifteen years' experience of writing in the areas of health, education and safety. Her articles have appeared in *Young Children, Children and Families, Firehouse, Fire Chief* and others. She is a co-author of *Juvenile Firesetting: A community guide to prevention and intervention* (Fireproof Children/Prevention First, 2006), and the author of *Mikey Makes a Mess* (Fireproof Children/Prevention First, 2004), a children's storybook incorporating fire safety education.

Contact details: Excelsior Editorial Consulting, Fireproof Children/Prevention First, 1 Grove Street, Suite 235, Pittsford, NY 14534, USA. *E-mail*: carolynkourofsky @fireproofchildren.com

Ian Lambie, PhD, is a senior lecturer in clinical psychology at the University of Auckland, New Zealand. His specialist clinical and research interests are youth forensic psychology, severe conduct disorder, adolescent sexual offending and arson. He is on the board of Youth Horizons Trust – a treatment programme for youths with severe conduct disorder. He is a member of the Ministry of Justice Independent Advisory Group on Youth Offending and the Ministry of Social Development Expert Group on the treatment of conduct disorder and is the consultant psychologist for the New Zealand Fire Service National Fire Awareness and Youth Intervention Programme.
Contact details: Psychology Department, University of Auckland Private Bag 92019, Auckland, New Zealand. *E-mail*: i.lambie@auckland.ac.nz

Daniel Le Grange, PhD, is Associate Professor and Director of the Eating Disorders Programme at the Department of Psychiatry, University of Chicago. His research concerns treatment outcomes and has, in particular, focused on family-based interventions for adolescents with eating disorders.
Contact details: Eating Disorders Program, University of Chicago, 5841 South Maryland Avenue, MC3077, Chicago, IL 60637, USA. *E-mail*: legrange @uchicago.edu

Brad Levingston is a psychologist who has worked in community and hospital-based services for the past thirty years, developing alcohol and drug programmes and clinical services with a special emphasis on the needs of young people. He has a Master's Degree in clinical psychology and was made a Fellow of the Australian Psychological Society in recognition of his work in the field of substance use and dependence. He currently manages clinical psychological services provided for general medical practitioners on the Sunshine Coast in Queensland, Australia.
Contact details: 2 Jarrah Road, Buderim, Qld 4556, Australia. *E-mail*: brakerry @optusnet.com.au

Jenny Melrose is a psychologist and member of the Australian Psychological Society who has worked with clients with alcohol and other drug and mental health issues since the early 1990s. She has worked clinically in both government and non-government sectors in Australia and the UK. She has also worked in Indonesia, providing drug and HIV information to a variety of health and community workers. Along with her clinical work, Jenny runs JEMECO Psychology, providing clinical supervision and training to people and organizations in Australia.
Contact details: PO Box 6237, Mooloolah Valley, Qld 4553, Australia. *E-mail*: jennymelrose@bigpond.com

Susan M. Moore, PhD, is Professor of Psychology at Swinburne University in Melbourne, Australia. Her research areas include adolescent development, sexuality and romance, risk-taking (including gambling) and health, particularly how individuals cope with chronic illness. She has published widely in these areas, with over 100 refereed journal articles, four books and several book chapters. Professor Moore's most recent book is *Sexuality in Adolescence: Current trends* (with D. Rosenthal, Taylor & Francis, 2006).

Contact details: 8 Alford Street, East Brighton, Victoria 3187, Australia. *E-mail*: smoore@swin.edu.au

Wendy Patton, PhD, is Executive Dean, Faculty of Education, at Queensland University of Technology, Brisbane, Australia. She is Series Editor of the Career Development Series with Sense Publishers. She has published extensively in the area of career development, including articles, book chapters, conference papers, one co-authored book (currently in its second edition) and seven co-edited books. She serves on the editorial boards of a number of journals.
Contact details: Faculty of Education, Queensland University of Technology, Victoria Park Road, Kelvin Grove, Qld 4059, Australia. *E-mail*: w.patton @qut.edu.au

Carole Rayburn is a clinical, research and consulting psychologist in Silver Spring, Maryland. Carole has worked in a comprehensive juvenile delinquency setting with adolescents and their families. She is a Fellow of 13 divisions in the American Psychological Association, including Clinical, Educational, Child, Youth, and Family Services, Psychotherapy, Media, International and Psychology of Women and of Religion.
Contact details: Loyola College, 2034 Greenspring Drive, Timonium, MD 21093, USA. *E-mail*: valentinecarole@copper.net

Lee J. Richmond, PhD, is Professor of Education at the Department of Education Specialties of Loyola College in Maryland where she teaches in both the school counselling and pastoral counselling programmes. A licensed psychologist, Dr Richmond serves on the Board of Educational Affairs of the Maryland Psychological Association and is a past president of the American Counseling Association and the National Career Development Association. Her publications are numerous – three of the most recent deal with young people who are, or have been, involved with cults.
Contact details: 8907 Greylock Road, Baltimore, MD 21208, USA. *E-mail*: leejri@aol.com

Cindy M. Schaeffer, PhD, received her doctorate in child–clinical psychology from the University of Missouri, Columbia, and completed a post-doctoral fellowship in Prevention Science at the Johns Hopkins Bloomberg School of Public Health. Dr Schaeffer is now an Associate Professor at the Department of Psychiatry and Behavioral Sciences, Medical University of South Carolina, and is a member of the Family Services Research Center faculty. Her work involves understanding the development of antisocial behavior across childhood and adolescence and developing ecologically based interventions for antisocial youths and their families.
Contact details: Family Services Research Center, Department of Psychiatry and Behavioral Sciences, Medical University of South Carolina, 67 President Street Suite CPP, PO Box 250861, Charleston, SC 29425, USA. *E-mail*: schaeffc@musc.edu

Jude Sellen is a CAMHS consultant and trainer for Young Minds, helping young people who self-harm.
Contact details: 2 Clarence Terrace, Henfield, West Sussex BN5 9EJ, UK. *E-mail*: jude_sellen@btinternet.com

Daryl L. Sharp, PhD, APRN, BC, FNAP, is Associate Professor of Clinical Nursing and Director of the Doctor of Nursing Practice Programme at the University of Rochester School of Nursing. Her clinical and research interests are focused on health behaviour change, especially for those with psychiatric illnesses. She is a consultant to Fireproof Children, Inc., where she collaborates in training multidisciplinary groups on fire-prevention and health-promotion strategies among youths and their families.
Contact details: Nursing Practice Program, University of Rochester School of Nursing, Box SON, 601 Elmwood Avenue, Rochester, NY 14610, USA. *E-mail*: daryl_sharp@urmc.rochester.edu

Ian Shochet, PhD, is Professor and Head of the School of Psychology and Counselling at the Queensland University of Technology in Brisbane, Australia. He developed the Resourceful Adolescent Programme, which has been trialled in 14 countries and found to be effective in building resourcefulness in young people.
Contact details: Faculty of Health, School of Psychology and Counselling, Queensland University of Technology, Victoria Park Road, Kelvin Grove, Qld 4059, Australia. *E-mail*: i.shochet@qut.edu.au

Peter K. Smith, PhD, is Professor of Psychology and Head of the Unit for School and Family Studies at Goldsmiths, University of London, and is a Fellow of the British Psychological Society. He is co-author and co-editor of several textbooks related to children, bullying, violence in schools and childhood social development. He chaired the Research and Advisory Group of the Anti-Bullying Alliance from 2006 until 2008. He is currently (2007–2009) a partner in a DAPHNE project, 'An investigation into forms of peer–peer bullying at school in pre-adolescent and adolescent groups: new instruments and preventing strategies'.
Contact details: Room 215, Whitehead Building, Psychology Department, Goldsmiths College, University of London New Cross, London SE14 6NW. *E-mail*: pss01pks@gold.ac.uk

Fran Thompson graduated from Goldsmiths in 2006 and is a researcher with Professor Peter Smith at the Unit for School and Family Studies. Publications include a Web-based resource for the Anti-bullying Alliance, *Tackling Bullying in Schools* (2008), and she co-authored an article on the use of the Support Group Method (2007). At present, she is principal UK researcher on both a DAPHNE project on cyberbullying (2007–2009) and a two-year project assessing the effectiveness of anti-bullying intervention strategies in English schools for the Department of Children, Schools and Families (2008–2010).
Contact details: 97 Leahurst Road, London SE13 5HY, UK. *E-mail*: ps201at@gold.ac.uk

Neil Tippett is a researcher at the Unit for School and Family Studies, Goldsmiths College, London. His research interests include school bullying and child aggression and he is currently investigating the nature and prevalence of cyberbullying within the UK, on which he has published two articles and given several conference presentations. He is also involved with the Anti-Bullying Alliance, for which he regularly writes literature reviews and briefing papers on subjects related to bullying.

Contact details: 5 Cotsland Road, Truro, Cornwall TR1 1YR, UK. *E-mail*: pss01nt@gold.ac.uk

Astrid Wurfl is a senior researcher at the School of Psychology and Counselling at the Queensland University of Technology. For the past ten years, Astrid has been involved in the development, research and evaluation of intervention programmes to build resilience across the lifespan. These include intervention programmes at the intrapsychic, familial and broader contextual levels.

Contact details: Faculty of Health, School of Psychology and Counselling, Queensland University of Technology, Victoria Park Road, Kelvin Grove, Qld 4059, Australia. *E-mail*: a.wurfl@qut.edu.au

Tara Young graduated from the University of Bristol with a First Class degree in sociology and completed a Master's degree in criminology at the London School of Economics and Political Science (LSE). She joined the Centre for Social and Evaluation Research as a research fellow in January 2004 after three years with the Mannheim Centre for Criminology and Criminal Justice Policy at the LSE. She is currently working on several national and international projects focusing on understanding the extent and nature of gang membership in the UK and a pan-European gang intervention project.

Contact details: *E-mail*: t.young@londonmet.ac.uk

Part I

Introduction

Engaging Young People Collaboratively

Kathryn Geldard

Because you are reading this book, I thought you might be interested to know what motivated me to invite a group of international authors to join with me in putting it together.

For many years, I have worked as a counsellor in both mental health systems and private practice. In these environments I have tended to specialize in working with young people and their families.

My work with young people has convinced me that they are not an homogeneous group. Each young person is an individual with their own attitudes, beliefs, constructs, behaviours and unique responses to the challenges presented to them. I have discovered that the strategies and interventions I use with a particular young person during counselling have to be not only relevant to that young person's situation and issues but also appealing to them so that they will be engaged in the therapeutic process. It is clear to me that what suits one young person may not suit another. Consequently, I developed a way of working collaboratively and proactively with each young person, valuing them as individuals and inviting them to be actively involved in the selection of counselling strategies and interventions that are of interest and use to them.

In my work, I began to recognize that there are a number of commonly identifiable challenges faced by young people. For example, one young person might be troubled by sexual issues, another might find it difficult to control a tendency to light fires, while another might be struggling with issues related to membership of a cult group. These challenges, combined with a notion affecting Western society that misbehaviour, even crime, among young people could grow to such an extent as to threaten the social fabric of society (Gregory, 2006), have led many people in our communities to become fearful, to some extent, of young people who do not have conventional lifestyles – those who do not live in a traditional family structure, are not employed or are not enrolled in a course of study, for example. In particular, homeless young people are regarded with discomfort and the lifestyles of delinquent young people tend to generate both fear and concern among members of the general public.

Fortunately, there is now increasing recognition that a young person can be both an 'offender' and a 'victim' and success in enabling them to learn and develop socially adaptive behaviours is most likely to be achieved through empowerment and helping them to take responsibility for the choices they make themselves when facing the challenges associated with the transition to adulthood.

When, as a counsellor, I met with a young person experiencing an issue related to challenges such as these, I would sometimes recognize that I did not have a well-informed background with regard to the nature of the challenges confronting them and might not be aware of the best possible strategies and interventions available. Naturally, in such instances, I would seek out the information that was required. However, I often wished that I had, at my fingertips, a single resource, from which I could access information with regard to the most common challenges confronted by young people, along with the strategies and interventions that have been found to be most useful for addressing these. Consequently, I decided to invite authors with special expertise to join with me in writing this book.

Rather than only looking for specialists in particular fields from my own country – Australia – I thought that it would be more useful to seek out international experts. In this way, solutions and interventions for change would be represented by a diverse group of authors with expertise in their selected fields of interest. By accessing such diversity, I believed that I would be honouring the diversity and uniqueness that exist among the young people in our communities and with whom we work. Consequently, I set about inviting internationally recognized authorities on particular challenges for young people to contribute to the book. I was delighted by the responses I received and the enthusiasm shown by the people I approached, who agreed to participate as authors and share their expertise in their areas of interest. The consequence is that contributors to this book include experts such as Alan Carr from Ireland, Scott Henggeler, Lee Richmond, Robert Cole, Susan Blaakman and Daniel Le Grange from the United States of America, Simon Hallsworth, Richard Ives, Peter Smith and Daryl Sharp from England, Ian Lambie from New Zealand and Ian Shochet, Wendy Patton and Susan Moore from Australia, together with many others with similar international profiles.

As a consequence of the international contributions to this book, my hope and expectation is that it will prove an extremely valuable resource for both practitioners and students with regard to strategies and interventions to help young people at risk.

I think it is important that, before considering specific strategies and interventions, we should have a clear understanding of what is meant by 'young people' and 'at risk'.

What do we mean when we refer to 'Young People'?

When I first planned to write this book, I was thinking in terms of the stage in life where young people experience a transition from childhood to adult life. Many publications on helping young people refer to this group as 'adolescents' – a term that might suggest all young people fit into an homogeneous group with similar patterns of thinking and behaving. This does not fit at all with my own experience of young people, whom I have found to be uniquely individual with regard to their attitudes, beliefs, constructs, reactions and general behaviour. Consequently I, and the other authors in this book, prefer to use the words 'young people' as they are both accurate and respectful when referring to those who may be helped by using the interventions described in this book. At times, however, reference will be made to the term 'adolescent' as it appears in the research and literature.

What do we mean by 'At Risk'?

Can you remember what it was like when you grew up? When I think about my own development, I realize that moving from being a child to being a young person and then an adult involves much more than a linear progression of change. It is multidimensional, involving a gradual transformation or metamorphosis of the person as a child into a new person as an adult. During this process, psychological, physiological, biological and social changes have to be confronted. I remember that, during this stage of life, I began to re-evaluate my identity and was confronted with moral and spiritual challenges, which is typically the case for most young people.

Every day, it is common to read of the demands and stresses increasingly faced by young people. For example, finding employment in competitive conditions, developing relationships with others, demands for self-organization and adaptation to technology all provide challenges and they are likely to be experienced as stressful. Additionally, many young people experience anxiety and stress related to personal safety and security in an age of national and international events that are often alarming and disturbing. It is important for us to recognize, however, that there are individual differences, some young people coping with these challenges more easily than others. Those who are not able to negotiate the challenges they confront successfully experience failure, which may result in emotional and psychological harm.

I will argue that, because of the many difficult challenges that young people are confronted with, often for the first time in their lives, all young people should be thought of as 'high risk individuals'.

It is important to remember that there are many young people who have specific needs or confront specific issues that make their lives particularly difficult to manage. Clearly, challenges that persist despite a young person's attempts to overcome them are likely to compromise their long-term well-being unless specific and informed help is provided.

The positive aspects of risk

When considering the interventions described in this book, I would like to suggest that it can be helpful to remember all young people are vulnerable to risk and risk-taking behaviours, as this is an inevitable part of their developmental stage. Rather than considering the idea that 'risk-taking' is primarily an indiscriminate response to earlier unresolved adversity or power struggles with parents and/or society, however, it might be helpful to redefine these struggles as contributing to a potentially positive growth process whereby challenge and risk are the primary tools young people use to find out who they are and determine who they will become. Understanding the way that young people make meaning of their lives through their own personal experiences is important when engaging with them collaboratively in interventions for solutions. Recognizing how those experiences are influenced by the family, wider society, culture, the environment, socio-economic and political factors, lifestyle and, most importantly, developmental issues is central to the collaborative process of selecting those interventions that will fit for each young person.

The Need for Collaborative Engagement

As discussed previously, in order to be respectful of young people as individuals who are capable of making their own decisions, it is important to work collaboratively with them in any process. Throughout this book, there is an emphasis on using a collaborative process.

In the counselling literature, it is well established that the relationship between the practitioner and client, more than any other factor, contributes to successful outcomes (Lambert, 1992). Consequently, if we are to work effectively with young people, we need to build relationships with them that are based on respect, trust and a non-judgemental stance. Creating such relationships enables us to engage in collaborative conversations and have a participatory and reciprocal dialogue with them. By doing this, we can bring alive practices and ideas from postmodern therapeutic approaches, such as narrative therapy and solution-focused counselling. Any control issues arising in the relationship can then be intentionally invited into the conversation so that the politics of 'roles' is worked out as practitioner and young person take up or resist calls to occupy positions of 'privilege' or 'the subject'.

Acceptance of diversity

Unfortunately, it is common for people in our contemporary society to regard differences from conventional standards as socially undesirable. I believe, however, that we will be more successful in our interventions with young people if we are able to accept such differences in the ways young people adjust to the challenges they confront. We need to recognize that what is considered a success by some may not be an optimal or attainable solution for others. It is important to identify adaptation patterns that are congruent with the experiences of young people in different circumstances and recognize and respect different solutions (Schoon, 2007). Throughout this book, therefore, there is a recognition of the need for an acceptance of diversity in solutions to the challenges facing young people and the importance of providing a diversity of opportunities in the community to build, maintain and sustain resilient and adaptive behaviour. Also, it is important to emphasize that it is essential to consult with young people themselves and work collaboratively with them. Failure to do so will inevitably affect the impact and usefulness of the strategies and interventions under consideration.

Recognition and building on strengths

An emphasis throughout this book is to focus on the young person's strengths rather than those things that are problematic or pathological. Clearly, important processes of change need to occur within a young person if they are to identify their strengths and adaptively confront the challenges that face them with suc-cess so that they can experience positive outcomes. One way to invite young people to begin this process is to understand the stories and narratives of young people. The stories that young people tell describe themselves and their lives. Sometimes these stories are unhelpful and, instead of enabling them to live sat-isfying lives, the stories that they live out cause problems for them. Collaborative conversations can be used to help practitioners understand and value the strug-gles encountered by young people and help them to replace problem stories with other more useful stories. Often young people can begin to understand them-selves and their relationship with the world if practitioners operate under the social constructionist assumption that problems are anchored and supported by dominant cultural discourses or taken-for-granted cultural prescriptions for how we should act and make sense of our world. Thus, engaging young people in col-laborative interventions is about deconstructing their dominant stories and bringing forth and thickening alternative, preferred accounts of how the young person would like to be.

By listening to the life stories of young people, as practitioners, we can begin to understand the ways in which they are confronting and experiencing challenge and risk along the path to self-discovery. We can then support and speak out for them, encouraging the community to accept collective responsibility for the importance, empowerment, rights, well-being and humanity of young people.

Making Use of a Diverse Range of Interventions

Throughout this book, a variety of practical intervention processes are discussed, including:

- health promotion as a primary intervention
- using young people to help each other as a secondary intervention
- tertiary interventions in the community.

Health promotion as a primary intervention

There are various ways to provide protective primary interventions for young people. Population-based health promotion can avoid the development of over-whelming and distressing outcomes for young people at risk and topics described in Chapters 1, 2, 4, 6, 8, 9, 10, 11, 12 and 13 highlight opportunities for the devel-opment of such programmes. They seek to buffer young people against the impact of stressors, and, as a result, can be a useful resource when considering interven-tions for them. Public information can be provided through a variety of media, such as print, radio, the Internet, television or film. Certainly, if we are to help young people, information that is useful to them on their journey through life needs to be freely available. It is particularly important that this information be presented in ways that appeal to them and that it is promoted through media that young people prefer to use. To help achieve this goal, it can be useful for practi-tioners to engage the young people with whom they work in collaborative endeavours to develop primary intervention initiatives that will suit them and their peers.

Using young people to help each other as a secondary intervention

One of the problems we face as practitioners working with young people is that it is well known that most young people prefer to seek emotional and psychological support from their peers in the first instance (Gibson-Cline, 1996). Many are reluctant to seek help outside of their peer group. Consequently, it can be useful to educate young people in ways to help each other. You will find that many of the interventions mentioned in this book can be adapted so that young people are enabled to do exactly that (see Chapters 3, 8, 10, 11, 12 and 13).

A basic ethos of peer education is that it is designed to be by and for young people – they themselves largely determine what is relevant in terms of information and how it is to be delivered (Backett-Milburn and Wilson, 2000). This concept can be disconcerting for some adult stakeholders because, if young people are left in control of what is happening, they can much less easily be made the mouthpiece for adult messages or exhortations. The fear that inaccurate information or the wrong messages will be given may also be of real concern.

Two important points flow from this observation when considering the peer education model as a template for training young people to educate their peers. First, workers need to confront their fear that the young people they train may use or suggest strategies that are considered to be unhelpful by adults. Second, it can be advantageous if trainers relinquish some control over what young people include in the training content, precisely in order to enable them to perform their role as peer educators in appropriate and relevant ways, which might be difficult to accept. Workers interested in adopting such a model need to be prepared to allow young people in general the space to make their own choices and mistakes with regard to the way that they provide education on specific topics to their peers. When young people do what they determine to be relevant and helpful with their peers, however, assessing the impact on the recipients can help in evaluating the appropriateness of the education.

While encouraging young people to make their own choices and mistakes with regard to the way that they provide education or support to their peers, it is important for them to be given information during their training to enable them to take into account important factors relating to educating and helping others. For example, issues concerning personal growth, the clarification of values, understanding and respecting difference, limits to confidentiality, ethical considerations, expectations/limitations and referral, are important inclusions that help to encourage ethical and moral practice in any training model.

Tertiary interventions in the community

It is important to recognize that community interventions can be helpful when working with young people who have been unable to negotiate risks adaptively. Interventions that reduce the negative impact of an already established condition by discouraging unhelpful behaviours and encouraging more helpful ones, restoring function and reducing related complications are many and are discussed through-out this book (see Chapters 4, 5, 6, 12, 14, 15 and 17).

The Importance of Evidence-based Practice

It is highly desirable that practical interventions intended to help young people at risk should involve evidence-based solutions and service delivery models. The authors in this book have ensured that the practical interventions described are those that have been demonstrated to produce positive outcomes. Wherever possible, intervention processes need to be evaluated with regard to their effec-tiveness and usefulness. In this regard, it is strongly recommended that such eval-uations recognize the value of various kinds of evidence, both qualitative and quantitative, and should not be limited to one specific model of research inves-tigation. Through the use of sound research practices, we can increase our knowledge regarding evidence-based practice so that interventions will be of benefit to young people and the possibility of successful outcomes will be maximized.

The Organization and Structure of the Book

In organizing the structure of this book, I decided on the risk factors that were to be included and, in consultation and collaboration with the other authors, finalized decisions on chapter titles. The chapters were then organized so that they are in groups under part headings as follows:

- Building on Strengths
- Suicide and Self-harm
- Confrontational Behaviour
- Substance Abuse
- Sexual Behaviour
- Mental Health
- Marginalized Young People

The advantages of diversity

I am delighted by the diversity that is offered throughout this book. I believe that this diversity makes the book a much more useful resource than it would have been otherwise.

First, there is diversity with regard to the style of writing of each author. While the authors have all complied with a particular structure for their chapters, they have used their own individual writing styles. This has made the book more inter-esting and, additionally, has enabled the authors to engage the reader in a personal way, so that the reader becomes aware of each author's attitudes and stance with regard to the nature of the risks discussed and the strategies and interventions sug-gested. Consequently, I expect that you will find that, at times, when reading the book you will be challenged to examine your own values, beliefs and attitudes. These are likely to influence your practice.

Second, within many chapters, there is diversity with regard to the strategies and intervention options available to address specific challenges. This is particularly advantageous when considering strategies and interventions suitable for young people. As explained previously, they need to be ones that will appeal to the young people concerned, consequently engage them and enable them to make helpful changes.

Concluding Remarks

I would like to take this opportunity to thank the authors who have contributed to this book. They are all internationally recognized as having expertise with regard to responding to the particular challenges encountered by young people. I very much appreciate their willingness to share their expertise in this way, suggesting practical interventions that are either preventative or a response to difficulties that arise for young people as they negotiate and navigate their transition to adulthood. As you will discover when you read this book, there is a continuing emphasis on the collaborative engagement and empowerment of young people through the use of evidence-based interventions. This reflects the commitment of the authors to promoting positive youth development.

My hope is that this book will be a useful resource for those practitioners who work with young people and for students who intend to work with young people in the future.

References

Backett-Milburn, K. and Wilson, S. (2000) 'Understanding peer education: insights from a process evaluation', *Health Education Research*, 15 (1): 85–96.

Gibson-Cline, J. (1996) *Adolescents: From crisis to coping: A thirteen nation study*. Oxford: Butterworth-Heinemann.

Gregory, H. (2006) *Giving Youth a Voice: The Youth Advocacy Centre, Brisbane 1981–2006*. Brisbane, Australia: The Supreme Court of Queensland Library.

Lambert, M.J. (1992) 'Implications of outcome research for psychotherapy integration', in J.C. Norcross and M.R. Goldfried (eds), *Handbook of Psychotherapy Integration*. New York: Basic Books.

Schoon, I. (2007) 'Life chances and opportunities in times of social change: evidence from two British birth cohorts', in R. Silbereisen and R. Lerner (eds), *Approaches to Positive Youth Development*. London: Sage.

Part II

Building on Strengths

1

Promoting Self-care Behaviours

David Geldard

Introduction

As we have seen in the Introduction, all young people are at a stage in life that involves learning new ways of thinking and behaving in order to cope with events adaptively. In this developmental stage, they will continually meet new challenges at home, school, work and with peers. Those new challenges will often involve risks for them and, additionally, they are likely to behave in ways that are risky in order to enlarge on their experience of life by experimenting with new behaviours.

During childhood, parents and/or carers look after their children, watch over them and make decisions on their behalf. As far as is possible, most children are protected from unnecessary exposure to risks or risk-taking. When a young person transitions into adulthood, however, they start to individuate and strive for a level of separation from their parents. Parents no longer monitor the young person's behaviour on an hour by hour basis and are not in a position where they either want or are able to be responsible for caring for them throughout the day. Moreover, it is not appropriate that they should do this. Consequently, the young person is left in a position where, to a large extent, they need to take responsibility for caring for themselves. Self-care doesn't come naturally to many young people, though. This is understandable because previously they have been under parental care.

If young people are to address the dilemmas of human relationships, develop healthy lifestyles, access the social systems they need and meet the demands of the workplace, they must learn certain basic skills for everyday life (Takanishi, 2000). The development of interpersonal, decision making and coping skills is required to enable young people to increase self-control, reduce stress and anxiety and enable them to make friends if they are isolated. There is much for young people to learn, but perhaps the most important behaviour they need to learn is to how to care for themselves.

How Do We Promote Self-care in Young People?

The promotion of self-care begins with the use of primary prevention strategies, such as providing public information and anticipatory guidance and offering opportunities for engagement in self-development activities such as those discussed in the Introduction. For example, the National Institute for Health and Clinical Excellence (NICE) is an independent organization in the UK responsible for providing national guidance on the promotion of good health and the prevention and treatment of ill health. NICE helps health professionals implement the guidance that they offer by providing tools such as cost templates, audit criteria and slide sets and is a valuable resource for them. As well as learning through primary prevention programmes, young people can acquire the skills they need for self-care in a number of differing ways – through trial and error, practice, by observing their peers and by modelling themselves on significant others.

If young people are to self-care, they must be capable of:

- developing and maintaining a social support system
- learning how to take responsibility for themselves
- managing and coping with stress
- caring for their physical and emotional well-being
- attending to their psychological health.

Developing and Maintaining a Social Support System

In developing and maintaining a social support system, young people need to:

- build positive peer relationships
- maintain positive relationships within their families
- develop appropriate boundaries.

Building positive peer relationships

The role peers play in young people's lives and their influence on psychosocial development during the transition to adulthood are well documented (Noak, 2000). Also, many research studies have shown that social relationships can buffer stress and poor social skills lead to rejection and isolation, which are major sources of stress (Argyle, 1999). It is therefore important for workers who are endeavouring to help young people to care for themselves to help them recognize that building effective social relationships makes an important contribution to self-care.

Because young people are in a developmental stage where, typically, they are starting the process of individuation from their family, it is helpful to their well-being if they are able to belong to a group of friends. As they rely less on family support, they are then able to replace this by support from their peers. To do this, though, they require social skills.

A useful way to help young people to develop social skills is through the use of group work. A group facilitated by skilled leaders can provide a safe environment in which young people can learn through experiential activities how to replace inappropriate social behaviours with more adaptive ones. A programme for developing social skills in a group setting is described by Geldard and Geldard (2001) in *Working with Children in Groups*. This programme can easily be adapted for use with teenagers.

As an alternative, or in addition, to group work, counselling strategies can help young people to develop social skills. The kinds of counselling strategies that are appropriate for helping young people build positive social relationships with peers are discussed in *Relationship Counselling for Children, Young People and Families* (Geldard and Geldard, 2009b).

Maintaining positive relationships within the family

Although the young person's life stage is the time when young people tend to become less dependent on their family, at crisis times it is helpful for them to be able to rely on their family for support. It is also advantageous for young people to learn how to access other resources outside the family for social support. These might include youth leaders, youth workers, school counsellors, teachers and other significant people in their lives. Useful counselling strategies for helping young people to build positive relationships within and outside of their families are discussed in *Relationship Counselling for Children, Young People and Families* (Geldard and Geldard, 2009b).

Developing appropriate boundaries

Some young people have difficulty in maintaining appropriate personal boundaries that are comfortable for them and will provide a sensible level of personal protection. They need to learn how to invite others to move into a closer relationship and how to push people away when this is required. A useful psycho-educational strategy to help young people learn how to manage boundary issues is the circle concept suggested by Champagne and Walker-Hirsch (1982) and described by Geldard and Geldard (2009a) in *Counselling Adolescents*.

Learning How to Take Responsibility for Themselves

During their transition to adulthood, young people need to learn how to take more responsibility for their actions and control of their lives. Some will become despondent, however, because, when things don't work out the way they want, they will either blame themselves or others.

An important message to be delivered within primary prevention programmes and when counselling young people is that blaming is unhelpful – it is more important for young people to take control of their lives by being solution-focused and replacing negative thinking with positive action. The use of resource books such as *Solution-focused Coaching* (Greene and Grant, 2003) can be helpful in encouraging solution-orientated positive action.

Managing and Coping with Stress

A meta-analysis of research findings on school programmes targeting stress management in children and young people confirmed that primary prevention programmes in schools targeting stress and coping are effective in promoting a positive overall effect with regard to stress and coping symptoms (Kraag et al., 2006). This confirms the value of providing education about stress and its effects and how to manage and control it.

Educational programmes related to stress need to highlight the possibility that stressful events may result in both positive and negative consequences. Positive consequences may be manifested by personal growth and negative consequences by distress reactions (Karlsen et al., 2006). Additionally, it is clear that a level of stress may be useful in promoting motivation. Consequently, it can be helpful for young people to recognize that, in many instances, experiencing stress can be an advantage. For example, the stress experienced before running a race might enhance their performance.

Because stress can sometimes be damaging, young people need to seek ways to reduce their stress level at times when being stressed is not helpful to their well-being. For example, it can be useful to let young people know that stress can be reduced by a number of strategies, including the following:

- using solution-focused strategies to deal with problems (as discussed above)
- making decisions so that their workload can be managed more easily
- talking to peers or others about their worries, as will be discussed later.

Cognitive behavioural strategies have been found to be relevant for managing stress in young people and include those from Rational Emotive Behaviour Therapy. An excellent description of useful strategies is provided by Dryden (2001).

An example of using a cognitive behavioural approach for promoting positive thinking is provided by Zager and Rubenstein (2002), who make the following suggestions:

- remember, no one is good at everything, so pay attention to your strengths – if you are doing your best, learn to accept your limitations
- if you want to improve your self-esteem and confidence, pursue stuff you like to do because motivation is the key to success
- practise your assertiveness skills
- measure success by your effort, not your performance – while you can't always control the outcome, you can control your input
- watch out for unrealistic expectations of yourself.

Caring for Physical and Emotional Well-being

There are various ways in which young people can care for their physical and emotional well-being. These will be discussed below under the following headings:

- involvement in physical and/or recreational activity
- healthy eating
- involvement in creative activities
- involvement in relaxing/recharging activities
- having a balanced lifestyle.

Involvement in physical activity and/or recreational activity

Regular exercise is something that some young people naturally engage with. These young people enjoy playing a variety of team games, such as football, cricket and basketball. There are those young people, too, who are interested in individual sporting activities, such as tennis, golf, swimming, athletics and gymnastics.

There are many other young people, however, who don't enjoy participating in sporting activities of any type. They are at risk of developing lifestyles that may compromise both their short-term and long-term physical health and may also have implications for their emotional well-being.

Educating young people about the benefits of physical activity is of some, but limited, use. Young people like to make their own choices and, if they don't like doing something, it can be very hard to succeed in encouraging them do it. Consequently, schools and community organizations need to provide facilities for young people that appeal to them in order to encourage them to undertake physical activity. Clearly, it is helpful if a wide range of activities is offered instead of just traditional sporting activities. For example, activities such as skateboarding, horse-riding, cycling, rowing, canoeing, camping, trekking, abseiling, exploring and scuba-diving may be of interest to some individuals. In deciding which activities to offer, it is important to take into account the financial costs of each particular activity and the ability of the young people or their parents or the social system to pay for them.

It needs to be recognized that physical activity is useful in a variety of ways and not just with regard to improving physical health. For example, physical activity can be useful in helping to reduce stress, manage weight and as way of dealing with anger.

Healthy eating

As will be discussed more fully in Chapter 15, it is very important for young people to adopt healthy eating habits. This can be particularly difficult for some and, unfortunately, advertising aimed at young people sometimes lures them into eating food that, although enjoyable to eat, is not necessarily helpful with regard to staying healthy.

There are clearly problems, too, with both overeating and eating too little. In extreme cases, obesity and anorexia have the potential to produce long-term health problems.

Once again, there is a strong case for the use of primary prevention education with regard to diet and eating habits. For details of other suitable interventions, see Chapter 15.

Involvement in creative activities

Some young people are particularly attracted to creative activities. These may include dance, drama, painting and sculpture. The benefits of such activities can be profound as they can take the young person into a new emotional and psychological space where they can recharge by separating themselves for a while from the normal stresses of their lives while fully entering into a creative experience. Often, a young person who is reserved and/or physically unsuited to sporting activities can, by participating in a creative activity, experience satisfaction, with consequent positive effects for their self-esteem and self-image.

Involvement in relaxing/recharging activities

Activities such as yoga, pilates, tai chi, meditation and others that involve self-reflection and spirituality allow young people to recharge their energy and experience a calmness, together with a sense of control of themselves and their lives. Offering these activities to young people can clearly be extremely useful in helping to enhance their emotional and psychological well-being.

Having a balanced lifestyle

Many children are raised by parents who have organized them in ways that have ensured they have a balanced life in which they eat healthy food, are encouraged to look after their personal hygiene and have regular bedtimes. Even for those parents who have reared their children in this way, however, when those children move towards adulthood, parental influence is generally reduced.

Now, there is an old saying, 'you can take a horse to water, but you can't make it drink'. It is the same with many young people. Because they are at a stage in life where they need to individuate, as is appropriate, they will naturally resist being told what to do. This creates a problem for many parents.

Perhaps the best way to deal with this problem is through primary prevention programmes in schools, youth and community organizations that promote the idea of having a balanced, healthy lifestyle.

Attending to their Psychological Health

All human beings have troubling issues at times, but, for many young people, moving towards adulthood is a period in their lives when they are most likely to become overwhelmed when confronted with situations and issues that they have not previously experienced. Consequently, it is a time when their psychological well-being is at risk. If they are to minimize that risk, they need to be aware of their options for addressing problems. Unfortunately, some young people are not well informed in this regard, so, once again, primary prevention education is important.

It is very important, too, that young people are taught how to recognize the normal ups and downs of daily life. Through this education they may be less likely to react despairingly and take undesirable action when they experience an emotional trough. A good example of a useful primary prevention programme is beyondblue, which is available on the Internet and takes the reader step by step through the symptoms of depression – how to recognize it, how to get help, how to help someone and how to stay well.

Useful ways in which young people can attend to their psychological health include:

- seeking help from peers
- using counselling.

Seeking help

Unfortunately, seeking professional help is generally not a preferred option for young people (Gibson-Cline, 1996). Additionally, it is well documented that young people generally prefer to seek help from their peers about their problems rather than from their parents or other adults (Buhrmester and Prager, 1995). Because of this, peer counselling training programmes are strongly recommended as they can give young people the skills to informally help each other talk about and resolve troubling issues. Additionally, well-trained peer helpers can encourage young people with serious problems to take the step of going to see a professional counsellor.

Chapter 3 describes a peer counselling training programme that enhances the natural helping conversational skills of young people. It is strongly recommended that such programmes be introduced in schools as part of the normal curriculum. This is essential if we are to reduce the number of young people who suffer preventable mental health problems.

Programmes focusing on the notion of peer support can be developed with the assistance of the Peer Mentoring Project UK. This organization can provide guidance to help you through the process of getting started, running your project and, finally, evaluating the impacts that the scheme has had in your school.

Using counselling

Despite the reluctance of young people to use professional counsellors, some will do so, particularly if they are encouraged by their peers. The advantages are that a counselling situation provides an opportunity for troubling issues and psychological problems to be addressed. Also, self-care strategies can be promoted to help address long-term needs.

When counselling a young person, it can be useful to start by making an assessment of their existing coping strategies as this will give an indication of their ability to self-care. A good way to make such an assessment is to use the Adolescent Coping Scale (Frydenberg and Lewis, 1993). This scale is a self-help instrument by means of which young people can come to understand their own coping behaviour and subsequently make self-initiated changes.

Conclusion

If we are to help young people to develop self-care behaviours, we need to proactively introduce primary intervention programmes that will promote these behaviours. Educational programmes can be used to teach young people to cope with and manage stress, build positive social relationships, take responsibility and learn how to care for their physical and psychological health.

Because they are in the process of individuation, young people do not like being told what to do. Consequently, programmes need to be inviting to them, meeting their personal preferences and offering them opportunities to self-care in ways that they find attractive.

As pointed out by Pittman et al. (2002), young people grow up in communities, not just schools and not just youth programmes. Community-based organizations, service agencies, businesses and other places of employment are settings where strategies can be used to contribute to a young person's development. Whereas these contexts tend to overlap to varying degrees, it is essential that social policies address the specific intersections between young people and the contexts that shape and inform their developmental experiences. Interventions should focus on support and opportunities related to self-efficacy, empowerment and positive identity formation.

Resources

National Institute for Health and Clinical Excellence www.nice.org.uk
Peer Mentoring Project www.peermentoring.org.uk

KEY POINTS

- Developing and maintaining a social support system involves building positive peer relationships, maintaining positive relationships with the family and developing appropriate boundaries.
- Primary prevention programmes in schools targeting stress and coping can have positive outcomes.
- Young people can care for their physical and emotional well-being by getting involved in physical, recreational, creative and relaxing/recharging activities, healthy eating and having a balanced lifestyle.
- Young people need to be aware of their options with regard to addressing their psychological health.

QUESTIONS FOR DISCUSSION

1. How would you set about designing a primary prevention programme to help young people develop self-care behaviours?
2. What young people do you work with now who might benefit from the ideas expressed in this chapter? Describe how they would benefit.

References

Argyle, M. (1999) 'The development of social coping skills', in E. Frydenburg (ed.), *Learning to Cope: Developing as a person in complex societies*. Oxford: Oxford University Press. pp. 81–106.

Buhrmester, D. and Prager, K. (1995) 'Patterns and functions of self-disclosure', in K.J. Rotenburg (ed.), *Disclosure Processes in Children and Adolescents*. New York: Cambridge University Press. pp. 10–56.

Champagne, M.P. and Walker-Hirsch, L.W. (1982) 'Circles: a self-organisation system for teaching appropriate social/sexual behaviour, to mentally retarded/developmentally disabled persons', *Sexuality and Disability*, 5: 172–4.

Dryden, W. (2001) *Reason to Change: A Rational Emotive Behaviour Therapy workbook*. Hove, Sussex: Brunner-Routledge.

Frydenberg, E. and Lewis, R. (1993) *Adolescent Coping Scale*. Melbourne, Australia: ACER.

Geldard, K. and Geldard, D. (2001) *Working with Children in Groups: A handbook for counsellors, educators and community workers*. Basingstoke, Hampshire: Palgrave Macmillan.

Geldard, K. and Geldard, D. (2009a) *Counselling Adolescents: The proactive approach* (3rd edn). London: Sage.

Geldard, K. and Geldard, D. (2009b) *Relationship Counselling for Children, Young People and Families*. London: Sage.

Gibson-Cline, J. (1996) *Adolescents: From crisis to coping: A thirteen nation study*. Oxford: Butterworth-Heinemann.

Greene, J. and Grant. A.M. (2003) *Solution-focused Coaching: Managing people in a complex world*. Harlow: Pearson Education.

Karlsen, E., Dybdahl, R. and Vitterso, J. (2006) 'The possible benefits of difficulty: how stress can increase and decrease subjective well-being', *Scandinavian Journal of Psychology*, 47 (5): 411–17.

Kraag, G., Zeegers, M.P., Kok, G., Hosman, C. and Abu-Saad, H.H. (2006) 'School programs targeting stress management in children and adolescents: a meta-analysis', *Journal of School of Psychology*, 44 (6): 449–72.

Noak, P. (2000) 'Adolescent peer relations in times of social change', in L.J. Crockett and R.K. Silbereisen (eds), *Negotiating Adolescence in Times of Social Change*. Cambridge: Cambridge University Press. pp. 137–56.

Pittman, K., Diversi, M. and Ferber, T. (2002) 'Social policy supports for adolescence in the twenty-first century: framing questions', in R.W. Larson, B.B. Brown and J.T. Mortimer (eds), *Adolescents' Preparation for the Future: Perils and promise*. Ann Arbor, MI: The Society for Research on Adolescence. pp. 149–58.

Takanishi, R. (2000) 'Preparing adolescents for social change: designing generic social interventions', in L.J. Crockett and R.K. Silbereisen (eds), *Negotiating Adolescence in Times of Social Change*. Cambridge: Cambridge University Press. pp. 284–93.

Zager, K. and Rubenstein, A. (2002) *The Inside Story on Teen Girls*. Washington, DC: American Psychological Association.

2

Building Resilience to Prevent Mental Health Problems in Young People: The Resourceful Adolescent Programme (RAP)

Ian Shochet, Rebecca Hoge and Astrid Wurfl

Introduction

This chapter describes an evidence-based programme called the Resourceful Adolescent Programme (RAP), which has been successful in building resilience in young people to prevent depressive symptoms developing. The programme adopts a strengths-focused approach. It aims to build a range of coping resources that foster teenagers' abilities to maintain a positive sense of self and regulate emotions in the face of the vicissitudes of everyday struggles and difficult life events. This group-based programme can be implemented routinely in schools or by counselling professionals as an early intervention or prevention programme.

While there is no universal definition, 'resilience' generally means the process of avoiding the negative trajectories associated with exposure to risk factors (Fergus and Zimmerman, 2005). Current models of resilience are also very clear that there 'are many pathways to resilience' (Bonanno, 2004) and there is no 'one size fits all approach'. Thus, each of us has the capacity to become resilient.

Why Build Resilience and Focus on Strengths?

Research has shown that only a small proportion of those who do not meet diagnostic criteria for a mental health disorders are actually mentally healthy – that is, flourishing (Keyes, 2007). For example, while 20 per cent of young people may be diagnosed with a mental illness before the age of 18, this does not imply that the other 80 per cent of young people are mentally healthy (Keyes, 2006). Keyes found that closer to 40 per cent of young people were mentally healthy and that this percentage declines with age (15–18 years). A study by Keyes (2006) indicated that flourishing youth function better than moderately mentally healthy youth, who, in turn, function better than languishing youth. Anything less than complete mental health results in increased impairment and a burden to self and society. Therefore, promoting mental health and resilience is seen as a worthwhile goal in itself and is associated with positive outcomes in many areas, including physical health, health behaviours, educational performance, employability, earnings and crime reduction (Friedli and Parsonage, 2007).

Proponents of population-based approaches to prevention also argue that there is great value in targeting not only the at risk group, but also in keeping the healthy from becoming at risk.

To assist with this process, one of the most promising findings of resilience research is that protective factors are more important than risk factors (Knight, 2007). Research has consistently shown that, regardless of the type of risk factor an individual is exposed to, internal and external protective factors can mitigate the risk (Knight, 2007). Therefore, interventions need to focus on strengths, not only deficits, and aim to develop assets and resources instead of focusing solely on risk amelioration (Fergus and Zimmerman, 2005).

It is clear that one of the key factors in building resilience is identifying and expanding on the strengths of individuals and those within their whole system (family, school, community and so on; Miller and Daniel, 2007). Thus, in this chapter, we will describe a strengths-based, resilience-building programme – the Resourceful Adolescent Programme (RAP). We will outline the theoretical basis, content, goals and methods for each session of the programme and provide evidence for its efficacy and effectiveness.

The Resourceful Adolescent Programme (RAP)

As mentioned the RAP is a strengths-focused, resilience-building programme for young people aged 12 to 15. The aim of the RAP is to facilitate the development of positive coping and interpersonal skills to build resilience in young people. It promotes intrapsychic and interpersonal protective factors that have been found to promote well-being and prevent mental health problems.

The RAP is primarily designed as a universal (that is, it can be used regardless of any particular risk factors), school-based programme, to be run as an integral part of the school curriculum. It is usually run with students aged 12 to 15 in groups of about 10 to 15 pupils. The universal approach of the RAP enables us to prevent healthy students from becoming 'at risk' and promote health in the 'at risk' group.

The programme has also been implemented successfully with indicated or selected groups that have some predetermined risk of mental health problems (such as mild symptoms of depression, family conflict, poor school connectedness). It is run by accredited counsellors, mental health professionals or teachers who have undergone the appropriate training. It also has a parent component – RAP-P – and a teacher's component – RAP-T – that promote parental and teacher protective factors identified in the literature. This chapter, however, will only focus on the teenage programme – RAP-A.

The theoretical basis of the RAP

The RAP integrates elements of cognitive behavioural therapy (CBT) with inter-personal therapy (IPT) and has the overarching aim of assisting teenagers in self-regulation and managing the daily vicissitudes of self-esteem. One of the essential features of the programme is that it is very positively focused and concentrates on building strengths rather than repairing deficits.

The RAP is based on the recognition and reinforcement of existing personal strengths and the development of additional skills and psychological resources. It was initially developed in 1997 by converting current knowledge at that stage about evidence-based practice for treatment of depression (drawn from cognitive behavioural therapy and interpersonal therapy), into a school-based preventative intervention. In addition, the programme draws extensively on the parallel research on intrapsychic and interpersonal risk and protective factors. Finally, we integrated the interpersonal and individual components through a common focus on the development of strategies to manage threats and ruptures to self-esteem and maintain a positive regulation of self.

The CBT components of the RAP include cognitive restructuring (maintain-ing positive self-talk), stress management (self-regulation and self-relaxation) and problem-solving. Over the past couple of decades, Beck and other researchers at the Center for Cognitive Therapy have provided extensive evidence of the link between what we think and how we feel (Burns, 1980), so cognitive restructur-ing is an integral component of building resilience. Stress management is also important because stressful life events increase risk for mental health problems and the ways in which individuals respond to stress can significantly impact on their future adjustment and psychopathology (Garber, 2006). Finally, a problem-solving component was included because a positive problem-solving orientation can reduce the impact of negative life circumstances (d'Zurilla and Maydeu Olivares, 1995; Werner, 1995).

The broad interpersonal and IPT components (Klerman and Weissman, 1993; Mufson et al., 1993) include material that encourages participants to establish and draw on a social support network, as well as develop the skills that are nec-essary to deal with role transitions and role disputes and prevent and manage conflict. Interpersonal skills promoted in the RAP include an improved ability to understand the perspectives of others, plus communication and other behav-ioural skills to prevent and manage conflict. The interpersonal components of the RAP were included because relationships are an important source of emo-tional well-being, providing a functional context that influences many, if not most, basic psychological processes (Reis and Gable, 2003). Interpersonal factors appear to be the most salient predictors of depression in particular and depres-sion is one of the most ubiquitous problems with teenagers and presents with it many problems – such as substance misuse, anxiety, suicide, educational out-comes and so on.

A central hinge of the RAP is to funnel the building of skills through a reg-ulation of the self. All the components of the programme converge on helping participants to maintain self-regulation and a positive sense of self in the face of stress or to recover a positive sense of self in the event of a 'rupture' in their

FIGURE 2.1   *The RAP house*

self-concept. The CBT and Interpersonal components of the RAP work in an integrated way to help young people achieve this individuated self-regulation or 'self-soothing' when there is a threat to their self-esteem.

In summary, the RAP draws on CBT and interpersonal perspectives to enhance the coping resources of young people and build resilience.

Intervention goals and methods

The RAP's positive philosophy and metaphors

The RAP focuses on the recognition and utilization of existing strengths and promotion of psychological skills and resources. Accordingly, positive language is used throughout and all the skills are framed in the positive – 'Keep the peace', 'Positive self-talk' and so on. While the programme was originally developed and funded as part of a national initiative to prevent depression and suicide, it does not mention depression or suicide at any point. Rather, the programme is promoted to teenagers as an opportunity to learn skills that will increase their self-esteem, help them to manage and solve problems and improve interpersonal relationships.

The RAP is written around a metaphor derived from the children's story, *The Three Little Pigs*. The 'resourceful little pig' built his house out of bricks rather than straw or sticks and, being strong and resilient, was able to withstand the onslaught of the wolf. Throughout the RAP, participants develop their own personal 'RAP house' (see Figure 2.1) by laying down personal resource bricks, such as personal strengths bricks, problem-solving bricks and so on.

In keeping with the strategy of funnelling coping skills through self-regulation and self-esteem, the RAP introduces students to the concept of the 'Selfenometer' (see Figure 2.2). This is a ten-point scale and it is introduced to students to help them regularly monitor their self-esteem level. At the beginning and end of each session, participants circle the Selfenometer number that represents the way they feel.

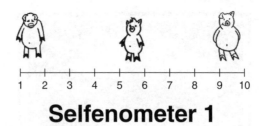

Selfenometer 1

FIGURE 2.2   *The Selfenometer*

The Selfenometer has two main aims. First, it increases participants' awareness of fluctuations in their feelings of well-being from day to day and situation to situation. Second, it normalizes this experience and encourages participants to be aware of their self-esteem and self-regulate in times of stress.

Implementing the RAP

The RAP consists of 11 sessions that last 50 to 60 minutes, designed to be implemented once a week as part of the school curriculum. Ideally, RAP groups are limited to 10 to 15 participants so that group leaders are able to provide attention and positive regard to each individual. Groups are usually created by dividing a regular class in half, but the RAP has been implemented in a wide range of other settings and formats (such as detention centres, community mental health centres, employment services, three-day camps and five-day residential programmes).

The RAP is facilitated by mental health professionals or teachers who have completed an approved one-day training course. Group leaders come from a range of professional backgrounds, including psychology, education, social work, human services and community mental health and must be skilled in communication and group facilitation, plus managing potentially difficult situations.

The group leader's role includes providing unconditional positive regard, focusing on strengths, modelling positive coping skills and prompting and rewarding the use of skills being introduced in the RAP. Each session consists of group activities that enable participants to practise the skills being taught, experience how the skills can help and relate each new skill to building their self-esteem. The group process is experiential and positive, creating many opportunities to validate and affirm participants. This process component is a vital factor in successfully implementing the RAP.

The programme's content

The theoretical basis, goals and methods for each session of the RAP have been summarized in Table 2.1.

As can be seen from the table, the sequence is carefully layered to progressively develop skills of affect and self-regulation, particularly in the context of interpersonal challenges.

Evidence for the efficacy and effectiveness of the RAP

The RAP has been endorsed at the Australian Commonwealth level as an evidence-based programme for preventing depression in young people and has

TABLE 2.1 *Theoretical basis, goals and methods for each session of the RAP.*

Session title and key message/s	Theoretical basis	Goals and methods
1. Getting to know you We're interested in you! Let's work together as a team.	Developing a working alliance with participants has been shown to correlate positively with therapeutic change (Castonguay et al., 2006). The working alliance made possible in small groups is an indispensable part of the RAP and distinguishes it from universal programmes that are conducted in large, class-sized groups.	Introduce programme. Establish rapport and build trust through games and activities.
2. Building self-esteem I'm OK. I'm building on my strengths.	The resiliency literature suggests that promotion of self-esteem and self-efficacy in young people is probably the key ingredient in any effective intervention process (Werner and Johnson, 2004). It has been suggested that we must bring strength-building to the forefront in the prevention of mental illness (Johnson, 2003).	Introduce the RAP metaphor (*The Three Little Pigs*), 'Selfenometer' and self-esteem. Help participants identify their existing strengths and coping resources by filling in 'personal strengths bricks'.
3. Introduction to the RAP model Our body clues and our self-talk affect the way we feel and behave.	This session is essentially an introduction to CBT. Participants are introduced to the RAP model, a Venn diagram that was derived from the cognitive model of emotion and behaviour (Burns, 1980).	Use the RAP model to explore links between body clues, behaviour, self-talk and emotions. Normalize problems that many teenagers experience. Use the RAP model to demonstrate 'risky' and 'resourceful' ways to manage situations.
4. Keeping calm Be a detective. Find your body clues and keep calm.	Stressful life events are a known risk factor for mental health problems. The way individuals respond to stress can significantly impact their future adjustment and psychopathology (Garber, 2006).	Explore body signals related to positive and negative feelings. Identify personal stress indicators. Discuss strategies for relaxing and managing stress and anger. Introduce common CBT relaxation techniques. Complete the 'keep calm bricks' with strategies (new and existing) for staying calm.
5. Self-talk I am what I think.	Drawing extensively on the work of Beck (see Burns, 1980), this session provides a user-friendly way for participants to identify negative automatic thoughts, learn appropriate ways to challenge those thoughts and replace them with more resourceful alternatives.	Explore how thoughts affect feelings and behaviour, challenge negative thoughts using the 'thought bricks' (e.g. Are you jumping to conclusions?) and practise cognitive restructuring.

(Continued)

TABLE 2.1 (Continued)

Session title and key message/s	Theoretical basis	Goals and methods
6. Thinking resourcefully You can change	The focus of Session 6 is on teaching cognitive restructuring skills. Based on Burns (1980), the technique employed involves completing a table consisting of seven columns: situation, risky thought, risky behaviour, risky feeling, resourceful thought, resourceful behaviour and resourceful feeling.	Continue focusing on challenging risky responses to situations and generating resourceful alternatives. Complete the table of risky and resourceful responses as a group, then individually.
7. Finding solutions to problems There are solutions to my problems.	A *positive* problem-solving orientation provides protective factors that reduce the impact of negative life circumstances (d'Zurilla and Maydeu Olivares, 1995; Werner, 1995).	Introduce a model for effective problem-solving using the 'problem-solving bricks'. Apply this process to a typical teenage interpersonal problem.
8. Support networks There is always help at hand.	The resiliency literature indicates that children who thrive despite adversity are skilled in establishing a support network that provides positive role models and affectional ties that encourage trust, autonomy and initiative (Werner, 1995). In addition to identifying social supports in difficult times, Session 8 also emphasizes the importance of sharing *positive* experiences. This is based on self-psychology's theory that we need people in our lives who can provide a mirror to reflect a sense of self-worth and value, creating internal self-respect (Baker and Baker, 1987).	Identify and develop a social support network for good times and difficult times. List these support people on the 'support network bricks'. Introduce humour as a strategy for managing stress.
9. Considering the other person's perspective There are two sides to every story. Take time out, stop and think.	Late adolescence is a particularly important time for maintaining strong relationships with family members (Galambos et al., 2004), and a time when peer relationships become increasingly complex and intense (Allen et al., 2006), so early adolescence is the optimal time to impart these skills. This session aims to help participants minimize and manage conflict in their relationships.	Apply the RAP model to interpersonal situations. Introduce the link between self-esteem and conflict, explaining that people fight when their Selfenometer is low and their ratings can go even lower as the conflict continues. Discuss the importance of the body clues, self-talk, emotions and behaviours of each person in the situation. Conclude that neither person is necessarily right or wrong, they just see things differently because there are usually two sides to every story.

TABLE 2.1 (Continued)

Session title and key message/s	Theoretical basis	Goals and methods
10. Keeping the peace and making the peace Keep the peace and make the peace.	While there is a commonly held myth that teenagers want nothing to do with their parents, the research literature indicates the opposite (Johnson, 2003). Teenagers need their parents, but the ways in which they need them evolves as they negotiate the major developmental task of adolescence: attaining autonomy while maintaining attachment. This session aims to increase participants' awareness and understanding of this developmental task, normalize the adolescent experience and encourage resourceful ways to 'keep the peace' and 'make peace' in relationships.	Continue exploring ways to see the other person's perspective and avoid going round in circles in conflict situations. Use the 'keep the peace' and 'make peace bricks' to find ways to deal with situations in more positive ways. Demonstrate through role playing.
11. Putting it all together Being a resourceful adolescent really works! Let's celebrate.	An important function of this session is to leave participants feeling that their contributions to the group were valuable and confident about using their new skills. The group leader personally thanks every young person for participating and provides positive feedback about each person's contributions.	Briefly review and discuss each session. Complete the RAP house with the 'resource bricks' gained throughout the programme. Celebrate the group's successes with a party.

become widely used throughout Australia and internationally, in 13 other countries. The programme has been translated into Chinese, Dutch, French and Braille and adapted for Maori students and indigenous Australians.

The RAP has been extensively evaluated internationally and a summary of the results from some of the major trials of the programme has been included on the website (www.rap.qut.edu.au, on the 'Research' page).

Summary of findings

The findings suggest that we can be confident about the RAP's efficacy in the short and medium term. There is good evidence of its efficacy when conducted by mental health professionals. The RAP is also effective when conducted in a controlled environment by trained or carefully selected teachers, but large, unsupervised implementation has demonstrated small, but not necessarily sustained effects. These findings suggest that there is a need for an increased focus on teacher selection and training to ensure they are comfortable in presenting the RAP as well as management of organizational issues that impact schools undertaking large-scale implementations.

Summary and Conclusion

The RAP is a positively focused, resilience-building group programme for young people. We believe that one of its strengths is that it integrates CBT and interpersonal perspectives. We have also been very mindful of the importance of the group process as good programme content is substantially more effective when delivered with warmth, vitality, autonomy, support and opportunities for individual connection.

The evidence suggests that, when delivered appropriately, either by mental health professionals or adequately trained and supervised teachers, the RAP is effective in preventing clinically meaningful depressive symptoms in the short and medium term.

Resources

How to access the RAP

Group leader manuals (Shochet, Holland and Whitefield, 1997) and participant workbooks (Shochet, Whitefield and Holland, 1997) are distributed via the RAP Office at the Queensland University of Technology, Queensland, Australia. Further details are available at the RAP website: www.rap.qut. edu.au

Further reading

Merry, S., McDowell, H., Wild, C.J., Bir, J. and Cunliffe, R. (2004) 'A randomized placebo-controlled trial of a school-based depression prevention program', *Journal of the American Academy of Child and Adolescent Psychiatry*, 43: 538–47.
Shochet, I.M., Dadds, M.R., Holland, D., Whitefield, K., Harnett, P. and Osgarby, S. (2001) 'The efficacy of a universal school-based program to prevent adolescent depression', *Journal of Clinical Child Psychology*, 30: 303–15.

KEY POINTS

- Promoting resilience in young people results in positive outcomes for them and society generally.
- The RAP concentrates on building strengths rather than repairing deficits and is a strengths-focused, resilience-building programme.
- The RAP integrates elements of cognitive behavioural therapy with interpersonal therapy.
- The RAP has been extensively evaluated internationally with regard to its efficacy.

QUESTIONS FOR DISCUSSION

1. Discuss how building resilience in teenagers can promote their well-being and prevent depression.
2. Can resilience be created? If so, how? If not, why not?

References

Allen, J.P., Insabella, G., Porter, M.R., Smith, F.D., Land, D. and Phillips, N. (2006) 'A social–interactional model of the development of depressive symptoms in adolescence', *Journal of Consulting and Clinical Psychology*, 74: 55–65.

Baker, H.S. and Baker, M.N. (1987) 'Heinz Kohut's self psychology: an overview', *The American Journal of Psychiatry*, 144: 1–9.

Bonanno, G.A. (2004) 'Loss, trauma and human resilience: have we underestimated the human capacity to thrive after extremely aversive events?', *American Psychologist*, 59: 20–8.

Burns, D.D. (1980) *Feeling Good: The new mood therapy*. New York: New American Library.

Castonguay, L.G., Constantino, M.J. and Grosse Holtforth, M. (2006) 'The working alliance: where are we and where should we go?', *Psychotherapy: Theory, Research, Practice, Training*, 43: 271–9.

d'Zurilla, T.J. and Maydeu Olivares, A. (1995) 'Conceptual and methodological issues in social problem-solving assessment', *Behavior Therapy*, 26: 409–32.

Fergus, S. and Zimmerman, M.A. (2005) 'Adolescent resilience: a framework for understanding healthy development in the face of risk', *Annual Review of Public Health*, 26: 399–419.

Friedli, L. and Parsonage, M. (2007) 'Building an economic case for mental health promotion: Part I', *Journal of Public Mental Health*, 6: 14–23.

Galambos, N.L., Leadbeater, B.J. and Barker, E.T. (2004) 'Gender differences in and risk factors for depression in adolescence: a 4-year longitudinal study', *International Journal of Behavioral Development*, 28: 16–25.

Garber, J. (2006) 'Depression in children and adolescents: linking research and prevention', *American Journal of Preventive Medicine*, 31: S104–S125.

Johnson, N.G. (2003) 'On treating adolescent girls: focus on strengths and resiliency in psychotherapy', *Journal of Clinical Psychology/In Session*, 59: 1193–203.

Keyes, C.L.M. (2006) 'Mental health in adolescence: is America's youth flourishing?', *American Journal of Orthopsychiatry*, 76 (3): 395–402.

Keyes, C.L.M. (2007) 'Promoting and protecting mental health as flourishing: a complementary strategy for improving national mental health', *American Psychologist*, 62: 95–108.

Klerman, G.L. and Weissman, M.M. (1993) 'The place of psychotherapy in the treatment of depression', in G.L. Klerman and M.M. Weissman (eds), *New Applications of Interpersonal Psychotherapy*. Washington, DC: American Psychiatric Association Press. pp. 51–71.

Knight, C. (2007) 'A resilience framework: perspectives for educators', *Health Education*, 107: 543–55.

Merry, S., McDowell, H., Wild, C.J., Bir, J. and Cunliffe, R. (2004) 'A randomized placebo-controlled trial of a school-based depression prevention program', *Journal of the American Academy of Child and Adolescent Psychiatry*, 43: 538–47.

Miller, D. and Daniel, B. (2007) 'Competent to cope, worthy of happiness?: How the duality of self-esteem can inform a resilience-based classroom environment', *School Psychology International*, 28: 605–22.

Mufson, L., Moreau, D., Weissman, M.M. and Klerman, G.L. (1993) 'Interpersonal psychotherapy for adolescent depression', in G.L. Klerman and M.M. Weissman (eds), *New Applications of Interpersonal Psychotherapy*. Washington, DC: American Psychiatric Association Press. pp. 130–66.

Muris, P., Bogie, N. and Hoogsteder, A. (2001) 'Effects of an early intervention group program for anxious and depressed adolescents: a pilot study', *Psychological Reports*, 88: 481–2.

Reis, H.T. and Gable, S.L. (2003) 'Toward a positive psychology of relationships', in C.L.M. Keyes and J. Haidt (eds), *Flourishing: Positive psychology and the life well-lived*. Washington, DC: American Psychological Association. pp. 129–59.

Shochet, I.M., Dadds, M.R., Holland, D., Whitefield, K., Harnett, P. and Osgarby, S. (2001) 'The efficacy of a universal school-based program to prevent adolescent depression', *Journal of Clinical Child Psychology*, 30: 303–15.

Shochet, I., Holland, D. and Whitefield, K. (1997) *The Griffith Early Intervention Depression Project: Group Leader's Manual*. Brisbane, Australia: Griffith Early Intervention Project.

Shochet, I., Whitefield, K. and Holland, D. (1997) *The Griffith Early Intervention Depression Project: Participant's workbook*. Brisbane, Australia: Griffith Early Intervention Project.

Werner, E.E. (1995) 'Resilience in development', *Current Directions in Psychological Science*, 4 (3): 81–5.

Werner, E.E. and Johnson, J.L. (2004) 'The role of caring adults in the lives of children of alcoholics', *Substance Use and Misuse*, 39: 699–720.

3

Enhancing Peer Support

Kathryn Geldard and Wendy Patton

Introduction

A useful way to enhance peer support among young people is to provide peer counsellor training programmes. Research has shown, however, that there are problems associated with typical peer counselling training programmes for young people. Most rely on teaching young people counselling skills that are commonly used by professional counsellors when counselling adults and these are not compatible with typical conversational behaviours used by young people. Another problem is that they suggest some commonly used communication processes evident in the conversations of young people are unhelpful, whereas research has shown that this is not the case (Geldard, 2006).

In order to overcome these problems, a peer counsellor training programme has been developed for young people as an outcome of research into training young people as peer counsellors (Geldard, 2006).

Challenges Facing Young People

Transitioning to adulthood is a stage of human development during which young people must move from dependency to independence and develop autonomy and maturity. Consequently, they are faced with many challenges (Dacey and Kenny, 1997; White, 1996) and some young people are more successful than others when confronting and dealing with the stress associated with them. Those who do better are more resilient and have better coping strategies (Frydenberg and Lewis, 2002; Patton and Noller, 1990; Schoon and Bynner, 2003) than others. Some young people, however, are unable to confront and deal with these challenges successfully.

During the transition to adulthood, young people experience many physiological and biological changes that also alter their emotional state. Additionally, they experience cognitive changes – they develop a capacity for abstract thinking, discern new ways to process information and learn to think creatively and critically. These changes are challenging and, when combined with the other stresses and demands of life, lead many young people to become disillusioned, overwhelmed and unable to cope.

The Use of Social Support for Coping with Stress

One possible approach to helping young people who experience difficulties with these challenges is to provide social support. An important theory that underpins the use of social support as a coping strategy is Hobfoll's (1988) conservation of resource (COR) theory, which views social support as 'the building block for successfully mastering environmental demands' (Freedy and Hobfoll, 1994: 320). Thus, social support is a coping resource, a social fund in the environment that people may draw on when handling stressors. Consequently, intentionally altering environments so that social support is more accessible contributes to the investment in resources in that environment.

Conversational helping behaviour is a form of social support that relies on the positive active social interaction between individuals in a particular environment. Consequently, if we are to improve the resources available for young people, a strong case can be made for providing training programmes in school and community environments that can enhance their ability to help each other through conversational interaction.

The Ways in Which Young People Seek Help

It is well documented that young people generally prefer to seek help from their peers (Buhrmester and Prager, 1995; Carr, 1984; Gibson-Cline, 1996; Turner, 1999), suggesting that it is unlikely they will seek adult counselling help in the first instance.

Consistent with previous research, Wilson and Deane (2001) have reported that young people repeatedly suggest strong positive relationships with potential help-givers are very important in influencing their seeking help from either peers or adults. Young people in their study also suggested that they were more amenable to receiving help from a helper who was perceived to have 'gone through the same sort of thing', so that they could describe how *they* went about resolving the problem. This situation is likely to occur when young people talk with other young people who are experiencing, or have experienced, similar troubles.

Prosocial behaviour and empathy-related responding have a genetic basis (Eisenberg et al., 1999), which suggests that some young people might be potentially more able to provide social support to their peers than others. Many young people, however, can be taught how to build and maintain interdependent relationships so that they can give and receive help and assistance to cope with the stressful events in their lives. In fact, Johnson and Johnson (2002) viewed the interpersonal theory of coping with stress as useful in teaching young people how to cope with stress. They consider the individual as being part of a network of relationships, so stress is dealt with within the social network, drawing on resources above and beyond that of the individual.

Current Approaches to Training Young People as Peer Counsellors

From the previous discussion it is clear that it is useful to provide programmes to teach young people how to help each other through the use of conversational skills. In order to meet the need for such skills, a number of peer counsellor training programmes for young people have been developed (Carr and Saunders, 1980; de Rosenroll, 1988; Morey and Miller, 1993; Myrick and Sorensen, 1988; Painter, 1989; Tindall, 1989; Turner, 1999). It is disappointing to find, however, that, when using these approaches, the peer helper training literature reports problems for young people trained as peer counsellors with regard to:

- skill implementation
- role attribution
- status differences.

With regard to skill implementation, Carr (1984) recognized that, once core counselling skills had been reasonably well mastered, young people 'may feel awkward, mechanical or phoney'. This is not surprising as research has shown, as mentioned above, that the counselling skills taught in typical programmes have not been compatible with the typical conversational processes of young people (Geldard, 2006).

Issues concerning to role attribution appear to be problematic, too, with regard to the helping activities or duties undertaken by young people (de Rosenroll, 1988) particularly if the term 'peer counsellor/helper' is used, which carries with it professional expectations. Once again, this is not surprising as, when a young person is labelled a 'peer counsellor', he or she will be seen as having a different role and this might interfere with his or her peers' expectations that relationships should be reciprocal and equal.

Similarly, issues with regard to status relate to the fact that some young people receive training and others don't and that the role of peer helper could imply elevated status. Interestingly, Carr and Saunders (1980: 21) suggest, 'student resentment of the peer counsellor is not a problem', but they go on to say, 'this is not to say that the problem does not exist', so they provide opportunities within their training for young people trained as peer counsellors to develop ways to manage resentment.

Most current programmes for training young people as peer counsellors ignore, actively discourage and censor some of their conversational helping behaviours, such as persuading, advising, recommending, praising, supporting, sympathizing, diverting and kidding. In these programmes, such behaviours are referred to as 'communication stoppers' or 'roadblocks' to communicating (Carr and Saunders, 1980; de Rosenroll, 1988) and it is strongly suggested that they are negative in effect and retard helpful interpersonal relationships. Research suggests, however, that these communication behaviours are, in fact, considered useful by young people when helping peers (Geldard, 2006). Additionally, they enable the young person trained as peer counsellor to engage comfortably in a conversation with the person being helped, as the behaviours are consistent with the typical communication processes and conversation of young people so it feels more comfortable and natural than the advocated behaviour.

Current programmes for training young people as peer counsellors rely on teaching microcounselling skills from adult counselling models. They teach these skills in discrete and finite blocks, each with a beginning and an end, then integrate all that has been learnt and include skills such as attentive listening, accentuating high facilitative responses of reflecting feelings and content, summarizing and clarifying, providing feedback with an emphasis on avoiding giving advice, judging or labelling, responsible decision making, values clarification and being accountable. Research shows, however, that there are problems with these approaches (Geldard, 2006).

Research into Training Young People as Peer Counsellors

We conducted research where the underlying goal was to prepare young people to be providers of social support. The research focused on enhancing the typical conversational helping behaviours of young people with a view to strengthening social support as a resource in a secondary school environment. By training young people using a programme that was compatible with their typical conversational helping behaviours as well as including counselling skills that were compatible with their communication processes, it was hypothesized that problems associated with existing programmes could be reduced. It was anticipated that young people would be more likely to approach these peers for support than is the case with those trained using the kinds of programme discussed above, making social support a more attainable resource for young people in their community.

The research project

The project focused on what young people typically do when they help each other conversationally, identifying which counselling skills and/or approaches appeal to young people and are easy for them to use. Additionally, the project explored how having been trained as a peer counsellor affected the participants' experience of helping with regard to skill implementation, role attribution and status difference.

The participants included 52 volunteer students aged from 13 to 17 in a secondary school, relating in a peer environment. The study utilized a phenomenological qualitative approach to data collection and analysis as well as quantitative methods. Focus groups were used to discover what young people typically do when they help each other conversationally. Transcripts from these groups were analysed using Krueger's (1998) thematic content analysis continuum model.

Self-selected students from the focus groups formed four groups, each of which was trained in a different set of counselling microskills. These were facilitative counselling skills, problem-solving skills, solution-focused skills and skills focused on enhancement of the typical helping behaviours of young people. Questionnaires were used to rate the ease and usefulness of each specific counselling microskill. Results from the questionnaires were analysed, using the statistical package for social sciences (SPSS) to set out the data descriptively.

A peer counsellor training programme for young people was then developed, using an intervention research approach (Bailey-Dempsey and Reid, 1996;

Reinharz, 1992; Rothman and Thomas, 1994). The training programme involved 15 hours of training and focused on the process of a helping conversation rather than training in discrete blocks.

Data were collected using questionnaires and focus groups during the training. The data were analysed using emergent theme analysis and organized into themes under the headings of skill implementation, role attribution and status.

What we learned from the research participants

The results provided confirmation of a number of findings that other studies have identified regarding the idiosyncratic nature of young people's communication between friends and the conversational and relational behaviours of young people (Chan, 2001; Turkstra, 2001; Young et al., 1999). These included listening, respect, mediation, making contact, collaborative problem-solving, understanding, confidentiality, trust, helping others to talk and the creation of a safe relationship.

The results extended previous research by identifying the specific conversational characteristics that young people use in helping conversations. It also confirmed that some typical conversational helping behaviours of young people that have been proscribed for use in other peer counsellor training programmes are actually useful when young people help each other. Typical examples illustrating these behaviours included:

- reassurance: 'Reassured him it was OK and that it is not the end of the world'
- endorsement: 'I am the sort of person who will back people up. Like you don't just keep going, "Oh, you suck" or "You stink" and everything'
- offering another point of view: 'Tell them how you solved that problem you might have had and, if it's worked for you, you can suggest that solution to them'
- giving advice: 'Sometimes [I] try to offer advice, who to see or something like that'
- distracting: 'I just like making [different] conversation with them, getting their mind off the bad things that they are thinking about usually'
- evaluative responses: 'I tell her it goes both ways to my friend when she complains of her friends turning against her. I suggest how her behaviour might affect her relationships with others'
- kidding/humour: 'I made a bit of a joke and she started laughing'
- persuasion: 'I just keep telling her to try it and see if it works'.

The project confirmed the researchers' expectations that some counselling microskills currently used in training young people to be peer counsellors are not easy to use and considered unhelpful by young people. Microcounselling skills of reflection and summarizing were perceived by young people as being not only difficult to use but also unhelpful in helping conversations with their peers. A problem-solving process and open and closed questions were found to be easy to use and considered useful.

With regard to how an adolescent-friendly peer counsellor training programme affects the participants' experience of helping (in particular with regard to skill implementation, role attribution and status differences), the results demonstrated that the training programme developed in the course of the project overcame the difficulties of skill implementation identified in the peer counselling literature (Carr, 1984). Most importantly, it was found that the participants did not feel deskilled with regard to their own typical helping behaviours during the training process. Results confirmed suggestions that acting in the role of peer counsellor creates relationship difficulties and group membership as a peer counsellor raised issues of status difference for the participants, based on the acquisition of counselling skills when compared with their peers.

The project identified the process used by young peer counsellors to deal with issues related to role attribution and status difference. Older participants responded and adjusted to negative feedback from peers by behaving in ways that indicated they were not part of a 'peer counsellor' group and were, in fact, 'peers'. Younger participants responded and adjusted to negative feedback from peers using strategies that enhanced and augmented their identity as peer counsellors, behaving in ways that raised their role and social profile. Thus, the processes used by peer counsellors to deal with issues related to role attribution and status difference were different for younger and older participant groups, indicating that the role of peer counsellor is closely associated with the developmental process of individual and social identity formation.

Implications for training

The findings of the research project described above suggest that the identified differences between older and younger participants in this cohort should be taken into account when recruiting young people for inclusion in peer counsellor training programmes. Whereas younger participants may respond positively to the prospect of acting in a designated role in their community, older participants are more likely to be committed to a process of providing social support for their peers through a role that agrees with their own self-identity, social role perception and their views about who they would like to become in the future. Training programmes should consider training and preparing younger and older youth separately in their own homogeneous groups.

The findings suggest that it might be useful to incorporate peer counsellor training programmes into the normal school classroom curriculum to minimize the negative effects of status difference. Because young people provide emotional and psychological support to peers informally, it is possible that training for *all* students in the provision of conversational social support would be useful. As a result of the training, young people could then choose whether or not to participate in specific programmes where they could use their peer support skills. It may be that when all students share the same social and skilled standing with regard to having acquired counselling skills to help their peers, status differences will be eliminated.

The findings from the current study highlight the temptation when conducting training with young people with regard to prosocial behaviour to discount and exclude prosocial attributes that are actually emphasized and valued by young people. Whether or not young people view a peer as a source of social support depends on the helper's overall behavioural repertoire and benevolent intent and should not be seen as dependent on those specific communication skills deemed appropriate and acceptable for adults in the counselling and communication literature.

The Adolescent-friendly Peer Counsellor Training Programme

A peer counsellor training programme for young people was developed as a result of the research described above (the training manual for the programme is available free at: www.geldard.com.au). The programme provides an alternative to current peer counsellor training programmes.

When compared with other training programmes it has the following advantages. First, it combines the use of typical helping behaviours and communication processes used by young people with those counselling skills from adult counselling models and approaches that have been identified by young people as valuable, helpful and easy to use.

Second, the programme follows the process of a helping conversation, beginning with typical joining behaviours, followed by teaching skills that maintain the conversation and then those that are useful in ending a helping conversation. This contrasts with most current training programmes, which are based on the assumption that teaching effective helping skills from adult counselling models is best done in discrete and finite blocks, each with a beginning and an end, then integrating all that has been taught by emphasizing the process of a helping conversation.

The programme involves three modules:

- skills practice
- values and self-discovery
- role and ethics.

The skills module focuses on discovering and enhancing the skills required to initiate a helping conversation, find out about the problem, encourage active participation in the conversation, clarify the main problem, explore options and choices, deal with emotions, then end a conversation.

The values and self-discovery module focuses on understanding and respecting difference, self-disclosure, values clarification, non-judgemental listening, helper expectations/limitations, hopes, inclusion and exclusion and expressing positive affirmations.

The role and ethics module includes discussion and decision making with regard to issues of confidentiality and referral, ethical considerations when using helping skills (such as power), developing a code of ethics and psycho-education relating to the topics of suicide, drugs/alcohol and sexual issues.

The training programme involves 16 to 18 hours of peer counsellor training run by two trainers experienced in facilitating groups with young people, usually spread over three consecutive days, with regular breaks for lunch and refreshments.

During the training sessions, the trainers make use of experiential and interactive role play exercises to illustrate the issues and topics being discussed. The role play topics are selected by the participants and agreed on by the whole group as being issues relevant to young people. Role play makes it possible for trainers and participants to reflect and seek specific feedback regarding the developmental stages of a helping conversation, identify which typical skills used by young people can be utilized and take into account the ease with which the participants can incorporate specific helpful counselling microskills into the helping conversation.

Feedback also focuses on whether the helping conversation was helpful or unhelpful with regard to whether or not the person being helped could self-disclose and feel comfortable and the peer counsellors' perceptions of whether they achieved positive outcomes as a result of the conversation or not. Two role play conversations are used to assess each participant with regard to peers', trainers' and participants' perceptions of helpfulness. Trainers provide feedback to participants on completion of each assessment conversation to ensure ethical accountability and award each subject accreditation as a peer counsellor in the school community.

Summary

The peer support training programme developed during the course of this project is a resource that enhances peer support for young people. A major advantage of the programme is that it enhances typical helping conversational skills rather than attempting to teach those counselling skills which are not comfortable for young people to use and cannot be easily incorporated into the typical conversations young people have. As a consequence, some of the problems associated with other peer counsellor training programmes for young people are ameliorated.

Similar programmes focusing on the notion of peer support can be developed with the assistance of the Peer Mentoring Project. It can provide guidance to help you in the process of getting started, running your project and, finally, evaluating the impacts that the scheme has had on your school.

Resources

The 'Adolescent Peer Support Training Manual' mentioned in this chapter is available for practitioners to download and use free of charge by visiting: www.geldard.com.au

The Peer Mentoring Project www.peermentoring.org.uk

KEY POINTS

- A useful way to enhance peer support among young people is to provide peer counsellor training programmes.
- Specific conversational characteristics that young people use in helping conversations include reassurance, offering endorsement, offering another point of view, giving advice, distracting, evaluative responses, kidding/humour and persuasion.
- Behaviours such as listening, respect, mediation, making contact, collaborative problem-solving, understanding, confidentiality, trust, helping others to talk and the creation of a safe relationship are typical helping behaviours of young people.

QUESTIONS FOR DISCUSSION

1. Discuss your beliefs as to whether or not programmes used to enhance the existing skills that young people have with regard to helping each other should be strengths-based or directed in other ways? Use anecdotal examples to illustrate your answer.
2. What resources would you need to deliver the programme described in this chapter? Consider the option of external funding and describe how you would evaluate the efficacy of the programme to secure ongoing funding.

References

Bailey-Dempsey, C. and Reid, W.J. (1996) 'Intervention design and development: a case study', *Research on Social Work Practice*, 6: 208–28.

Buhrmester, D. and Prager, K. (1995) 'Patterns and functions of self-disclosure', in K.J. Rotenberg (ed.), *Disclosure Processes in Children and Adolescents*. New York: Cambridge University Press. pp. 10–56.

Carr, R. (1984) *The Theory and Practice of Peer Helping*. Victoria, BC: Peer Resources.

Carr, R. and Saunders, G. (1980) *The Peer Counsellor Starter Kit*. Victoria, BC: Peer Systems Consulting Group, Inc.

Chan, C.K. (2001) 'Peer collaboration and discourse patterns in learning from incompatible information', *Instructional Science*, 29: 443–79.

Dacey, J. and Kenny, M. (1997) *Adolescent Development*. Chicago: Brown & Benchmark.

de Rosenroll, D.A. (1988) 'Peer counselling: implementation and program maintenance issues', paper presented at the Annual Meeting of the National Peer Helpers Association, Fort Collins, CO.

Eisenberg, N., Guthrie, I.K., Murphy, B.C., Shepherd, S.A., Cumberland, A. and Carlo, G. (1999) 'Consistency and development of prosocial dispositions: a longitudinal study', *Child Development*, 70 (6): 1360–72.

Freedy, J.R. and Hobfoll, S.E. (1994) 'Stress inoculation for the reduction of burnout: a conservation of resources approach', *Anxiety, Stress and Coping*, 6: 311–25.

Frydenberg, E. and Lewis, R. (2002) 'Adolescent well-being: building young people's resources', in E. Frydenberg (ed.), *Beyond Coping: Meeting goals visions and challenges*. London: Oxford University Press. pp. 175–94.

Geldard, K. (2006) 'Adolescent peer counselling', unpublished doctoral dissertation, Queensland University of Technology, Brisbane, Australia.

Gibson-Cline, J. (1996) *Adolescents: From crisis to coping: A thirteen nation study*. Oxford: Butterworth-Heinemann.

Hobfoll, S.E. (1988) *The Ecology of Stress*. New York: Hemisphere.

Johnson, D.W. and Johnson, R.T. (2002) 'Teaching students how to cope with adversity: the three C's', in E. Frydenberg (ed.), *Beyond Coping: Meeting goals visions and challenges*. London: Oxford University Press. pp. 195–216.

Krueger, R.A. (1998) *Analysing and Reporting Focus Group Results: Focus 1 Group Kit 6*. Thousand Oaks, CA: Sage.

Morey, R.E. and Miller, C.D. (1993) 'High school peer counselling: the relationship between students' satisfaction and peer counsellors' style of helping', *School Counsellor*, 40: 293–301.

Myrick, R.D. and Sorenson, D.L. (1988) *Peer Helping: A practical guide*. Minneapolis, MN: Educational Media Corporation.

Painter, C. (1989) *Friends Helping Friends: A manual for peer counselors*. Minneapolis, MN: Educational Media Corporation.

Patton, W. and Noller, P. (1990) 'Adolescent self-concept: effects of being employed, unemployed or returning to school', *Australian Journal of Psychology*, 42: 247–59.

Reinharz, S. (1992) *Feminist Methods in Social Science Research*. New York: Oxford University Press.

Rothman, J. and Thomas, E. (1994) *Intervention Research*. New York: Haworth Press.

Schoon, I. and Bynner, J. (2003) 'Risk and resilience in the life course: implications of interventions and social policies', *Journal of Youth Studies*, 6 (1): 21–31.

Tindall, J.A. (1989) *Peer Counselling: An in-depth look at training peer helpers* (3rd edn). Muncie, IN: Accelerated Development Inc.

Turkstra, L.S. (2001) 'Partner effects in adolescents' conversations', *Journal of Communication Disorders*, 34: 151–62.

Turner, G. (1999) 'Peer support and young people's health', *Journal of Adolescence*, 22: 567–72.

White, F.A. (1996) 'Parent, adolescent communication and adolescent decision-making', *Journal of Family Studies*, 2: 41–56.

Wilson, C.J. and Deane, F.P. (2001) 'Adolescent opinions about reducing help-seeking barriers and increasing appropriate help engagement', *Journal of Educational and Psychological Consultation*, 12 (4): 345–64.

Young, R.A., Antal, S., Bassett, M.E., Post, A., DeVries, N. and Valach, L. (1999) 'The joint actions of adolescents in peer conversations about career', *Journal of Adolescence*, 22: 527–38.

Part III

Suicide and Self-harm

4

Combatting Depression

Alan Carr

Introduction

Major depression is an episodic disorder characterized by major depressive episodes and intervening periods of normal mood. This is distinguished from dysthymia, which is a milder but more persistent mood disorder, characterized by chronic low mood for at least a year in young people, accompanied by fewer additional cognitive or behavioural symptoms than are required for a diagnosis of a major-depressive disorder. The diagnostic criteria for a major depressive episode are described in ICD-10 (World Health Organization, 1992) and DSM-IV-TR (American Psychiatric Association, 2000).

Epidemiology, course and sex differences

In a review of 18 epidemiological studies, Costello et al. (2004) found prevalence rates for major depression in youngsters under 18 to range from 0.2 to 12.9 per cent, with a median of 4.7 per cent. Depression is more common among young people than children, more common among teenage girls than boys and very common among clinical populations (Costello et al., 2002).

The majority of young people recover from a depressive episode within a year, about a tenth relapse during the following year, about a third relapse within four years and inter-episode intervals decrease as more episodes occur (Lewinsohn et al., 1994). Depression often persists into adulthood and it is a risk factor for suicide (Harrington and Dubicka, 2001). Treatment of depressed young people with tricyclic antidepressants (TCAs) is ineffective (Hazell et al., 2002). Treatment with selective serotonin reuptake inhibitors (SSRIs) is effective in some cases (Cheung et al., 2005), but there is still controversy about the potential for SSRIs to increase suicide risk in young people (Gibbons et al., 2006). Children and young people with depression are at a higher risk of suicide than youngsters with other disorders, so the assessment and management of suicide risk is a priority when dealing with depressed young people (NICE, 2004).

Aetiology

Environmental factors that place undue stress on youngsters, outstripping their coping capacities and occurring in the absence of social support, interact with genetic factors and may initially render youngsters psychologically vulnerable to depression. Later, they may precipitate the onset of depressive episodes and prevent recovery or lead to a relapse (Goodyer, 2001). Loss of important relationships, failure experiences, bullying, illnesses and injuries, and disruptive life transitions such as moving house or the onset of puberty, all constitute stressful life events.

Non-optimal early parenting environments are particularly important sources of environmental stress and deserve special mention. Such environments include those characterized by lack of parental attunement, parental psychopathology (notably maternal depression and paternal substance use), family conflict, stressful parental separation, domestic violence and child maltreatment, all of which may be influenced by wider sociocultural factors, such as poverty and social isolation (Shortt and Spence, 2006).

On the positive side, personal and contextual protective factors may reduce the likelihood of depression or contribute to recovery from it. These include intelligence, problem-solving skills, an active coping style, the capacity for self-reflection, self-esteem, an internal locus of control and sense of mastery, higher levels of physical activity, good social skills, a supportive cohesive family, a positive school environment, supportive peer relationships and a supportive community (Shortt and Spence, 2006).

Prevention of Depression in Young People

In a systematic review of the primary prevention programmes for depression in young people aged 5 to 19 years old, Merry et al. (2004) identified 21 well-designed studies. They found that the psychological, but not educational, prevention programmes showed some evidence of efficacy. In the studies of psychological interventions, a range of programmes was evaluated, including the PENN Resiliency Programme (Freres et al., 2002), Coping with Stress Course (Clarke and Lewinsohn, 1995), Resourceful Adolescent Programme (Shochet, 2002), Problem Solving for Life programme (Sheffield et al., 2006) and FRIENDS programme (Barrett et al., 2000).

These programmes share a number of features. They are brief (under 20 sessions), manualized, structured interventions that can be delivered to groups of young people in classroom settings. They are all theoretically-based, and draw on social learning theory, cognitive behaviour therapy and a diathesis stress model of depression. They all involve skills training, as well as didactic teaching methods and group discussion.

Within these courses, young people learn a coherent framework within which to conceptualize factors affecting low mood and the self-regulation of emotional states. They also learn and practise skills for the self-monitoring of mood and related thoughts, behaviour patterns, interpersonal transactions and stressful events.

The development of a variety of coping skills and strategies for regulating negative mood states is also central to all of these programmes, although the precise subset of skills varies from programme to programme. These skills and strategies include challenging depressive and pessimistic thinking styles, using relaxation skills to control anxiety, systematic problem-solving skills to manage stressful situations, soliciting social support from family and friends, scheduling pleasant events and preventing the build-up of life stresses.

Merry et al. (2004), found that psychological prevention programmes led to significant reductions in depressive symptoms in studies that targeted youngsters at risk of depression (effect size = .26), but to non-significant reductions in depressive symptoms in those delivered to whole populations (effect size = .21). They also found that, averaging across all types of studies, prevention programmes had signif-icant short-term effects and reduced depressive symptoms (effect size = .26) or rates of depressive syndromes when improvement was assessed immediately after pro-gramme completion. Over follow-up periods of one to three years, however, these positive effects 'washed out' and the programmes overall did not have a significant long-term benefit for young people in terms of reducing depression.

The Assessment and Treatment of Depression

When young people present with low mood, a preliminary assessment is essential to determine if depression is the core issue.

Assessment

Assessment for depression should begin with a broad screening for psychological dif-ficulties. If this suggests that there are mood problems, a more detailed assessment of depressive symptoms may be conducted. If appropriate, this may be followed by structured interviewing about depressive syndromes. Then, a wider interview cover-ing risk and protective factors mentioned in the previous section, along with a sui-cide risk assessment, should be conducted. Guidelines for such broader interviews are given in Carr (2006).

For screening school-aged young people for any type of psychological disorder, including depression, the Achenbach System of Empirically Based Assessment (ASEBA) (Achenbach and Rescorla, 2001) and the Behavioural Assessment System for Children (BASC) (Reynolds and Kamphaus, 2004) are very useful.

If they screen positive for mood disorders on the brief ASEBA or BASC depression scales, a more detailed assessment of depressive symptoms may be obtained with more comprehensive mood-evaluation instruments, such as the Beck Depression Inventory for Youth (BDIY) (Beck et al., 2005).

Where elevated scores occur on depressive symptom assessment instruments, it is appropriate to conduct a structured interview with schedules, such as the Development and Well-being Assessment (DAWBA) (Goodman et al., 2000) or Diagnostic Interview Schedule for Children (DISC-IV) (Shaffer et al., 2000) to assess depression from a syndromal perspective.

The Effectiveness of Different Treatments

In a comprehensive meta-analysis of 35 randomized controlled studies of psy-chotherapy for depression in young people, Weisz et al. (2006) found that the average treated case fared better than 63 per cent of untreated cases. They also found that there were no significant differences in outcome between cognitive behavioural treatments and other treatments or between treatments conducted under optimal or routine clinical conditions. Treatment gains were maintained at six months, but not at a one year follow-up.

Cognitive behavioural therapy (CBT)

There is evidence from reviews by Harrington et al. (1998), Lewinsohn and Clarke (1999) and Reinecke et al. (1998) to support the effectiveness of CBT in the treatment of depression in young people. Collectively, the results from these reviews indicate that just over 60 per cent, to just over 70 per cent of young people diagnosed with a depressive disorder benefited from CBT. CBT for depression rests on the hypothesis that low mood is maintained by a depressive thinking style and constricted lifestyle that entails low rates of response-contingent positive reinforcement.

CBT programmes for young people evaluated in treatment trials have two main components that target these two maintaining factors: challenging depressive thinking and behavioural activation (Compton et al. 2004). In challenging depressive thinking, young people learn mood monitoring and how to identify and challenge depressive negative automatic thoughts and cognitive distortions that accompany decreases in mood.

With behavioural activation, youngsters reorganize their daily routines so that they involve more pleasant events, physical exercise and social interaction. They also develop skills to support this process, including social skills, relaxation skills, communication and problem-solving skills and relapse prevention skills.

Some CBT programmes for depression in young people include concurrent intervention with parents, which helps them understand factors that maintain depression and support youngsters in following through on the behavioural activation and cognitive components of the child-focused part of the programme. CBT usually spans 10 to 20 young person-focused sessions and may be offered on an individual or group basis. Where concurrent parent sessions occur, usually about five to ten of these are offered. Stallard's (2002, 2005) Think Good, Feel Good programme is a useful clinical resource that combines many aspects of effective cognitive behavioural approaches to depression in young people.

In an important comparative trial, Weersing and Brent (2003) found that, immediately after treatment, more youngsters who received CBT (60 per cent) were in remission compared with those who received family therapy (38 per cent) or supportive therapy (39 per cent). At two years' follow-up, however, there were no significant differences between the outcomes of the three groups. The positive effects of CBT arose predominantly from changes in depressive cognitive distortions. The results of this study suggest, however, that it may be worthwhile combining individually orientated, CBT and family therapy, aiming to address both intrapsychic and interpersonal depression-maintaining factors and extend therapy beyond 16 sessions so that additional services are not required.

Psychodynamic therapy

Only a single, randomized controlled trial provides evidence for the effectiveness of psychodynamic psychotherapy with depressed young people. In the trial,

72 youngsters aged 9 to 15 were assigned to psychodynamic or family therapy and Trowell et al. (2007) found that about 75 per cent of cases in both groups were fully recovered after therapy. All of those who received psychodynamic therapy and 81 per cent of those who received family therapy were fully recovered at six months' follow-up (but this group difference was not significant). Psychodynamic and family therapy also led to a significant reduction of double depression (major depression with comorbid dysthymia) and rates of other comorbid conditions.

In the study, psychodynamic therapy involved an average of 25 individual sessions and 12 concurrent parent sessions spanning nine months, following a manual based on Malan's (1995) model of brief psychodynamic psychotherapy. In this model, the focus is on interpreting the links between defences, anxiety and unconscious feelings and impulses within the context of the transference relationship with the therapist, relationships with significant people in the young person's current life and early relationships with parents or carers. Family therapy involved an average of 11 sessions spanning nine months.

Interpersonal therapy (IPT)

There is evidence from a number of studies that interpersonal psychotherapy is an effective treatment for depression in young people that leads to recovery in more than 75 per cent of cases. Interpersonal therapy for depression in young people targets five interpersonal difficulties that are assumed to be of particular importance in maintaining depression:

- grief associated with the loss of a loved one
- role disputes involving family members and friends
- role transitions, such as starting or ending relationships within family, school or peer group contexts, moving houses, graduation or diagnosis of an illness
- interpersonal deficits, particularly poor social skills for making and maintaining relationships
- relationship difficulties associated with living in a single-parent family.

In IPT, the specific focal interpersonal factors that maintain the young person's depressive symptoms are addressed within a series of child-focused and conjoint family sessions. Mufson et al.'s (2004) *Interpersonal Psychotherapy for Depressed Adolescents* provides detailed guidance on this approach to therapy.

Family therapy

There is evidence from several studies of the effectiveness of family therapy for treating depression and suicidal tendencies in young people (Curry et al., 2003; Diamond et al., 2002; Sanford et al., 2006; Trowell et al., 2007; Weersing and Brent, 2003).

In a comparative study, Trowell et al. (2007) found that having 11 sessions of family therapy was as effective as part of a programme that included 25 sessions of psychodynamic therapy, coupled with 12 adjunctive parent sessions. The therapy helped families understand the links between the young person's depression, problematic family scripts and insecure family attachment patterns.

In another comparative study, Weersing and Brent (2003) found that only 38 per cent of depressed young people recovered immediately after family therapy, but, at two years' follow-up, 77 per cent no longer met the criteria for depression. Family therapy was less effective in the short-term, but as effective in the long-term as CBT. Improvements in family functioning accounted for the young people's recovery.

A behavioural systems approach to family therapy was used in the trial. This involved using family-based behavioural interventions, such as problem monitoring, communication and problem-solving skills training, contingency contracting and relapse prevention to reduce family conflict, enhance family relationships and promote better mood management.

In a controlled study of attachment-based family therapy for depression with 32 young people, Diamond et al. (2002) found that, after treatment, 81 per cent of treated cases no longer met the criteria for depression, whereas 47 per cent of the waiting list control group did. At six months' follow-up, 87 per cent of people were not depressed.

Attachment-based family therapy involves the following sequence of interventions: relational reframing, building alliances with the young person first and then with the parents, repairing attachment relationships between parents and young people and building family competency (Diamond, 2005).

In a controlled trial involving the families of 31 young people, Sanford et al. (2006) evaluated the incremental benefit of adding psycho-educational family therapy to a routine treatment programme involving predominantly supportive counselling and SSRI antidepressant medication. Three months after treatment, 75 per cent of the family therapy group and 47 per cent of controls no longer met the criteria for depression and relationships between parents and the young people in the family therapy group were significantly better than in the control group. A 13-session, home-based, family therapy model was used in this study, which included psycho-education about depression, communication and problem-solving skills training, plus relapse prevention.

A single group outcome study with young people with comorbid depression and substance abuse found that, after a combined programme of CBT and family therapy, 50 per cent of cases recovered from depression and 66 per cent from substance abuse. The programme spanned 10 weeks, with weekly family therapy sessions and twice-weekly CBT group sessions. Robin and Foster's (1989) model of family therapy for negotiating conflict between parents and young people was used in this programme.

Collectively, these studies lend support for both attachment-based and psycho-educationally-orientated cognitive behavioural approaches to family therapy as effective treatments for depressed young people.

Conclusion

Depression is a problem for a significant minority of young people. It is caused and maintained by both biological and psychosocial factors. Prevention programmes that facilitate the development of mood management and self-regulation skills, targeting young people shown to be at risk of depression, have significant positive short-term effects. Such programmes may be offered within a school context. In clinical settings, where young people present with a low mood, psychological treatment may be offered following a thorough assessment. Effective protocols for mild to moderate depression have been developed within the cognitive behavioural, interpersonal, psychodynamic and family therapy traditions. These protocols should be flexibly applied in clinical practice, taking due account of the clinical formulations of clients' unique profiles of personal and contextual predisposing, precipitating, maintaining and protective factors. In light of such clinical formulations, a case may be made for combining components of treatment protocols for the young person and the family that have been shown to be effective, to address specific elements within a client's formulation (Carr, 2006).

The available evidence suggests that family-based interventions for depression in young people should include family psycho-education, facilitating family understanding and support of the depressed young person and organizing a home–school liaison to help them re-establish normal home and school routines.

Evidence suggests that interventions focused on the young person involve an exploration of contributing factors, some of which may be outside their awareness – facilitating mood monitoring, increasing physical exercise, social activity and pleasant events, the modification of depressive thinking styles, depression-maintaining defence mechanisms and depression-maintaining patterns of social interaction, the development and use of social problem-solving skills, and the development of relapse prevention skills.

The evidence also suggests that a dozen family sessions and twice as many individual sessions are probably necessary to treat mild to moderate depression in young people. With severe depression, where clients show no response to a brief trial of psychotherapy, a trial of SSRIs combined with psychotherapy may be appropriate. Caution is warranted regarding using SSRIs to treat young people, however, as they may increase the risk of suicide.

These conclusions are broadly consistent with international guidelines for best practice (American Academy of Child and Adolescent Psychiatry, 1998; NICE, 2005).

Resources

Therapy manuals

Byng-Hall, J. (1995) *Rewriting Family Scripts: Improvisation and change*. New York: Guilford Press. (A family therapy approach that may be used for depression in children and adolescents.)

Langelier, C. (2001) *Mood Management Leader's Manual: A cognitive-behavioural skills-building program for adolescents*. Thousand Oaks, CA: Sage.

Malan, D. (1995) *Individual Psychotherapy and the Science of Psychodynamics* (2nd edn). Oxford: Butterworth-Heinemann. (A psychodynamic approach that may be used for adolescent depression.)

Mufson, L., Dorta Pollacle, K., Moreau, D. and Weissman, M. (2004) *Interpersonal Psychotherapy for Depressed Adolescents* (2nd edn). New York: Guilford Press.

Stallard, P. (2002) *Think Good – Feel Good: A cognitive behaviour therapy workbook for children and young people.* Chichester: Wiley.

Stallard, P. (2005) *A Clinician's Guide to Think Good – Feel Good: The use of CBT with children and young people.* Chichester: Wiley.

Self-help books

Fitzpatrick, C. (2004) *Coping with Depression in Young People: A guide for parents.* Chichester, UK: Wiley.

Langelier, C. (2001b) *Mood Management: A cognitive-behavioural skills-building program for adolescents: skills workbook.* Thousand Oaks, CA: Sage.

Websites

Adolescent Coping with Stress Class: Leader Manual www.kpchr.org/public/acwd/CWS_MANUAL.pdf

Brent's therapy manuals www.Starcenter.pitt.edu or BrentDA@upmc.edu

FRIENDS Programme www.friendsinfo.net

Problem Solving for Life Programme jeanie@psy.uq.edu.au

Resourceful Adolescent Programme www.hlth.qut.edu.au/psyc/rap/

Royal College of Psychiatrists www.rcpsych.ac.uk

Weisz's therapy manuals weisz@psych.ucla.edu

KEY POINTS

- Depression is commoner among young people than children and among teenage girls than boys and very common in clinical populations.
- Primary prevention programmes that are psychological rather than educational in nature have shown evidence of efficacy.
- Where mood problems are identified, a more detailed assessment of depressive symptoms may be indicated.
- Cognitive behavioural therapy, psychodynamic therapy, interpersonal therapy and family therapy have all been demonstrated as being useful for some young people with regard to treating depression.

QUESTIONS FOR DISCUSSION

1. Why do you think prevention programmes have a significant short-term effect on adolescents at risk of depression, but less effect on populations that are not at risk and little effect in the long-term?
2. Why do you think cognitive behavioural therapy, interpersonal therapy, family therapy and psychodynamic psychotherapy all 'work' for adolescent depression when they are so different from each other?

References

Achenbach, T. and Rescorla, L. (2001) *Manual for ASEBA School-Age Forms & Profiles.* Burlington, VT: University of Vermont, Research Centre for Children, Youth, & Families.

American Academy of Child and Adolescent Psychiatry (1998) 'Practice parameters for the assessment and treatment of children and adolescents with depressive disorders', *Journal of the American Academy of Child and Adolescent Psychiatry,* 37: 63.

American Psychiatric Association (2000) *Diagnostic and Statistical Manual of the Mental Disorders* (4th edn) (*DSM-IV-TR*). Washington. DC: APA.

Barrett, P., Lowry-Webster, H. and Turner, C. (2000) *FRIENDS Programme for Youth: Group leader's manual.* Brisbane: Australian Academic Press.

Beck, J., Beck, A., Jolly, J. and Steer, R. (2005) *Beck Youth Inventories: For Children and Adolescents* (2nd edn) (BYI-II). San Antonio, TX: Harcourt Assessment.

Byng-Hall, J. (1995) *Rewriting Family Scripts: Improvisation and change.* New York: Guilford Press.

Carr, A. (2006) *Handbook of Child and Adolescent Clinical Psychology* (2nd edn). London: Routledge.

Cheung, A., Emslie, G. and Mayes, T. (2005) 'Review of the efficacy and safety of antidepressants in youth depression', *Journal of Child Psychology and Psychiatry,* 46 (7): 735–54.

Clarke, G. and Lewinsohn, R. (1995) *Adolescent Coping with Stress Class: Leaders manual.* Portland, OR: Kaiser Permanente Centre for Health Research.

Compton, S., March, J., Brent, D., Albano, A., Weersing, V. and Curry, J. (2004) 'Cognitive-behavioural psychotherapy for anxiety and depressive disorders in children and adolescents: an evidence-based medicine review', *Journal of the American Academy of Child and Adolescent Psychiatry,* 43: 930–59.

Costello, E., Mustillo, S., Keeler, G. and Angold, A. (2004) 'Prevalence of psychiatric disorders in childhood and adolescence', in L. Luborsky, J. Petrila and K. Hennessy (eds), *Mental Health Services: A public health perspective.* New York: Oxford University Press. pp. 111–28.

Costello, E., Pine, D., Hammen, C., March, J., Plotsky, P., Weissman, M., Biederman, J., Goldsmith, H., Kaufman, J., Lewinsohn, P., Hellander, M., Hoagwood, K., Koretz, D., Nelson, C. and Leckman, J. (2002) 'Development and natural history of mood disorders', *Biological Psychiatry,* 52: 529–42.

Curry, J., Wells, K., Lochman, J., Craighead, W. and Nagy, P. (2003) 'Cognitive-behavioural intervention for depressed, substance-abusing adolescents: development and pilot testing', *Journal of the American Academy of Child and Adolescent Psychiatry,* 42 (6): 656–65.

Diamond, G. (2005) 'Attachment-based family therapy for depressed and anxious adolescents', in J. Lebow (ed.), *Handbook of Clinical Family Therapy.* Hoboken, NJ: Wiley. pp. 17–41.

Diamond, G., Reis, B., Diamond, G., Siqueland, L. and Isaacs, L. (2002) 'Attachment-based family therapy for depressed adolescents: a treatment development study', *Journal of the American Academy of Child and Adolescent Psychiatry,* 41 (10): 1190–6.

Fitzpatrick, C. (2004) *Coping with Depression in Young People: A guide for parents.* Chichester, UK: Wiley.

Gibbons, R., Hur, K., Bhaumik, D. and Mann, J. (2006) 'The relationship between antidepressant prescription rates and rate of early adolescent suicide', *American Journal of Psychiatry,* 163: 1898–904.

Goodman, R., Ford, T., Richards, H. Gatward, R. and Meltzer, H. (2000) 'The Development and Well-being Assessment: description and initial validation of an integrated assessment of child and adolescent psychopathology', *Journal of Child Psychology and Psychiatry and Allied Disciplines,* 41 (5): 645–55.

Goodyer, I. (2001) 'Life events: their nature and effects', in I. Goodyer (ed.), *The Depressed Child and Adolescent* (2nd edn). Cambridge: Cambridge University Press. pp. 204–32.

Hankin, B.L. and Abramson, L.Y. (2001) 'Development of gender differences in depression: an elaborated cognitive vulnerability-transactional stress theory', *Psychological Bulletin,* 127: 773–96.

Harrington, R. and Dubicka, B. (2001) 'Natural history of mood disorders in children and adolescents', in I. Goodyer (ed.), *The Depressed Child and Adolescent* (2nd edn). Cambridge: Cambridge University Press, pp. 353–81.

Hazell, P., O'Connell, D., Heathcote, D. and Henry, D. (2002) 'Tricyclic drugs for depression in children and adolescents', *Cochrane Database of Systematic Reviews 2002,* Issue 2, Art. No.: CD002317. DOI: 10.1002/14651858.CD002317.

Langelier, C. (2001a) *Mood Management Leader's Manual: A cognitive-behavioural skills-building program for adolescents.* Thousand Oaks, CA: Sage.

Langelier, C. (2001b) *Mood Management: A cognitive-behavioural skills-building program for adolescents, skills workbook.* Thousand Oaks, CA: Sage.

Lewinsohn, P. and Clarke, G. (1999) 'Psychosocial treatments for adolescent depression', *Clinical Psychology Review,* 19 (3): 329–42.

Lewinsohn, P.M., Clarke, G.N., Seeley, J.R. and Rohde, P. (1994) 'Major depression in community adolescents: age at onset, episode duration, and time to recurrence', *Journal of the American Academy of Child & Adolescent Psychiatry,* 33: 809–18.

Luthar, S. (2003) *Resilience and Vulnerability: Adaptation in the Context of Childhood Adversities.* Cambridge: Cambridge University Press.

Malan, D. (1995) *Individual Psychotherapy and the Science of Psychodynamics* (2nd edn). Oxford: Butterworth-Heinemann.

Merry, S., McDowell, H., Hetrick, S., Bir, J. and Muller, N. (2004) 'Psychological and/ or educational interventions for the prevention of depression in children and adolescents', *Cochrane Database of Systematic Reviews 2004,* Issue 1, Art. No.: CD003380. DOI: 10.1002/14651858.CD003380.pub2.

Mufson, L., Dorta Pollack, K., Moreau, D. and Weissman M. (2004) *Interpersonal Psychotherapy for Depressed Adolescents* (2nd edn). New York: Guilford Press.

NICE (2004) *Self-harm: The short-term physical and psychological management and secondary prevention of self-harm in primary and secondary care.* London: National Institute for Clinical Excellence.

NICE (2005) *Depression in Children and Young People: Identification and management in primary, community and secondary care.* London: National Institute for Clinical Excellence.

Reinecke, M., Ryan, N. and Dubois, D. (1998) 'Cognitive-behavioural therapy of depression and depressive symptoms during adolescence: a review and meta-analysis', *Journal of the American Academy of Child and Adolescent Psychiatry,* 37 (1): 26–34.

Reynolds, C. and Kamphaus, R. (2004) *Behaviour Assessment System for Children* (2nd edn) (BASC-2). Circle Pines, MN: American Guidance Service Publishing.

Robin, A. and Foster, S. (1989) *Negotiating Parent – Adolescent Conflict: A behavioral-family systems approach.* New York: Guilford Press.

Sanford, M., Boyle, M., McCleary, L., Miller, J., Steele, M., Duku, E. and Offord, D. (2006) 'A pilot study of adjunctive family psychoeducation in adolescent major depression: feasibility and treatment effect', *Journal of the American Academy of Child and Adolescent Psychiatry,* 45 (4): 386–95.

Shaffer, D., Fisher, P., Lucas, C.P., Dulcan, M.K. and Schwab-Stone, M.E. (2000) 'NIMH diagnostic interview schedule for children version IV (NIMH DISC-IV): description, differences from previous versions, and reliability of some common diagnoses', *Journal of the American Academy of Child and Adolescent Psychiatry,* 39: 28–38.

Sheffield, J., Spence, S. and Rapee, R. (2006) 'Evaluation of universal, indicated, and combined cognitive-behavioural approaches to the prevention of depression among adolescents', *Journal of Consulting and Clinical Psychology,* 74: 66–79.

Shochet, I. (2002) 'The Resourceful Adolescent Program (RAP): building resilience and preventing depression in adolescents through universal school-based interventions', in L. Rowling, G. Martin and L. Walker (eds), *Mental Health Promotion in Young People: Concepts and practice.* Sydney: Mcgraw-Hill. pp. 172–84.

Shortt, A. and Spence, S. (2006) 'Risk and protective factors for depression in youth', *Behaviour Change,* 23 (1): 1–30.

Stallard, P. (2002) *Think Good – Feel Good: A cognitive behaviour therapy workbook for children and young people.* Chichester: Wiley.

Stallard, P. (2005) *A Clinician's Guide to Think Good – Feel Good: The use of CBT with children and young people.* Chichester: Wiley.

Trowell, R., Joffe, I., Campbell, J., Clemente, C., Almqvist, F., Soininen, M., Koskenranta-Aalto, U., Weintraub, S., Kolaitis, G., Tomaras, G., Anastasopolous, D., Grayson, K., Barnes, J. and Tsiantis, J. (2007) 'Childhood depression: a place for psychotherapy: an outcome study comparing individual psychodynamic psychotherapy and family therapy', *European and Adolescent Psychiatry,* 16: 157–67.

Weersing, V. and Brent, D. (2003) 'Cognitive behavioural therapy for adolescent depression', in A. Kazdin and J. Weisz (eds), *Evidence-Based Psychotherapies for Children and Adolescents.* New York: Guilford Press. pp. 135–47.

Weisz, J., McCarty, C. and Valeri, S. (2006) 'Effects of psychotherapy for depression in children and adolescents: a meta-analysis', *Psychological Bulletin,* 132: 132–49.

World Health Organization (1992) *The ICD-10 Classification of Mental and Behavioural Disorders: Clinical descriptions and diagnostic guidelines.* Geneva: WHO.

5

Empowering Young People Who Self-harm

Jude Sellen

Introduction

It is widely recognized that professionals working in children's services frequently feel uncomfortable and lack confidence when it comes to supporting children and young people who self-harm (Mental Health Foundation, 2006). Self-harm provokes a wide range of strong emotional responses. It is argued here that, while it may be useful for staff to attend training courses offering facts and figures, these alone do very little to build professionals' confidence. Leaving a training day knowing that one young person every 30 minutes tries to take their life, that on average two children in every secondary school class self-harm, that ice cubes and elastic bands can be useful harm-minimization techniques and so forth, does not address the attitudes a professional may hold about self-injury.

Acknowledging one's attitude to self-harming behaviour and, in turn, encouraging workers to understand how their attitude impacts on their work with young people who self-harm is essential in developing a positive working relationship with a young person who self-harms. Attitudinal change can contribute to positive relationships that optimize future work with young people.

This chapter outlines a training programme developed for workers that specifically addresses attitude and attitudinal change towards young people who self-harm (Sellen, 2006). It also describes how the training has been adapted for young people who self-harm, with the goal of influencing their attitude to self-harming behaviour. Materials for the training workshop described were developed in collaboration with groups of young people who self-harm (Sellen, 2006).

A Model to Support Attitudinal Change

An attitude is 'a state of readiness, a tendency to respond in a certain manner when confronted with certain stimuli' (Oppenheim, 2001).

For many workers who meet with young people who self-harm, the self-harming behaviour and its consequences are a disturbing stimulus, evoking responses that are often not useful when providing help. Such responses are related to the workers' attitude. The quotes below are statements of attitude made by participants during an introductory session in a training workshop entitled, 'Empowering young people who self-harm and those who seek to support them' (Sellen, 2006).

> I work in a school and, quite frankly, I don't have any time for these young people who self-harm. I know I shouldn't probably say this, but they make me feel cross and I'm not sure if its nothing but 'copy cat' behaviour.

> I work in a busy A&E department and they [the young people who have self-harmed] take up time I should be spending on people who have a genuine need for nursing care and what I came into nursing for.

Many will recognize the above quotes as the kinds of comments that they have heard from colleagues with regard to self-harm. It can be useful to examine these statements and explore the attitude that they express.

Constructs of attitude

The training workshop aims to gradually construct a framework for understanding one's personal attitude to young people who self-harm by exploring the components of this attitude. We begin by looking at where our attitudes derive from, how they are fuelled and how they manifest themselves. This is done by examining how attitudes are constructed. For example, we explore three components that construct an attitude (Oppenheim, 2001):

- cognitive
- emotional
- action tendency.

'Cognitive' here refers to the component of an attitude that is reinforced by our thoughts and beliefs. The 'emotional' component is the part of an attitude that can attract strong feelings. The 'action tendency' component of an attitude leads to particular behaviours or intentions.

Participants complete exercises encouraging them to build a picture of their attitude to self-harm that will enable them to support their future work with young people. It is proposed that this framework can also be used to underpin a programme of work with young people who self-harm. At the end of the training workshop, participants review the attitude they held at the start with that held at the end of the training, and are encouraged to consider how they might apply a 'model of attitudinal change' in their future work with young people.

Exercises to explore changes in attitude to self-harming behaviour

During the workshop training, participants are first asked to state why they have attended the workshop (voluntarily or mandatory) and what they hope to get out of it. Ideally, participants will come from a wide range of children's services and mental health professional backgrounds. Such a cross-section ensures that there are representatives from a variety of the agencies working in the local geographical area – from schools (both primary and secondary), children's social services, youth services, juvenile justice, primary and secondary health services, adult mental health, A&E departments and a variety of local voluntary-sector services targeting young people who experience a wide range of expressions of mental distress.

The quotes cited above are the starting point – they represent the many attitudes participants bring to the day. It is important to return to them at the end of the training so that participants can reflect on any changes to these positions. For many participants, the change in their attitude can be quite significant.

The cognitive component of attitude

The first exercise in the workshop considers the 'cognitive' component of an attitude. The exercise was designed by the Bristol Crisis Service for Women who self-injure (Arnold, 1997), the group kindly giving their permission for its inclusion in my training materials (Sellen, 2006).

Participants are divided into small groups (no larger than five people per group). Each group is invited to consider six 'acts' of self-harm and then to list them in what they think is the order of severity. The 'acts' include bingeing and vomiting, people cutting their arms, drinking alone, insomnia through overwork, regular gambling and smoking (cigarettes).

Deliberately, no contextual details are given as they would be likely to distract participants' attention away from examining the constructs that underpin their attitude to looking for causal factors for the acts. They are encouraged to focus on their own attitude towards the acts, as reflected in their perceptions of their relative severity, rather than the behaviour of the young person.

The participants are requested to share and make notes about the decision making process used within their groups. This will be informed by the diversity of personal attitudes with regard to each of the acts.

This exercise usually provokes a wideranging discussion, leading to conclusions ranging from concern about the self-destructive impacts on the individuals described – 'They [the acts] are all as bad as each other for a person' – to conclusions that consider the impacts of the act on the wider community – 'Well, in terms of the cost to the health service, it's gotta be smoking [judged the most serious] hasn't it?' – and, interestingly, to a consideration of definitions of self-harm that are not generally seen as being self-inflicted – 'When I came here this morning, I would have put cutting arms at the top, but now, thinking about it, I think a person drinking alone is harming themselves potentially far more'.

Some groups separate the acts into those that are 'socially acceptable', 'hidden', 'carried out in isolation' and '[those that] can provoke more fear in the professional'.

Interestingly, when young people who self-harm complete this exercise and are pushed to cite the one act that they consider the most serious, they will usually conclude that it is 'smoking'. Otherwise, as with some of the groups of professionals, young participants will mostly list the acts as being broadly equally self-harming.

When training workers, this exercise seeks to remind participants of the extent to which our attitude informs both the lesser and more significant judgements that we make about behaviours we support or reject. What we assume to be a judgement based on a 'rational attitude' may in fact not be rational at all, but, rather, a response informed by specific socially constructed discourses that influence the way we make sense of the world and how we think people should live.

It is likely that, by not exploring the foundations for the attitude we hold, we are at risk of ignoring the individual beliefs and foundations that contribute to the way young people develop their attitude with regard to self-harming behaviour. As a result, our behaviours in relationships with young people who self-harm may be affected. For example, on meeting a young person who smokes and who at times may drink alone, our own attitude may allow us to accept this as being normal behaviour for many young people. This, in turn, can lead to a more relaxed way of relating to the young person. In contrast, when faced with a young person with scars and cuts on their arms, we can feel less relaxed as our attitude might be that this is not normal. Yet, in both instances, the acts are intentional, have motivations and lead to similar outcomes – mainly mood changes. For example, many young people who self-harm describe feelings of relief from the anxiety associated with depression when they do so.

Being open to exploring our attitude encourages an openness to exploring the attitudes held by the young people we work with. It can be particularly useful for young people and practitioners alike to share their own processes of attitudinal change when working together.

The emotional component of attitude

In order to explore the 'emotional' component of an attitude, participants are invited to complete a number of 'feelings' exercises. One such exercise is described below. It requires participants, still in their small groups, to remain silent while listening to a scenario, then, individually and in silence, they write down, on a large piece of flipchart paper, single words to describe the feelings that it provoked.

Scenario example

> You are waiting to meet a young woman aged 14 years. You've not met her before. As she comes into the room to meet you, she is wearing knee-high boots, a very short denim skirt, she is slender in build with shoulder-length blond hair. She has a long-sleeved white T-shirt with both the sleeves coming to just below the elbow, over which is a black vest T-shirt.
>
> You notice beneath the edge of her skirt on her left thigh that there are a number of marks that resemble burns. On her left wrist and arm there are both fresh scratches and some old scars, most probably caused by deeper wounds.

How do you feel?

The participants quietly write down their feelings. Some find it hard not to start writing words that reflect the *actions* they wish to take. While participants write down their feelings, the trainer turns the flipchart board away from the group and writes the following list of feelings: helpless, angry, frustrated, embarrassed, sad, lonely, horrified, concerned.

A representative from each small group reads out to the other groups all the words on its sheet of paper. It's important to note the words that come up repeatedly. Feelings that come up time and time again whenever this exercise has been completed in the UK include anxious, worried, frightened, maternal, angry, concerned, unsure, sad, while many say they feel curious.

The group is then asked to compare the two lists. The feelings most consistently expressed by participants are sad, concerned, angry and helpless. The trainer's list is a list of feelings that young people who self-harm say they feel most frequently – feelings they struggle to contain when meeting professionals.

The value of sharing these respective lists and seeing the similarities cannot be overstated. It usefully leads the workshop on to explore the third component of an attitude – the action tendency.

The action tendency component of an attitude

What do we do with the feelings evoked in us when working with a young person who self-harms? We act.

Both the professional and young person will in part act in ways to manage their feelings. It is within this context that their relationship begins. Both parties will make certain decisions about the ways in which they will behave towards each other and the chosen 'action tendency' that manifests itself will be the outcome of the two previous components – cognitive and emotional.

For professionals, the initial contact with the young person frequently commences in a context framed by a risk assessment. That risk assessment context influences the relationship climate and is in direct contradiction to the relationship climate hoped for by the young person when they enter the room – one of non-judgemental support.

At this stage in the training the impact of possible different positions between the worker and the young person is explored. It is helpful for the trainer to illustrate these positions pictorially on a continuum as polarized responses. The dominant message encourages professionals to be transparent and honest by sharing their attitude to self-harm.

Following the exercises described above, workshop participants are encouraged to explore ways in which they might in the future begin to have a conversation about attitude to self-harm with a young person with a view to providing a less threatening starting point than they did before.

Workshop discussion: how can cognition, emotion and action components work together to contribute to attitudinal change?

Having examined the three components of an attitude, the next task is to explore the possibilities of attitudinal change occurring in both the young person and the worker. It is useful at this point in the workshop for the trainer to remind the participants that young people often say they do not feel heard. Similarly, professional workers repeatedly express concern that young people find it hard to share their feelings with them.

Because young people who self-harm have often developed strong attitudes about their self-harming behaviours – for example, attitudes regarding the role it serves in their life or about the reception they expect to experience from others who do not self-harm – it is important at this point in the workshop to try and find a rationale for the respective experiences of both the young person and the professional. Furthermore, it also becomes an opportunity to understand the potential role that self-harm can play in maintaining feelings of separateness, both experienced and acted out by the young person and, at times, the professional.

Discussions in workshops have led to some enlightening discoveries. For example, it seems that professionals work very hard at trying to make sense of often very complex and alien presentations of behaviour by young people, while also trying to provide an environment in which the young person feels comfortable to talk openly. Participants have recognized the potential for miscommunication between themselves as a professional and the young person. Additionally, they have realized that, in many cases, both young person and professionals will be working very hard to disguise their feelings and may feel vulnerable.

> There is no room for my feelings. That would be unprofessional.
> *School counsellor*

Reports from participants often indicate that the professional will work hard to maintain a sense of separateness between their personal feelings and their professional stance – a stance that often involves asking the young person a number of questions, usually associated with trying to establish whether or not they are at risk of either significantly harming themselves and/or suicide.

Equally, professionals often focus on the external, physical manifestations of the self-harm, thinking do their injuries require treatment, are they likely to lose consciousness, what and how many tablets have they taken, should they be taken to the local hospital, do the cuts look like only scratches, indicating that the young person can't be that distressed, and maybe it's just copy cat behaviour?

In this way, the professional strives to make sense of how someone could want to hurt themselves, while also seeking to manage their own sense of personal and professional vulnerability:

> I see a lot of this these days, I know it's just their way of coping, but what if I get it wrong?

Participants begin to gain greater insight into how their responses can lead to a state of separateness between them and the young person they are trying to help as they (the professional) seek to push their feelings to one side. Perhaps, like the school counsellor quoted above, they consider it 'unprofessional' to express their own feelings and do not wish to burden the young person by showing any of their own anxieties and concerns. This dynamic is reinforced by the risk assessment framework, where the professional is required to focus on a mechanistic assessment of the likelihood of further self-harm.

I would argue that the risk assessment framework can itself also amplify the professional's need to focus on the external landscape of the young person; that is, the visible impact of self-harm on the young person's body. Seeing a young person's external pain and mental and emotional distress manifested in physical cuts, wounds, burns, scalds and so on can be very distressing for the professional. This often results in the professional needing to manage the feelings evoked by separating them from their actions. Such practice appears to be common and an example of how an 'action tendency' is adopted. The need for the professional to manage their feelings of distress, concern and vulnerability (their 'internal landscape') is manifested in their 'externalized landscape' (the ways in which the professional behaves towards the young person). This is frequently perceived and experienced by the young person as detached, distanced behaviour. As some young people say, 'they [the professional] just seem aloof'. The relationship between the professional and young person becomes one where each manages their respective internal landscapes without recognizing that both are allowing the impact of self-harm to further suppress their feelings. This, in turn, perpetuates a state of disconnectedness or separation.

The act of self-harm can also, however, provide a bridge across which communication between the professional and young person can be negotiated. Indeed, any acts of self-harm by the young person arguably become the instrument of negotiation – they are, after all, what has led to them meeting with the professional. We frequently hear of young person who always takes an overdose when they know a nurse who is kind to them at their local A&E department is on duty.

Participants are encouraged to consider how a professional and young person can develop a shared understanding of the role self-harm can play in each of their lives. This is the crux of creating a supportive working relationship, underpinned by a shared attitude with regard to self-harm that, I would argue, ultimately defuses the potency of the self-harming behaviour and, in time, renders it ineffective.

By recognizing the externalizing role self-harm plays in perpetuating a state of separateness, both individually within the professional and the young person, and between them in the therapeutic relationship, both parties can discover ways to manage their respective external landscapes, thereby feeling empowered, not helpless. The challenge for the professional is to understand how the 'action tendency' component of an attitude can in itself perpetuate and/or reinforce a state of 'separateness'.

If participants then return to the exercise that explored the emotional component of an attitude, they begin to see that both the professional and the young person come to their meeting with some fundamentally similar feelings. Similarly, when examining the action tendency component, both the professional's and the young person's actions appear to be similarly motivated.

Most participants acknowledge that professionals want to encourage young people to explore the feelings that they believe to be masked by the self-harming behaviours, with the aim of helping them to recognize what is going on in their internal landscape. I would argue, however, that, if a professional does not have sufficient, if any, opportunities to examine their own internal landscape and how their own attitudes about self-harm shape these, it is likely that they may inadvertently mirror the young person's state of detachment. Menninger (1938; 1985), for example, argues convincingly that self-harm is experienced by a young person as being valuable in maintaining a state of separateness between their external and internal worlds. As a consequence, it is likely that the young person may have very little sense of safety or confidence in connecting with emotions and considering emotional strategies for managing difficult situations and instead will have adopted physical strategies.

Participants are therefore encouraged to explore ways in which a relationship with a young person can be created that does not place the physical manifestations of the self-harming behaviour centre stage and, instead, to consider how they can engage with the inner world of their own feelings and those of the young person, by means of a change in attitude.

The training workshop concludes with a consideration of how participants can apply this model of attitudinal change in their work with young people. Feedback from participants indicates that such an attitudinal change provides an opportunity to expand the focus of their engagement with a young person, as illustrated by a comparison of the views expressed by participants at the start of workshops and at the end. For example:

View 1

> I work in a school and, quite frankly, I don't have any time for these young people who self-harm. I know I shouldn't probably say this, but they make me feel cross and I'm not sure if it's nothing but copy cat behaviour.

This participant found that the workshop led them to question what they now saw to be a punitive position, founded in the cognitive components of their attitude. A lack of information about how a young person can learn to separate their internal and external landscapes had, in the past, increased the likelihood of this participant mirroring the young person's sense of helplessness.

This participant also came to see that the emotional component of their attitude included feelings of helplessness provoked by the visible manifestations of self-injury; for example cuts, scratches and so on.

As a result of examining these components, the participant concluded their future action tendency would significantly change – that they would need further supervision, but that they would be far more sympathetic to young people who self-harm.

View 2

> I want to understand more [about self-harm] so I can spot the ones who might try to commit suicide.

This participant identified herself as someone who was working hard to make *herself* feel safe by ensuring the safety of the young person.

On reflection, she could see that, despite the focus on safety being appropriate, it was a way of disguising her own high levels of anxiety within the emotional component of her attitude towards self-harm. Having recognized this and explored the origins of the cognitive component, she concluded that her action tendency would in future include a greater capacity to explore the internal land-scape with a young person as a consequence of having a greater understanding of her own.

Summary

The training workshop described in this chapter aims to encourage professionals to take a step back – an opportunity that is welcomed by many participants. The workshop provides a model that can be used to explore what shapes and under-pins our attitudes about self-harm, enabling professionals to adopt a similar process of exploration in their work with young people.

It is argued that acts of self-harm disguise a young person's internal landscape and engender strong emotional responses in those seeking to support them. In a parallel way, acts of self-harm by young people can lead to professionals working equally hard to disguise the impact on their own internal landscapes.

Adopting a model of attitudinal change can support professionals as they explore the components of their attitude to self-harm and, in turn, enable them to explore with the young person the components of *their* attitude to their par-ticular self-harming behaviours.

Supporting young people in this way offers both professionals and young people the opportunity to share and own their respective internal landscapes within the context of a safe, non-judgemental relationship.

Resources

Further reading

Arnold, L. (1997) *Working with People Who Self-injure*. Bristol: Bristol Crisis Service for Women.
National Self harm Network www.nshn.co.uk and info@nshn.co.uk
NICE, Self-harm: the short-term physical and psychological management and secondary pre-vention of self-harm in primary and secondary care www.nice.org.uk/Guidance/CG16
Young People and Self-harm, information resource www.selfharm.org.uk

---

KEY POINTS

- It is advantageous if training courses for workers who wish to work with young people who self-harm focus on attitudinal change.
- Being confronted by self-harm is a stimulus that may result in inappropriate responses by professionals due to their attitude.
- Constructs of attitude include cognitive, emotional and action tendency components.
- It can be helpful for the worker to create a supportive working relationship, underpinned by an attitude to self-harm that is shared with the young person concerned.

QUESTIONS FOR DISCUSSION

1. Discuss your beliefs with regard to the extent to which you believe that you can join with a young person who self-harms. What personal issues are relevant for you? Also, consider any issues that could arise for you with regard to other people's expectations.
2. Discuss the importance of supervision for workers who are involved with young people who self-harm. Why is supervision necessary and how can it be useful in helping to promote the best outcomes for a young client who self-harms?

References

Arnold, L. (1997) *Working with People who Self-injure*. Bristol: Bristol Crisis Service for Women.

Menniger, K. (1938; 1985) *Man Against Himself*. New York: Harcourt.

Mental Health Foundation/Camelot Foundation (2006) 'Truth hurts: report of the National Inquiry into Self-harm among Young People'. London: Mental Health Foundation.

Oppenheim, A.N. (2001) *Questionnaire Design, Interviewing and Attitude Measurement*. London/New York: Continuum.

Sellen, J. (2006) *See Beyond the Label: Empowering young people who self-harm and those who seek to support them*. London: Young Minds.

Sellen, J. (2008) 'Attitudes matter: working with children and young people who self-harm', in C. Jackson, K. Hill and P. Lavis (eds), *Child and Adolescent Mental Health Today: A handbook*. Brighton: Pavilion Publishing.

6

Preventing Suicide

Alan Carr

Introduction

The term 'suicidality' refers to all suicide-related behaviours and thoughts on the suicide risk spectrum, which range from passive thoughts of death at one extreme to completed suicide at the other (Bridge et al., 2006). It needs to be recognized that young people who engage in repeated non-suicidal self-harm may also become suicidal or unintentionally kill themselves. Self-harm was discussed in detail in the previous chapter.

Epidemiology

Suicide rates vary with country of residence, age and gender. They increase from childhood (World Health Organization, 2002). This may be due to the increased incidence of risk factors, such as mood and substance use disorders in young people compared with children (Bridge et al., 2006). It may also be due to an increased cognitive capability for planning self-harm, independence from parental supervision and access to the means for committing suicide.

In late adolescence, two to five times more males than females commit suicide (World Health Organization, 2002). In contrast, attempted suicide is far more common among females than males (Bridge et al., 2006). Parasuicide or non-suicidal self-harm is far more common than suicide or attempted suicide, especially among young females.

The pattern of higher rates of completed suicide among males and higher rates of attempted suicide and self-harm among females probably occurs because of the preponderance of suicide risk factors among males (Shaffer and Gutstein, 2002). Young males who complete suicide typically are impulsive, aggressive risktakers with a history of conduct disorder and comorbid mood and substance abuse who respond to precipitating stresses with lethal, self-harming reactions, such as hanging or shooting themselves. In contrast, females typically have a history of mood, anxiety or eating disorders and respond to precipitating stresses by contemplating suicide or engaging in less lethal, self-harming reactions, such as taking an overdose.

Risk and Protective Factors for Suicide

The risk and protective factors associated with completed suicide discussed below are based on extensive literature reviews (Berman et al., 2006; Bridge et al., 2006; de Wilde et al., 2001; Evans et al., 2004; Gould, 2003; Shaffer and Gutstein, 2002).

Suicidal intention and ideation

Suicidal intention may be distinguished from suicidal ideation, with the former being a risk factor for completed suicide. Suicidal intention is characterized by advanced planning, taking precautions against discovery, using a lethal method, such as hanging or using a firearm, avoiding seeking help and carrying out a final act, such as writing a suicide note. With suicidal ideation, in contrast, young people report thinking about self-harm and possibly engaging in non-lethal self-harm, such as superficial cutting of their wrists, but have no concrete plans about killing themselves. Suicidal intention and ideation reflect two ends of a continuum, with states that approximate suicidal intention reflecting a higher level of risk and those approximating suicidal ideation reflecting a lower level of risk.

The absence of suicidal intentions may be considered a protective factor. The acceptance by the young person of a verbal or written contract during a suicide risk assessment not to attempt suicide is also a protective factor. The commitment on the part of the parents or carers to monitor the young person constantly until all suicidal intention and ideation have abated is a further important protective factor. This commitment may take the form of an oral or written contract between the clinician and the parents or carers.

Method lethality

The lethality of the method used or threatened is a risk factor for suicide, with more lethal methods being associated with greater risk. Using a firearm, hanging, jumping from a great height and self-poisoning with highly toxic drugs are more lethal than cutting or overdosing on non-prescription drugs.

The availability of a lethal method, such as access to a firearm or highly toxic drugs, also constitutes an important risk factor. The unavailability of such lethal methods is an important protective factor. Such a protective factor can be created by inviting parents or carers to remove guns, drugs and other lethal methods from the household or hospitalizing the young person so that they have no access to such things.

Precipitating events

Suicide attempts are commonly precipitated by interpersonal conflicts or loss, involving a parent or romantic attachment.

Ongoing conflicts with parents, particularly if this entails physical, sexual or emotional child abuse, are strongly associated with completed suicide. More severe abuse, combined physical and sexual abuse and chronic abuse are all associated with higher levels of risk.

Conflict over disciplinary matters, rule-breaking, particularly if this involves court appearance, and imprisonment are also associated with suicide attempts. In fact, for imprisoned young people, the risk of suicide attempts is greatest during the early part of their detention.

The loss of parents or a romantic partner through death, long-term separation or severe chronic illness may also precipitate attempted suicide. Other loss experiences, such as the diagnosis of a severe illness or exam failure, may precipitate self-harm. Pregnancy in young people may also precipitate attempted suicide and may reflect a loss of innocence and a potential focus for intense conflict between young people and their parents.

Suicide arising from the imitation of others may be precipitated by suicides within the peer group, school or locality or media coverage of suicides.

Repeated attempts at suicide (as distinct from completed suicide) are associated with impulsive separation following romantic relationship difficulties or recent court appearances associated with impulsive or aggressive, antisocial behaviour.

Protective factors in this domain include the resolution of interpersonal conflicts with parents or romantic partners that may precipitate suicide, acceptance and mourning of losses that may precipitate suicide and physical and psychological distancing from peers or others who might precipitate imitative suicide. Clinical interventions may aim to facilitate the development of these protective factors.

Motivation

Young people may be motivated to attempt suicide for a wide variety of reasons. Suicide is usually perceived by them as the only feasible solution to a difficult problem involving interpersonal loss or conflict. It may be construed by some as a means of escaping from the psychological pain entailed by that loss or conflict. It may, alternatively, reflect an attempt to obtain revenge, express aggression, retaliate or punish a parent or romantic partner for their hostility or for leaving them through death, separation or illness. In other instances, suicide represents self-punishment, arising from guilt for not living up to perfectionistic self-expectations or expectations that youngsters perceive parents or others to have of them. For example, young people who fail exams or become unintentionally pregnant may see suicide as a way of atoning for their failure to meet academic or moral standards.

Attempted suicide may represent a way to obtain care and attention, particularly for young people who repeatedly make self-harming gestures.

Finally, young people from disorganized conflictual families may view their suicide as a necessary sacrifice that must be made to preserve the integrity of their family. That is, they may fantasize that their suicide will serve as a rallying point that will unite a fragmented family.

The potential for finding alternative ways to fulfill the functions of attempted suicide is a protective factor. Thus, flexibility about developing new coping styles for solving the problem for which the suicide attempt was a destructive solution places young people at a lower risk for suicide.

Understanding suicidal motives and the functions that suicidal gestures are intended to fulfil is important in planning treatment. When the functions of an attempted suicide are understood, the treatment plans should help the young person find other ways to fulfil those functions. That is, the plans should help them find less destructive ways to regulate difficult psychological states, modify painful situations, express anger assertively, resolve conflicts productively, mourn losses, manage perfectionistic expectations, solicit care and attention from others and cope with family disorganization.

Personality-based risk factors

Personality traits that place young people at risk for suicide include:

- hopelessness
- perfectionism
- impulsivity
- hostility and aggression
- neuroticism
- an inflexible coping style.

Those who attempt suicide view themselves as incapable of changing their situation, so the future, to them, looks hopeless.

Perfectionism is a risk factor for suicide probably because it leads to heightened self-expectations that may be difficult to achieve.

Suicidal young people tend to be inflexible in their coping styles and have difficulties drawing on memories of successfully solving problems in the past, so have a limited repertoire of coping strategies to draw on. Thus, they resort to strategies that may be ineffective. Their neuroticism, aggression and impulsivity may lead them to engage in self-directed aggression with little reflection on other possible alternatives for regulating their distressing emotional states and resolving their difficulties.

Having low levels of these personality traits that place young people at risk of suicide are protective factors in this domain – that is, low levels of hopelessness, perfectionism, impulsivity, aggression, neuroticism and inflexibility.

Disorder-related risk factors

An increased risk for suicide is strongly associated with multiple comorbid, chronic, severe psychological and physical disorders. With regard to psychological disorders, depression, bipolar disorder, alcohol and drug abuse, conduct disorder, borderline personality disorder, panic disorder and anorexia nervosa are risk factors for suicide. Comorbid, mood, conduct and substance use disorders greatly increase the risk of suicide. With regard to physical disorders, epilepsy and chronic painful illness place young people at such an increased risk.

The absence of psychological or physical disorders is an important protective factor in this domain. So, too, is the capacity to form a good therapeutic alliance and engage in a contract for the treatment of psychological disorders and physical illnesses.

Historical risk factors

A history of previous suicide attempts is the single strongest historical risk factor for future suicide. The risk of repetition is highest in the first six months after an attempt and remains elevated for up to two years.

Other historical risk factors include the loss of a parent in early life, previous psychiatric treatment and a history of involvement in the juvenile justice system. These three factors are particularly strongly associated with repeated suicide attempts or parasuicide.

The absence of these historical events is a protective factor, as is a history of good premorbid adjustment.

Family risk factors

A family history of a range of problems – notably, suicide attempts, depression, drug and alcohol abuse and assaultive behaviour – places young people at risk of suicide. In addition, they are placed at increased risk of suicide if their families are socially isolated, live in stressful, overcrowded conditions and they deny the seriousness of the young people's suicidal intentions or are unsupportive of them.

A family history that does not include suicide attempts, depression, drug and alcohol abuse and assaultive behaviour is a protective factor. Also, where the family is well-organized and supportive of the young person and there are low levels of stress and a high level of social support for the family as a whole, these may be considered as protective factors.

Demographic risk factors

Males are at greater risk for completed suicide while females are at greatest risk of attempted suicide and parasuicide. Males tend to use more lethal methods (guns and hanging) whereas females use less lethal methods (cutting or self-poisoning).

Membership of social class 5 (unskilled workers with low incomes and educational levels) is a risk factor for completed suicide and repeated parasuicide, while membership of social class 1 (professional and higher managerial employees) is a risk factor for completed suicide only.

With respect to ethnicity, in the USA, suicide rates are higher for white than black young people. With respect to religion, young people from communities with lower levels of religious practice are at greater risk of suicide. With respect to seasonality, completed suicide is most common in early summer.

Protective demographic factors include being female, membership of social classes 2, 3 and 4, being black (not white) in the USA, and having a strong commitment to religious values and practices.

Suicide Prevention

In an extensive systematic review of suicide prevention strategies that involved an international panel of suicidology experts, Mann et al. (2005) concluded that there was evidence for the effectiveness of two main strategies for reducing suicide rates for the population at large:

- interventions that trained physicians to recognize and treat depression and suicidality
- interventions that restricted access to lethal means, such as drugs used for overdosing and firearms.

Reviews of educational, school-based suicide prevention programmes show that they can improve suicide knowledge, referral skills and well-being (Gould, 2003; Hickey and Carr, 2002). With one exception, there have been no investigations of the impact of school-based programmes on suicide rates.

Currently, the Signs of Suicide (SOS) prevention programme, is the only school-based intervention that has been shown to reduce suicide risk. The SOS programme is manualized and supported by staff and participant training videos (it is available online at: www.mentalhealthscreening.org/highschool/index.aspx).

Assessment and intervention with suicidal young people

An assessment of suicide risk is necessary when young people have attempted suicide recently, threaten self-harm or show signs of severe depression. The overriding objective of consultation in such cases is to prevent harm or death.

Certain broad principles for assessment and crisis intervention may be followed (Carr, 2002, 2006). First, offer immediate consultation. Second, use the consultation process to develop a comprehensive understanding of the situation surrounding the suicide threat or attempt. Third, during the consultation process, establish or deepen the working alliance with the young person and significant members of their family or social network. Fourth, assess all of the risk and protective factors listed in Table 6.1.

Check if the factors were present in the past, the extent to which they were present during the recent episode and whether or not they are immediately present. Where possible, obtain information relating to risk factors from both the young person and members of their family or social network (including previously involved social or healthcare professionals).

Fifth, identify people within the young person's social network who may be available to help implement a management plan.

Sixth, draw the information gleaned from the assessment together into a clear formulation on which a management plan can be based. The formulation must logically link together the risk factors identified in the case to explain the occurrence of the episode of self-harm and the current level of risk. It is important to specify predisposing factors and triggering factors that led to an escalation from suicidal ideation to intention or from suicidal intention to self-injury. The management plan must specify the short-term action to be taken in the light of the formulation. The plan must also logically indicate that the changes it specifies will probably lower the risk of self-harm and increase the number of protective factors present. It is also vital that, until the risk of suicide has reduced, the young person and their parents make a contract at the conclusion of each session to return to meet the clinician at a specified time. For the young person, such a contract involves them making a commitment to not make further suicide attempts. For the parents or carers, the contract involves making a commitment to monitor their young person so as to prevent further suicide attempts. Where such arrangements cannot be made, hospitalization or a residential placement with staff who can fulfil this supervision role is essential.

TABLE 6.1   *Risk and protective factors for suicide*

Risk factors	Domain	Protective factors
• Suicidal intention. • Advanced planning. • Precautions against discovery. • Lethal method. • Absence of seeking help. • A final act.	**Suicidal intention and ideation**	• Suicidal ideation, not intention. • Acceptance by young person of 'no suicide' contract. • Acceptance by parents and carers of suicide monitoring contract.
• Availability of lethal methods.	**Method lethality**	• Absence of lethal methods.
• Loss of parents or partner by death, separation or illness. • Child abuse. • Conflict with parents or partner. • Involvement in judicial system. • Severe personal illness. • Major exam failure. • Unwanted pregnancy. • Imitation of other suicides.	**Precipitating factors**	• Resolution of interpersonal conflict with parents or partner that precipitated the attempted suicide. • Acceptance and mourning of losses that precipitated the attempted suicide. • Physical and psychological distancing from peers or others who precipitated an imitative attempted suicide.
Suicide attempted to serve the function of: • escaping an unbearable psychological state or situation • gaining revenge by inducing guilt • inflicting self-punishment • gaining care and attention • sacrificing the self for a greater good.	**Motivation**	Capacity to develop non-destructive coping styles or engage in treatment to be better able to: • regulate difficult psychological states • modify painful situations • express anger assertively • resolve conflicts productively • mourn losses • manage perfectionistic expectations • solicit care and attention from others • cope with family disorganization.
• High level of hopelessness. • High level of perfectionism. • High level of neuroticism. • High level of impulsivity. • High levels of hostility and aggression. • Inflexible coping style.	**Personality-based factors**	• Low level of hopelessness. • Low level of perfectionism. • Low level of neuroticism. • Low level of impulsivity. • Low levels of hostility and aggression. • Flexible coping style.
• Multiple comorbid chronic, severe disorders. • Depression. • Bipolar disorder. • Alcohol and drug abuse. • Conduct disorder. • Borderline personality disorder. • Panic disorder. • Anorexia nervosa. • Epilepsy. • Chronic painful illness	**Disorder-related factors**	• Absence of multiple comorbid chronic, severe disorders. • Absence of psychological disorders. •· Absence of physical disorders. • Capacity to form therapeutic lliance and engage in treatment for psychological and physical disorders.

TABLE 6.1   (Continued)

Risk factors	Domain	Protective factors
• Previous suicide attempts. • Loss of a parent in early life. • Previous psychiatric treatment. • Involvement in the juvenile justice system.	Historical factors	• No history of previous suicide attempts. • No history of loss of a parent in early life. • No history of previous psychiatric treatment. • No history of involvement in the juvenile justice system.
• Family history of suicide attempts. • Family history of depression. • Family history of drug and alcohol abuse. • Family history of assaultive behaviour. • Disorganized, unsupportive family. • Family deny seriousness of suicide attempts. • Family has high levels of stress and crowding. • Family has low level of social support and is socially isolated.	Family factors	• No family history of suicide attempts. • No family history of depression. • No family history of drug and alcohol abuse. • No family history of assaultive behaviour. • Well-organized, supportive family. • Family has low levels of stress. • Family has high levels of social support.
• Male. • Social class 5. • White (not black) in the USA. • Weak religious commitment. • Early summer.	Demographic factors	• Female. • Social classes 2, 3 or 4. • Black (not white) in the USA. • Strong religious commitment.

Engaging suicidal young people in psychotherapy

Attempted suicide is a risk factor for subsequent suicide attempts, so engaging young people who have attempted suicide in psychotherapy is an important step in preventing future self-harm.

Because this process can be challenging, procedures to enhance an engagement with psychotherapy have been developed and evidence from two trials supports their effectiveness. One intervention involved the young people and their parents or guardians making a verbal agreement to attend at least four psychotherapy sessions and take part in three phone interviews over an eight-week period that focused on reducing suicidal ideation and engaging in psychotherapy. This intervention led to significantly fewer missed psychotherapy appointments and fewer suicide attempts (Donaldson et al., 1997).

In a later randomized controlled trial of young people who had attempted suicide, Spirito et al. (2002) found that young people who received an intervention to enhance engagement in psychotherapy attended significantly more treatment sessions than those who received standard care.

Multisystemic therapy

Multisystemic therapy is an evidence-based, manualized approach to treatment, originally developed for young people with conduct disorder, but has been adapted for use with young people with severe mental health problems, including attempted suicide. The application of multisystemic therapy to such problems is described in Henggeler et al.'s book, *Multisystemic Treatment of Children and Adolescents with Serious Emotional Disturbance* (2002).

Multisystemic therapy combines intensive family therapy with individual skills training for the young person, and intervention in the wider school and inter-agency network. It involves regular, frequent, home-based family and individual therapy sessions, with additional sessions in the school or community settings, over three to five months. The effectiveness of this model of therapy was evaluated by Huey et al. (2004).

Dialectical behaviour therapy for suicidal young people

Dialectical behaviour therapy was originally developed as a comprehensive approach for treating adults with borderline personality disorder. An adaptation of this approach for use with young people who have attempted suicide is described in Miller et al.'s book, *Dialectical Behaviour Therapy with Suicidal Adolescents* (2007).

The approach involves individual therapy for young people combined with multi-family psycho-educational therapy. Individual behavioural assessment and therapy focuses on the use of change directed techniques (such as problem-solving) and acceptance techniques (such as validation) to achieve personal goals. Multi-family psycho-educational therapy helps family members understand self-harming behaviour and develop skills for protecting and supporting their suicidal offspring. Dialectical behaviour therapy for suicidal young people includes modules on mindfulness, distress tolerance, emotion regulation and interpersonal effectiveness skills to address problems, in the areas of identity, impulsivity, emotional liability and relationship problems, respectively. The effectiveness of this model of therapy was investigated by Miller et al. (2000), Rathus and Miller (2002) and Katz et al. (2004).

Youth-nominated support team

The youth-nominated support team is a manualized systemic intervention for young people who have attempted suicide. They nominate a parent or guardian and three other people from their family, peer group, school or community to be members of their support team (King et al. 2000).

For each case, support team members receive psycho-education, explaining how the young person's psychological difficulties led to the suicide attempt, the treatment plan and the role that support team members can play in helping the young person towards recovery and managing situations where there is a risk of further self-harm.

Support team members are encouraged to maintain weekly contact with the young person and are contacted regularly by the treatment team to facilitate this process.

The youth-nominated support team programme was evaluated for its effectiveness by King et al. (2006).

Family therapy

Two studies have evaluated the impact of specialized family therapy interventions for suicidal young people.

Rotheram-Borus et al. (2000) evaluated a programme in which suicidal girls and their mothers, during their initial attendance at a hospital emergency department, were engaged in a family therapy session after watching a video drama focused on suicidality. Hospital emergency staff were also trained in inducting these families into the programme.

Compared with standard care, the emergency department's family therapy programme led to a significant reduction in adolescent depression in young people over an 18-month follow-up period. Also, in families of girls with the greatest psychological difficulties, it led to a significant reduction in maternal distress.

In a randomized trial of 162 young people who had attempted suicide, Harrington et al. (1998) compared those who received a specialist assessment followed by four sessions of home-based, problem-solving family therapy, along with routine medical care, with a control group who received routine medical care only.

Parents in the group that received family therapy were more satisfied with the treatment than those in the control group, but the family therapy only led to a significantly greater reduction in suicidal ideation for young people who did not have major depression.

Individual cognitive behavioural and client-centred therapy for suicidal young people

Donaldson et al. (2005) found that both cognitive behavioural skills-based and client-centred supportive therapy protocols led to similar and significant decreases in suicidal ideation and depressed mood at three- and six-month follow-ups.

Group therapy for self-harming and suicidal young people

There is evidence from studies by Wood et al. (2001) and Esposito-Smythers et al. (2006) that group therapy may have a beneficial impact on self-harming and suicidal young people.

In the second study, participants found the construction of a 'Reasons to live' list the most helpful therapeutic activity, while the creation of a 'Safety list' was the least helpful.

Conclusions

For a significant minority of young people, suicide risk is a serious concern. There is evidence for a complex constellation of risk factors in the aetiology of suicide. There is also evidence for the effectiveness of the SOS programme, a school-based preventative intervention.

In the management of suicidal young people, careful assessment, crisis intervention, guided by the available evidence of the various risk factors, is essential.

The engagement in psychotherapy of young people who have attempted suicide may be enhanced by facilitating a verbal agreement between them and their parents or carers to attend psychotherapy sessions and conducting follow-up phone interviews with the young people over two months, with a focus on reducing suicidal ideation and psychotherapy attendance.

A number of psychotherapy protocols, particularly those that include individual therapy for young people combined with systemic therapy for members of their family and social support networks, may be more effective than routine care, so should be considered when treating young people who have attempted suicide.

Multisystemic therapy for young people with severe mental health problems, dialectical behaviour therapy for suicidal young people and nominated support network therapy are other well-developed protocols that show particular promise.

These conclusions are broadly consistent with international best practice guidelines (Shaffer and Pfeffer, 2001).

Resources

Further reading

Carr, A. (2006) *Handbook of Child and Adolescent Clinical Psychology* (2nd edn). London: Routledge.

The *Beck Scale for Suicide Ideation* (Beck & Steer, 1991) and Reynold's (1991) semi-structured interview are useful resources when evaluating suicide risk.

Treatment manuals

Berman, A., Jobes, D. and Silverman, M. (2006) *Adolescent Suicide: Assessment and intervention* (2nd edn). Washington, DC: American Psychological Association.

Henggeler, S.W., Schoenwald, S.K., Rowland, M.D. and Cunningham, P.B. (2002) *Multisystemic Treatment of Children and Adolescents with Serious Emotional Disturbance*. New York: Guilford.

King, C., Kramer, A. and Preuss, L. (2000) *Youth-nominated Support-Team Intervention Manual*. Ann Arbor, MI: University of Michigan, Department of Psychiatry.

Miller, A., Rathus, J. and Linehan, M. (2007) *Dialectical Behaviour Therapy with Suicidal Adolescents*. New York: Guilford.

Websites

American Foundation for Suicide Prevention (AFSP) www.afsp.org

National Institute for Health and Clinical Excellence (NICE) www.nice.org.uk

National Self Harm Network www.nshn.co.uk and info@nshn.co.uk

Signs of Suicide (SOS) programme www.mentalhealthscreening.org/high school/index.aspx

Suicide Awareness, voices of Education (SAVE) www.save.org

Suicide Prevention Action Network USA (SPAN USA) www.spanusa.org

Young People and Self-harm information resource www.selfharm.org.uk

KEY POINTS

- 'Suicidality' is a term used to refer to all suicide-related behaviours and thoughts on the suicide risk spectrum, which ranges from passive thoughts of death at one extreme to completed suicide at the other.
- Suicidal *intention* is characterized by advanced planning, taking precautions against discovery, using a lethal method, such as hanging or a firearm, avoiding seeking help and carrying out a final act, such as writing a suicide note.

- With suicidal *ideation*, in contrast, young people report *thinking* about self-harm and possibly engaging in non-lethal self-harm, such as superficial cutting of their wrists, but have no concrete plans to kill themselves.
- Currently, the Signs of Suicide (SOS) prevention programme is the only school-based intervention that has been shown to reduce the risk of suicide in young people.

QUESTIONS FOR DISCUSSION

1. Discuss why you think that the SOS programme, dialectical behaviour therapy, mutisystemic therapy, youth-nominated support team, family therapy, individual therapy and group therapy programmes described in the chapter all 'work' for adolescent suicidality when they are so different from each other?
2. What research question would you most like to address on adolescent suicidality? Design a research study to answer that question.

References

Berman, A., Jobes, D. and Silverman, M. (2006) *Adolescent Suicide: Assessment and intervention* (2nd edn). Washington, DC: American Psychological Association.

Bridge, J., Goldstein, T. and Brent, D. (2006) 'Adolescent suicide and suicidal behaviour', *Journal of Child Psychology and Psychiatry,* 47: 372–94.

Carr, A. (2002) *Depression and Attempted Suicide in Adolescence.* Oxford: Blackwell.

Carr, A. (2006) *Handbook of Child and Adolescent Clinical Psychology* (2nd edn). London: Routledge.

de Wilde, E., Kienhorst, I. and Diekstra, R. (2001) 'Suicidal behaviour in adolescents', in I. Goodyer (ed.), *The Depressed Child and Adolescent* (2nd edn). Cambridge: Cambridge University Press. pp. 267–91.

Donaldson, D., Spirito, A., Arrigan, M. and Aspel, J.W. (1997) 'Structured disposition planning for adolescent suicide attempters in a general hospital: preliminary findings on short-term outcome', *Archives of Suicide Research,* 3: 271–82.

Donaldson, D., Spirito, A. and Esposito-Smythers, C. (2005) 'Treatment for adolescents following a suicide attempt: results of a pilot trial', *Journal of the American Academy of Child and Adolescent Psychiatry,* 44: 113–20.

Esposito-Smythers, C., McClung, T. and Fairlie, A. (2006) 'Adolescent perceptions of a suicide prevention group on an inpatient unit', *Archives of Suicide Research,* 10 (3): 265–75.

Evans, E., Hawton, K. and Rodham, K. (2004) 'Factors associated with suicidal phenomena in adolescents: a systematic review of population-based studies', *Clinical Psychology Review,* 24: 957–79.

Gould, M. (2003) 'Youth suicide risk and preventive interventions: a review of the past 10 years', *Journal of the American Academy of Child and Adolescent Psychiatry,* 42: 386–405.

Harrington, R., Kerfoot, M., Dyer, E., McNiven, F., Gill, J., Harrington, V., Woodham, A. and Byford, S. (1998) 'Randomized trial of a home-based family intervention for children who have deliberately poisoned themselves', *Journal of the American Academy of Child and Adolescent Psychiatry,* 37: 512–18.

Henggeler, S.W., Schoenwald, S.K., Rowland, M.D. and Cunningham, P.B. (2002) *Multisystemic Treatment of Children and Adolescents With Serious Emotional Disturbance.* New York: Guilford Press.

Hickey, D. and Carr, A. (2002) 'Prevention of suicide in adolescence', in A. Carr (ed.), *Prevention: What works with children and adolescents?: A critical review of psychological prevention programmes for children, adolescents and their families.* London: Routledge. pp. 336–58.

Huey, S., Henggeler, S., Rowland, M., Halliday-Boykins, C., Cunningham, P. and Pickrel, S. (2004) 'Multisystemic therapy effects on attempted suicide by youths presenting psychiatric emergencies', *Journal of the American Academy of Child and Adolescent Psychiatry,* 43: 183–90.

Katz, L., Cox, B. and Gunasekara, S. (2004) 'Feasibility of dialectical behaviour therapy for suicidal adolescent inpatients', *Journal of the American Academy of Child and Adolescent Psychiatry,* 43 (3): 276–82.

King, C., Kramer, A. and Preuss, L. (2000) *Youth-nominated Support Team Intervention Manual.* Ann Arbor, MI: University of Michigan, Department of Psychiatry.

King, C., Kramer, A., Preuss, L., Kerr, D., Weisse, L. and Venkataraman, S. (2006) 'Youth-nominated support team for suicidal adolescents (Version 1): a randomized controlled trial', *Journal of Consulting and Clinical Psychology,* 74: 199–206.

Mann, J., Apter, A. and Bertolote, J. (2005) 'Suicide prevention strategies: a systematic review', *Journal of the American Medical Association,* 294: 2064–74.

Miller, A., Rathus, J. and Linehan, M. (2007) *Dialectical Behaviour Therapy with Suicidal Adolescents.* New York: Guilford Press.

Miller, A., Wyman, S., Glassman, S., Huppert, J. and Rathus, J. (2000) 'Analysis of behavioural skills utilized by adolescents receiving dialectical behaviour therapy', *Cognitive and Behavioural Practice,* 7: 183–7.

Rathus, J. and Miller, A. (2002) 'Dialectical behaviour therapy adapted for suicidal adolescents', *Suicide and Life-Threatening Behaviour,* 32: 146–57.

Rotheram-Borus, M., Piacentini, J., Cantwell, C., Belin, T. and Juwon, S. (2000) 'The 18-month impact of an emergency room intervention for adolescent female suicide attempters', *Journal of Consulting & Clinical Psychology,* 68: 1081–93.

Shaffer, D. and Gutstein, J. (2002) 'Suicide and attempted suicide', in M. Rutter and E. Taylor (eds), *Child and Adolescent Psychiatry* (4th edn). Oxford: Blackwell. pp. 529–54.

Shaffer, D. and Pfeffer, C. (2001) 'Practice parameter for the assessment and treatment of children and adolescents with suicidal behaviour', *Journal of the American Academy of Child and Adolescent Psychiatry,* 40: 24S–51S.

Spirito, A., Boergers, J., Donaldson, D., Bishop, D. and Lewander, W. (2002) 'An intervention trial to improve adherence to community treatment of adolescents following a suicide attempt', *Journal of the American Academy of Child and Adolescent Psychiatry,* 41: 435–42.

Wood, A., Trainor, G., Rothwell, J., Moore, A. and Harrington, R. (2001) 'Randomized trial of group therapy for repeated deliberate self-harm in adolescents', *Journal of the American Academy of Child and Adolescent Psychiatry,* 40: 1246–53.

World Health Organization (2002) *Suicide rates and absolute numbers of suicide by country,* available online at: www.who.int/mental_health/prevention/suicide-country-reports/en/index.html

Part IV

Confrontational Behaviour

7

Working with Gangs and Other Delinquent Groups

Simon Hallsworth and Tara Young

Introduction

Until recently, gangs have been seen as a uniquely American problem. In recent years, however, gangs appear to have migrated across the Atlantic to a range of European societies, including the UK, where it now appears that they have taken root and flourished.

As gangs have not been considered a public enemy to the extent that they have in the USA, European societies do not possess any established anti-gang strategies or, indeed, industry to confront the risks posed by street collectives (Hallsworth, 2007). As fears about gangs have grown in countries such as the UK, driven forward, not least, by sensational reporting of alleged gangland killings, policymakers in the UK have, in recent years, been turning to the USA and its well-established gang suppression industry for inspiration.

In recent years in the UK, a range of anti-gang policies has been initiated that borrows heavily from the USA model. Among them are the formation of dedicated gang-busting units and the creation of dispersion zones where law enforcement personnel are conceded powers to forcibly disperse groups of young people congregating together. In its latest action plan to confront violent crime the UK government publicly identified gangs as public enemies and outlined yet more powers to suppress them (HM Government, 2008). These included sanctioning the use of covert intelligence on gang members and creating dedicated policing operations with a mandate to crack down on gangs with the aim of suppressing them.

Given the sensational coverage gangs receive, it pays to rethink precisely how we might want to respond to problems posed by street collectives of various forms. Ought we to seek solutions to homegrown problems posed by youth collectives by looking towards the USA, with its large and well-established gang-suppression industry or is another order of intervention preferable and more desirable? If so, what might its features be? In this chapter, we address these questions.

Criminal Gangs or Street Collectives?

The way that a gang is defined in the USA has changed considerably in recent decades and this has affected how the state has responded to it.

One of the earliest attempts to understand gangs was the work conducted by Thrasher in the 1930s (Thrasher, 1936). Thrasher saw a gang as an 'interstitial entity' that formed spontaneously among young migrants in the burgeoning industrial city of Chicago. He did not view gangs as essentially criminal entities, though he did believe that they were 'integrated through conflict'.

In the 1970s, the way that gangs were perceived and defined began to change as their non-criminal dimensions began to diminish. The term 'gang' became criminalized and it is as a systematically criminal, not to say pathological, entity that it is now understood. This is particularly evident if we consider the widely accepted definition of a gang provided by Malcolm Klein in 1971.

> A juvenile gang is any denotable group of youngsters who (a) are generally per-
> ceived as a distinct aggregation by others in their neighbourhood (b) recognize
> themselves as a denotable group (almost invariably with a group name), and
> (c) have been involved in a sufficient number of delinquent incidents to call
> forth a consistent negative response from neighbourhood residents and/or
> enforcement agencies.

Though the debate about what constitutes a street gang still continues today, most practitioners and policymakers perceive gangs as pathological units that must be suppressed. Gang-affiliated members commit more crime, it is argued, than non-gang-affiliated members and, once in a gang, will engage in even more extreme criminality than would have been the case had they not joined (Decker and Van Winkle, 1996; Klien and Maxson, 2006; Thornberry, 2003).

Gangs, from this perspective, are the harbingers of social destruction. If you accept this thesis – and many certainly do – then the only solution to the problem is gang suppression, which, by and large (with considerable variation), is the dominant current response.

Punitive Responses to Gang Management – Do They Work?

The hallmarks of this intervention philosophy contain variations on the following themes. Gang researchers are employed by state bodies to map the gangs and assess the risk factors associated with them. Typically, this is accomplished using surveys. The knowledge produced is also tactical, in the sense that its function is to pave the way for suppression. This commences in different ways and with different levels of punitive response.

At the less punitive end, we find various education programmes such as GREAT (the Gang Resistance, Education and Training Programme) that attempt to dissuade people from being involved in gangs. This is considered to be 'primary prevention'.

As we move towards the more punitive dimensions of gang suppression, interventions include a range of punitive control programmes and organizations. Among these there are the development of gang intelligence and control units, such as the LA Community Resources Against Street Hoodlums (CRASH), which specialized in street gang suppression programmes.

The initiation of civil injunctions that target gang members and their activities has also become a popular anti-gang measure in several states. Variations can also be found here with regard to responses targeting individual gang members. They include making gang membership a mitigating factor in sentencing, removing the right to benefits for gang members, passing laws that prohibit gang members from congregating in particular areas, and banning the wearing of gang insignia and colours.

Then we have the arrest and imprisonment of gang members for various felonies by dedicated prosecution units and, last but not least, dedicated gang-busting operations, often involving paramilitary police units, which have resulted in mass arrests of suspected gang members. An excellent example of this would be Operation Hammer, unleashed by the LAPD in South Central Los Angeles, which involved 1000 police officers in a couple of weekend operations (Davis, 1990).

Despite the huge investment that the USA's repressive response has devoted to gang suppression, the problem of the gang appears to have grown across the USA, *despite* falls in crime nationally over recent years.

While the evaluation literature on gang intervention programmes is principally concerned with the relative success or failure of various individual projects in suppressing or preventing gangs from forming, it also pays to consider the wider social impact of the anti-gang crusade on the communities in which the targeted gang members live. This means assessing social policy not in terms of studying how far the risks posed by gangs have been effectively reduced, but considering instead the social costs attendant on such repression by the state.

The costs are huge, among which must be included:

- the mass criminalization of young people
- the further racialization of the crime problem
- the wholesale assault on the rights and civil liberties of individuals targeted through repressive tactics
- the mass incarceration of ethnic minority men in the expanding American Gulag
- the negative experiences of communities targeted by paramilitary policing
- the importance of the gang-suppression industry in helping to forge the 'deadly symbiosis' that Luke Wacquant has charted between the ghetto and the penitentiary (Wacquant, 2004).

Benevolent Responses to Gang Management – Can They Work?

While we ought not to lose sight of the fact that there remain more benevolent attempts to work with gang members in the USA, it must be pointed out that these are very much outside the mainstream – they are not part of the general policy paradigm, which aspires to gang suppression. We need to be very careful about adopting the suppression model, which leads us to the very first of our intervention strategies – beware American gang-suppression specialists bearing gifts. What might an alternative approach be? This is what we will now consider.

While street collectives come in a myriad of different shapes and sizes and the aetiology of urban violence has many causes (Hallsworth and Young, 2005), what we tend to find in the American gang-suppression industry is a filtering gaze that either focuses attention on ethnic street-based gangs alone or, alternatively, reduces the problem of urban violence to a problem of gangs.

This takes us to our second policy recommendation – be careful of gang talk and gang talkers, for the street and its violence will invariably escape the definitional straightjacket that they want to impose on it.

While we do not want to dispute that entities called gangs may be part of the problem of urban street-based violence, we contend that the problem of violence is not reducible to gangs alone and, consequently, seeking to confront the violence of the street by suppressing gangs is a misguided exercise. To begin with, gang members may commit crimes independent of those that are clearly gang-related (Jankowski, 1991). Much of the violence in an area may well be committed by individuals or duos who are not in gangs, while there are many who commit violence in peer groups that ought not to be labelled gangs. We need to see the gang as one part of the street puzzle and not concede to it an importance that it does not possess. In practice, that means making clear distinctions between what we may really want to term 'a gang' and groups that are not gangs, such as organized crime groups and peer groups. It also means understanding that different collectives require interventions that recognize their differences and do not entail imposing blanket, indiscriminate gang-suppression interventions on them, such as curfews or street clearance operations. Rather than beginning with the gang as your unit of analysis, begin with the street, its violence, and only then see if it has anything to do with gangs. This is beguilingly easy to say in theory, we accept, but difficult to apply in social contexts where people often want to find gangs everywhere.

By defining the problem of violent street worlds as essentially one of gangs, the control agents and gang researchers too often resolve the inherently amorphous reality of street life by imposing a form on it that gives it a shape they can comprehend and, they believe, control. In effect, they apply the term 'gang' and it is as if, in one fell swoop, the muddy, messy reality of volatile street worlds is magically resolved. It is as if, once the gangs have been identified by reference to their risk factors, all that is left to do is reach for gang solutions that often have their origins and justifications in US literature and research. The trouble with this, however, is that, on the one hand, the reality of the street described in the language of administrative gang talk and, on the other, street life as it is, are very different things. Far from clarifying street reality, it becomes misrepresented in the very language used to describe it.

As an example, control agents often express various roles of street life members in what remains a highly stereotypical vision of the gang. They refer to 'the leader', 'wanabees', 'a lieutenant', 'a foot solider' and so on. The trouble with this is that these terms, although they might help us understand the nature of military organizations, do not capture the informal, amorphous nature of street life, which is much more fluid than these categories can ever capture. Likewise, when people deploy terms such as 'initiation ceremonies' and 'recruitment strategies' to define gang realities, they are concepts that, typically, emanate from the world of control agents and do not capture the reality of the street, which is elsewhere.

As we found in our interviews, those often identified as gang members by con-trol agents did not accept that they were members of a gang, and did not talk about initiation rituals or recruitment strategies. That is not how they experience their gang realities.

Against this tendency to reification, we pose as a policy injunction the need to think carefully about what you are evoking when trying to articulate the world of the street in an attempt to define and control it. Are you capturing its life as its inhab-itants live their gang realities or are you imposing on it a conceptual discourse that misrepresents precisely what it claims to represent?

As an alternative, we stress the importance of finding out how the people themselves define their own street reality. Listen to what they say and work back from that. The importance of this came through powerfully to us in the course of research we con-ducted into a poor, deprived, inner London borough, where we had been tasked with the mission to uncover the gang reality that, we were told, was fuelling the violence within it (Hallsworth and Young, 2008).

We certainly did find evidence of things that approximated gangs, but, from talk-ing to violent men, residents and control agents, we did not find them identifying the gang as the source of the problem of violence. The gangsters we interviewed spoke instead of living life 'on road' and had a clear-cut sense of what that involved and how they had ended up there. Rather than attempt to reflect this back in the reified language of gang talk, we tried instead to explain and theorize the processes that led to people being 'on road'. In other words, we tried to frame our under-standing of the violent street worlds that we were attempting to uncover by listen-ing without prejudice to those who were immersed in them. The policies we abstracted to confront violence were shaped by this interpretation.

In the 1960s, the authorities in the USA typically believed that the best way to confront gangs was to intervene benignly to change them. Gangs were considered transformable and youth workers were considered the right kind of people to help facilitate that change. This kind of intervention, however, was strongly criticized in an influential intervention by Malcolm Klein in 1971, who saw such practices as only helping to cement gang identity further. This he felt was counterproductive to the need to curtail the gang and prevent entry into it. Before we too take this path, though, we would question the wisdom behind this intervention. If you do not reason with gangs or groups in ways that respect that they are a group, then what you are doing is simply leaving the way open for naked suppression.

We live in fragmenting and individualizing societies. The impact of free mar-ket principles on the self is to progressively atomize it. Given this, if youth show signs of collective efficacy by having the temerity to organize themselves with the goal of confronting the problems they encounter in the world around them, it is essential for us as practitioners to listen to and respect an alternative discourse. 'Take them as they come' constitutes our next policy recommendation.

Rather than approach street collectives, as most state-sponsored administrative researchers do, simply as a pathologic group that must be suppressed, instead work with the group to find out what its members believe themselves to be and what they may represent.

If that sounds like idealism, then consider what happens when this approach is adopted. Take the case of the pioneering work undertaken by David Brotherton and Louis Barrios in the case of the Almighty Latin Kings and Queens Nation in New York (Brotherton and Barrios, 2004).

To all intents and purposes, the Latin Kings represented, to average white Americans, the quintessential, stereotypical vision of their worst nightmare. This was a large, armed, violent street gang, populated by Hispanics. It was a gang that had spread on a national and international scale and, it was alleged, was heavily immersed in illegal drug distribution. It literally was considered the extreme edge of delinquency. In relation to the all-American way of life, the group was viewed as fit only for suppression, which is the policy that the state adopted.

Rejecting zero tolerance and the mass incarceration of ethnic outsiders, Brotherton and Barrios adopted an ethnographic approach and worked closely with the group. Rather than seeking to understand the group by reducing it to the impoverished language of risk variables, they sought to learn the life histories of the group members and the evolving history of the group itself. They approached the gang, in other words, as a cultural producing entity that needed to be understood.

By trying to humanize rather than demonize the Latin Kings, they sought to understand the gang's dynamics and position within American society. In so doing, they were able to highlight the many positive functions it served, while also retaining a realistic assessment of the violence its members were capable of.

As Brotherton and Barrios discovered, this was a group that was far more than a collection of violent outsiders. It also acted as a therapeutic community, not least by helping its members overcome the trauma of incarceration. The gang sought to provide a range of welfare services to its members and their families.

Rather than adopt the typical gang suppression fix, what Brotherton and Barrios sought to do was bridge the abyss between a criminalized group and the wider society that had excluded and criminalized it. As part of this approach, they organized a conference that bought together members from different gangs and practitioners and researchers as part of an attempt to find common ground.

More recently, they have been engaged in convening public meetings where local communities and gang members are given an opportunity to publicly debate issues that concern them. This is an American initiative that is outside of and opposed to the general fixation with the suppression of such groups.

The idea that one might actually humanize stigmatized outsiders as part of a strategy of intervention is not something that typically informs efforts to control gangs. Nor too is the attempt beyond that of recognizing street collectives as political actors who have a right to be involved in decisions that affect them. We offer however as another policy injunction the need to work with and engage with street collectives as political actors in their own right.

Rather than lead such groups to accentuate their most negative features by single-mindedly conspiring in their destruction, we propose working with the many positive features that group life can bestow. As an example of where this approach can lead, consider the lesson of Barcelona and the arrival there in the 1990s of the Latin Kings and Queens.

To begin with, the authorities in the city positioned the group as a public enemy that had to be suppressed. That original perspective began to change, however, in favour of seeking to work with the Latin Kings, considering them as a social movement in their own right. Far from trying to criminalize the group, they were recognized as a cultural movement by the local state and the state made money available to them to support their work.

More recently, a similar approach has been adapted to good effect in the case of Genoa, which has also witnessed an inward flux of Ecuadorian migrants who brought the Latin Kings with them. Far from casting them as social pariahs, through the pioneering efforts of dedicated researchers working at Genoa University and street-level practitioners, efforts were made to include the gang as a recognized social movement. Treating street collectives with respect, rather than as social pariahs, it could be observed, can go a long way.

If, as we demonstrated above, the problem on the street is not one of gangs, then, self-evidently, it is important that we do not place anti-gang programmes at the centre of any intervention strategy. Even if the street collectives that exist are volatile and dangerous, it is important to resist the temptation to use punitive and suppressive solutions.

We conclude here by suggesting that practitioners work with what they have. If, for example, a group of youths commit a spate of street robberies, utilize the usual ordinances and practices law enforcement agencies have evolved to tackle this particular crime rather than generate new gang suppression instruments to tackle the problem. Suppress the crime, not the gang.

As we have seen, street life and the violence within it operate in fast time. As violent street actors and the collectives to which they may be aligned often have no trust in the criminal law and evince a strong dislike and distrust of law enforcement agencies, the violence they do unfolds in street worlds that are often disconnected from formal society and its institutions. Reciprocal tit for tat reprisals may lead to a spiralling of violence. Given this situation, for an intervention effort to succeed, practitioners must be able to:

- provide a response in fast time, not in the ponderous slow time that bureaucratic organizations typically take to work
- build a bridge between the often separate worlds of the street and formal society.

Involving those who come from the street and holding the respect of street actors and street collectives are of fundamental importance if the trust necessary to make a difference is to be established.

Conclusion

We tend to live in societies today that, increasingly, seek to manage social problems by a recourse to crime control. Not only have our societies become more punitive but they have also become far more exclusionary in the nature of the practices they adopt. The current American fixation with suppressing gangs illustrates this tendency neatly. Where once, in the 1960s (a more benevolent and hopeful age), gangs were thought of as entities that could be reasoned with and transformed through benevolent intervention, by the 1980s and since, as we have seen, they have been thought fit only to be suppressed. Despite the fact that the programmes Klien and Maxson (2006) evaluated failed, this has not prevented the establishment from coming back and suggesting more of the same. At no point have people stopped to think that an alternative paradigm might be preferable. Despite the failure of suppression tactics, more and more European societies are turning to the USA for ways to confront what they believe and define as their growing gang problem.

Before we too wholeheartedly embrace gang talk and gang suppression, it is our contention that we really do need to think more carefully about the kind of society we are. From the survey that we have attempted here, we have tried to suggest that another order of intervention is necessary and also tried to articulate what the foundations of an alternative progressive paradigm of intervention might look like when it comes to the business of engaging with street collectives.

KEY POINTS

- Don't reduce violent street worlds to a problem of gangs.
- Recognize that street collectives exist which are not gangs and do not try to treat them as if they are.
- Be careful about imposing on to the messy world of the street a language that misrepresents its nature.
- Work back from the testimonies of street actors and derive your interventions from them.
- Work with the groups as you find them and do not make oppression the beginning, middle and end of what constitutes your strategy.

QUESTIONS FOR DISCUSSION

1. Imagine that you want to build helpful relationships with members of a street collective. Discuss the approach that you would take and any difficulties you think you might encounter.
2. Discuss what you think might be the advantages and disadvantages for a young person who is a member of a street collective.

References

Brotherton, D. and Barrios, L. (2004) *The Almighty Latin King and Queen Nation: Street politics and the transformation of a New York City gang.* New York: Columbia University Press.

Davis, M. (1990) *City of Quartz: Excavating the future in Los Angeles.* London, New York: Verso.

Decker, S.H. and Van Winkle, B. (1996) *Life in the Gang: Family, friends and violence.* Cambridge, New York: Cambridge University Press.

Hallsworth, S. (2007) 'Confronting the European gang'. European Commission.

Hallsworth, S. and Young, T. (2005) 'Interpreting the gang and other criminal groups', report produced for the Metropolitan Police Service.

Hallsworth, S. and Young, T. (2008) *Confronting Gang, Gun and Knife Related Violence in Hackney.* Hackney: Safer and Cleaner Partnership.

HM Government (2008) *Saving Lives. Reducing Harm. Protecting the Public: An action plan for tackling violence 2008–11.* London: HM Government. Also available online at: www.homeoffice.gov.uk/documents/violent-crime-action-plan-08/violent-crime-action-plan-180208?view=Binary

Jankowski, M.S. (1991) *Islands in the Street: Gangs and American urban society.* Berkeley, CA: University of California Press.

Klein, M.W. (1971) *Street Gangs and Street Workers.* Englewood Cliffs, NJ: Prentice Hall.

Klien, M. and Maxson, C.L. (2006) *Street Gang Patterns and Policies.* Oxford: Oxford University Press.

Thornberry, T.P. (2003) *Gangs and Delinquency in Development Perspective.* Cambridge: Cambridge University Press.

Thrasher, F.M. (1936) *The Gang: A study of 1,313 gangs in Chicago.* Chicago, IL: University of Chicago Press.

Wacquant, L. (2004) *Deadly Symbiosis: Race and the rise of neoliberal penalty.* Oxford: Polity.

8

Prevention and Responses to Bullying

Fran Thompson, Neil Tippett and Peter K. Smith

Introduction

'Bullying' can be defined as an aggressive, intentional act or behaviour that is carried out by a group or an individual repeatedly and over time against a victim who cannot easily defend him or herself (Olweus, 1991) or as a 'systematic abuse of power' (Sharp and Smith, 1994). The criteria of repetition, intention and a systematic imbalance of power make bullying a particularly undesirable form of aggression. It can occur in many contexts, including the workplace, but has been most investigated in young people.

Bullying can be both direct and indirect. Direct forms include physical or verbal attack and relational/social exclusion. Indirect bullying (for example, spreading nasty rumours or damaging belongings) includes, more recently, cyberbullying, which is bullying using mobile phones or the Internet (Smith et al., 2008a). Bullying can be based on a young person's race, religion or culture, sex, sexuality or disability.

Both bullying and more general antisocial behaviour have similar background risk factors: biological, personal, family, peer group, school/institution and community. For example, involvement in bullying others is associated with family predictors, such as insecure attachment, harsh physical discipline and being a victim of overprotective parenting (Espelage et al., 2000; Smith and Myron-Wilson, 1998). Parental maltreatment and abuse are likely risk factors in the bully or victim or aggressive victim group (Schwartz et al., 2000; Shields and Cicchetti, 2001). The peer group and the general school environment or climate also have powerful effects (Anderson et al., 2001; Utting et al., 2007). It is through the school and peer group that most anti-bullying interventions have tried to operate, although work with parents and families is clearly also relevant.

Interventions to Reduce Bullying

Many sources of advice and support exist for anti-bullying work, notably the Department for Children, Schools and Families (DCSF) in England has issued guidelines in *Safe to Learn* (DCSF, 2007). These describe the aims of effective anti-bullying strategies and intervention systems as:

- preventing, de-escalating and/or stopping any continuation of harmful behaviour
- reacting to bullying incidents in a reasonable, proportionate and consistent way
- safeguarding pupils who have experienced bullying and triggering sources of support for them
- applying disciplinary sanctions to pupils causing bullying and ensuring that they learn from the experience, possibly through multi-agency support.

Proactive strategies in school

Since 1999, it has been a legal requirement in England and Wales for all schools to have some form of anti-bullying policy. School policies vary in scope (Smith et al., 2008b), but provide a framework for each school's response, involving the whole school community – pupils, teachers, learning mentors, school support staff, governors and parents/carers. In Welsh schools, a significant association was reported between lower levels of bullying and pupils reporting that the school had clear rules on bullying (Lambert et al., 2008), although Woods and Wolke (2003) found few associations of policy scores with measures of bullying in 34 English primary schools.

School councils

School councils involve pupils from all age ranges, usually in the form of elected representatives. They meet regularly with members of school staff to discuss and decide on policy issues, which can include the issue of bullying.

Curricular materials/approaches

Classroom activities can be used to tackle issues associated with bullying, progressively and in age, gender and culturally appropriate ways. These can include literature, audiovisual materials, videos, drama/role play, music, debates, workshops, puppets and dolls (in the early years) and group work. Such curricular approaches can raise awareness of bullying and schools' anti-bullying policies and develop skills, empathy and assertiveness in confronting bullying.

There is some evidence that such approaches have positive effects, but only temporarily if curriculum work is not backed up by continuing anti-bullying work and supporting the policies (Smith and Sharp, 1994). Ofsted (2003) reported that schools with the most successful approaches to bullying canvassed and took full account of pupils' views and dedicated curriculum and tutorial time to discussing relationships and matters such as bullying.

The curriculum-based Social and Emotional Aspects of Learning (SEAL) resource directly addresses behavioural issues (including bullying) at whole-school and individual levels. The SEAL resource is a whole-school approach to developing social and emotional skills, to promote positive behaviour, attendance, learning and well-being.

The primary SEAL programme is based on seven themes, one of which is 'Say no to bullying'. This focuses on what it is, how it feels, why people bully, how schools can prevent and respond to it and how children can use their social and emotional skills to help them.

An external evaluation of the primary SEAL pilot (Hallam et al., 2006) found evidence of improvement in pupils' social skills, relationships and awareness of emotions, although the lack of a control group meant that these findings could not be fully validated.

Quality circles

Quality circles are small groups of pupils that are formed to take part in regular classroom sessions. The groups problem-solve particular issues – such as bullying – using standard procedures, including gathering information, and present their findings to a wider audience.

One evaluation undertaken in primary schools found that 95 per cent of pupils liked the experience and felt that the quality circle groups had worked well together. Over half stated that they had become more aware of bullying and now tried to stop it (Sharp and Smith, 1994).

Working in the playground

Pupil to pupil bullying predominately takes place outside the classroom, in corridors, school grounds and outside the school gates (Blatchford, 1998). An effective playground policy and well-designed play area can significantly help to reduce bullying (DCSF, 2007; Sharp and Smith, 1994). Ofsted (2003) identified features of good practice, including the efficient checking of the school site, setting up safe play areas or quiet rooms and close supervision at the start and finish of the school day.

Playground policy

A playground policy includes a strategy for appropriate behaviour in breaks and playtimes, liaison between teaching staff and lunchtime supervisors and encouraging prosocial playground games and activities.

The Birmingham Framework for Intervention scheme (Daniels and Williams, 2000) includes useful guidance for teachers to use when checking the constituent parts of their school's behaviour environment and how they might improve it.

Improving the playground environment

Work on the physical environment of the playground includes structuring or redesigning it to provide more creative opportunities for pupils during break- and lunchtimes, and so reduce boredom and bullying.

This can be a participatory and inclusive process for pupils. Strategies include playground design exercises, mapping existing use, identifying danger areas and bullying hotspots (Sharp and Smith, 1994). One study found that improvements to the school grounds resulted in a 64 per cent reduction in bullying (Learning through Landscapes, 2003).

Training lunchtime supervisors

Lunchtime supervisors have a pivotal role in implementing any playground or school anti-bullying policy, but often receive little or no training for this. Holding training sessions can provide them with additional skills in organizing games, recognizing bullying behaviours, interviewing pupils and dealing with bullying and conflict situations. An important aspect is distinguishing bullying from playful fighting. Such training can also raise the self-esteem of lunchtime supervisors and their status in the school community.

One study found that trained lunchtime supervisors brought about a clear decrease in bullying in the playgrounds of primary schools (Boulton, 1994).

Reactive strategies

Reactive strategies deal with bullying situations when they have arisen. Their success/effectiveness is dependent on clear and effective pupil reporting systems that enable pupils to report bullying incidents, including confidential and varied routes for doing so, effective and fair investigation, listening strategies and follow-up systems to ensure that agreements are sustained (DCSF, 2007).

Reactive strategies range from punitive or direct sanctions-based approaches, through restorative practices to more indirect and non-punitive approaches. In the UK, the DCSF recommends that bullying should always incur some form of sanction. Many professionals, however, prefer less direct approaches – at least for less severe cases of bullying. A school's philosophy on this should be evident in its anti-bullying policy.

Direct sanctions

Direct sanctions may vary in their severity and be used on a graded scale if bullying persists. They can range from reprimands/serious talks, involving parents or carers, temporary removal from class, withdrawal of privileges and rewards, disciplinary measures, such as detentions, school community service, such as picking up litter or school clean-ups, through to temporary or permanent exclusion. Direct sanctions are expected to impress on perpetrators that what they have done is unacceptable and promote understanding of the limits of acceptable behaviour, give an opportunity for those who bully to face up to the harm they have caused and learn from it, deter them from repeating that behaviour, signal to other pupils that the behaviour is unacceptable and deter them from doing it and demonstrate publicly that school rules and policies are to be taken seriously.

Milder sanctions can be implemented by all school staff, but only the head and deputy head teachers can temporarily and permanently exclude students. There is no evidence of the effectiveness of milder sanctions and a small amount of evidence of the effects of exclusion. Case studies of hard-to-reach children and young people who had been excluded from school concluded that there are no quick fix solutions (Frankham et al., 2007).

Restorative approaches

Direct sanctions are seen as a form of retributive justice. This contrasts with the idea of restorative justice (Braithwaite, 2002). The latter term refers to a range of practices that focus on offenders or bullying children being made aware of victims' feelings and the harm that they have caused and making some agreed reparation. Direct sanctions could still be resorted to if an individual refuses to make restorative approaches or does not abide by the decisions made using such a process.

In the UK, restorative approaches were originally developed in the area of youth justice and criminal behaviour, based on three main principles:

- responsibility – the offenders, along with their parents, learn to accept responsibility for the offence caused through their actions
- reparation – the victim is involved through consultation, mediation and participation, and reparative activities are devised to help the offender alleviate some of the damage and distress that they have caused
- resolution – successfully ending a dispute so that pupils and their families are free to interact without the threat of further conflict.

These approaches can also be applied to bullying in schools. In practice, restorative approaches are wide ranging and can be used for a variety of incidents in schools, including bullying, vandalism, theft, assault and conflicts between teachers and pupils.

The actual restorative practices used will depend on the nature and severity of the bullying incident, ranging from simple pupil-based discussions through to a full, restorative conference. An effective use of restorative justice depends on pupils being able to talk about feelings and relationship issues.

A good seedbed for this is problem-solving circles or circle time. Circle time experiences will facilitate simple, restorative approaches, such as restorative reminders, restorative discussions and restorative thinking plans. Under teacher supervision, pupils arrange their chairs in a circle and discuss a problem that needs to be resolved. All pupils are given the opportunity to speak, but only one is able to talk at any given time.

Pupils are largely positive about circle time, reporting that it helps them to learn about and express feelings and solve problems. If teachers have not had sufficient training or experience of good practice, however, it can be problematic (Taylor, 2003).

In a short or 'mini' conference, an informal meeting is held between the pupils involved, led by a trained member of staff. Incidents and the harm caused are examined and the offender(s) are asked to discuss possible means of reparation.

In a full restorative conference, a formal, structured meeting takes place involving pupils, their parents or carers, friends and school representatives, who are brought together to discuss and resolve an incident.

The staff member leading the conference needs to be highly trained and, prior to such a large meeting, will hold individual interviews with the participants to ensure that such a full conference is appropriate and everyone is completely prepared for it.

Restorative approaches are being increasingly used in schools and some evaluations are becoming available. Tinker (2002) evaluated 105 conferences carried out in schools in Nottingham and found that 78 per cent finished fully successful, while a further 16 per cent were partially successful. A pilot study evaluation in Lambeth schools also found that such conferences showed promising signs of resolving serious incidents (Edgar et al., 2002). A national evaluation found that 92 per cent of conferences were resolved successfully and, three months later, that 96 per cent of the agreements achieved in them remained intact (Youth Justice Board, 2004). Most school staff reported that their school had benefited, although no general improvements in pupils' attitudes were found at a whole-school level. A Scottish study has indicated that restorative justice 'can offer a powerful and effective approach to promoting harmonious relationships in school and to the successful resolution of conflict and harm' (Kane et al., 2007).

The method of shared concern

The shared concern, or Pikas, method was developed in Sweden by Pikas (1989, 2002) as a non-punitive, counselling-based approach to overcoming school bullying. It uses a combination of individual and group meetings, structured around five consecutive phases:

- individual talks with suspected bullies
- individual talks with the victim
- preparatory group meeting
- summit meeting
- follow-up of the results.

This approach is expected to sensitise bullying children to the harm that they are doing to their victims (enabled by a lack of hostile blaming attitude on the part of the interviewer), encourage positive behaviours towards the victim, and also encourage provocative victims to change their behaviour in positive ways.

   In an independent evaluation (Smith et al., 1994), 21 primary and secondary school teachers were trained in the method. All felt that it was an appropriate and helpful response to bullying and, among pupils who experienced it, three-quarters reported that bullying had decreased following the intervention. This improvement was attributed to pupils being given the chance to openly express their feelings and formulate their own solutions to resolve the situation. In some cases, however, the bullying child(ren) had switched their attention from the initial victim to another child outside of the group.

   The authors of the evaluation concluded that shared concern is a useful, short-term intervention for reducing bullying behaviours, but, in the case of very persistent bullying, further interventions may be required.

Support group method – the seven steps approach

The support group method (formerly called the no blame approach) was developed by Robinson and Maines (2007). It is a non-punitive approach that aims to change problem behaviours through a mixture of peer pressure to elicit a pro-social response and self-realization of the harm and suffering caused to the victim.

   There are seven steps:

- the facilitator talks individually to the bullied pupil
- a group meeting of six to eight students is then set up, some suggested by the victim but without his/her presence
- the facilitator explains to the group that the victim has a problem, but does not discuss the incidents that have taken place
- the facilitator assures the group that no punishment will given, but, instead, all the participants must take joint responsibility to make the victim feel happy and safe
- each group member gives their own ideas on how the victim can be helped

- the facilitator ends the meeting, with the group being given responsibility for improving the victim's safety and well-being
- individual meetings are held with group members one week after the meeting to establish how successful the intervention has been.

The support group method works on the premise of achieving lasting change rather than retribution and is expected to develop emotional awareness, peer support, social skills and empathy in the pupils involved. Young (1998), in a slight adaptation of the method, reported that, of 51 support group sessions studied, 80 per cent resulted in immediate success and 14 per cent experienced delayed success. The remaining 6 per cent had only limited success.

Smith et al. (2007) ascertained the use of and support for the support group method in schools across the UK. Most schools (83 per cent) rated the effectiveness of the method as either rather satisfactory or very satisfactory.

The method was found to be adapted considerably when in use, so that the 'seven steps' were not always followed as above. No direct evidence was provided as to whether or not the support group method was able to support and improve the behaviour of children who bullied others.

Peer support

Peer support uses the knowledge, skills and experience of the children and young people themselves in a planned and structured way to tackle and reduce bullying, using both proactive and reactive strategies. It takes a wide variety of forms, many of which involve some training of the peer supporters – for example, by ChildLine in their CHIPS (ChildLine in Partnership with Schools) programme. It is important that peer support projects involve the active commitment of staff, clear objectives and established ground rules for all aspects of the process.

Circles of friends, circles of support and supportive friends

In these kinds of circles, volunteer pupils are trained to befriend and support other pupils who are identified as being isolated or rejected by their peers and, hence, vulnerable to bullying.

Training involves increasing the pupils' empathic skills, developing a flexible and creative method to form positive relationships with peers and ingenuity in devising practical strategies to support victims.

Ofsted (2003) reported significant effects, with pupils feeling less isolated in the knowledge that some peers would not remain passive if they were intimidated or troubled.

Befriending

In befriending schemes, peer supporters are trained to offer support and friendship to pupils in everyday situations. Some schemes are based on having playground buddies (clearly identifiable by special caps or other clothing) to help lonely or bullied children during break- or lunchtimes. Others focus on organizing playground games or running lunchtime clubs that are open to all but offer companionship to lonely pupils.

Befrienders can be the same age or older than their target group. They are supported or supervised by school staff and need to receive training in listening skills, confidentiality issues, assertiveness and leadership.

Playground buddy schemes can be helpful, but may be underused if users feel exposed or stigmatized. Buddies may be teased about their special caps or clothes. Usually, running lunchtime activities can avoid these kinds of problems (Smith and Watson, 2004).

Peer mentoring

Peer mentoring schemes aim for a supportive relationship between two pupils, combining practical advice and encouragement. They are especially used to support pupils at challenging times, such as when they join a new school, suffer bereavement or experience bullying.

Peer mentors are known to the rest of the school (through assemblies, PSHE, newsletters and so on) and are contactable via a 'bully box', schools' intranets or referral by members of staff. In secondary schools, older pupil mentors can help train younger ones (Ofsted, 2003).

Mentoring is most effective when agreed ways of working are clear and there is good staff supervision and support given to the mentors (Cowie and Wallace, 2000; Smith and Watson, 2004).

Peer counselling or listening

Peer counselling or listening schemes are open to all students or target year groups as a drop-in or appointment service. Usually, pairs of students provide a 'listening ear' for student problems, including bullying-related issues (Cowie and Wallace, 2000).

Peer mediation

Peer mediation is a problem-solving process. It encourages pupils to:

- define the problem
- identify and agree key issues and discuss and brainstorm possible options
- negotiate a plan of action, agree on a follow-up process and evaluate outcomes.

Pupil mediators are trained in conflict resolution skills and helping individuals resolve disputes.

There is little hard evidence for the efficacy of such schemes (Baginsky, 2004). A peer mediation scheme in three Canadian primary school playgrounds, however, helped reduce physically aggressive playground behaviour by over a half (Cunningham et al., 1998).

Bystander (defender) training

This involves intervention action on the part of pupil bystanders when they witness peer victimization. They try to intervene to stop the bullying or comfort pupils who have experienced bullying.

Rigby and Johnson (2006) showed a video depicting bullying in the presence of bystanders to late primary and early secondary school students in Australia and 43 per cent of them indicated that they would be likely to help the victim.

General evaluation of peer support schemes

Reviews of peer support schemes (Cowie and Smith, 2006; Smith and Watson, 2004) have found that there are definite benefits for peer supporters and improvements are made in the schools' ethos. Reductions in bullying have been identified for particular cases, but are not yet substantiated at a broad level.

Issues that have been identified as crucial to the effectiveness of peer support schemes include:

- the selection and training of peer supporters
- recruiting boy as well as girl peer supporters
- recruiting peer supporters with high status in the peer group
- good and continuing supervision
- high level of awareness of the scheme
- sufficient take-up so that peer supporters feel positive about their role.

Resources

Further reading

McGrath, H. and Noble, T. (eds) (2006) *Bullying Solutions: Evidence-based approaches to bullying in Australian schools*. Frenchs Forest, NSW: Pearson.

Available online

The DCSF *Safe to Learn* materials www.teachernet.gov.uk/bullying

Websites

Anti-bullying Alliance	www..anti-bullyingalliance.org.uk
Child Line	www.childline.org.uk
Peer Mediation Network	www.peermediationnetwork.org.uk
School Councils UK	www.schoolcouncils.org
UK Observatory for the Promotion of Non-Violence	www.ukobservatory.com

KEY POINTS

- Bullying can be direct or indirect. The main types are physical, verbal, relational and indirect, which includes cyberbullying, and is sometimes based on a young person's race, sex, sexuality or disability.
- Interventions to address bullying in schools include proactive, reactive and peer support strategies.
- Restorative approaches help children who bully to become aware of the feelings and harm they do to the children they have bullied and make some form of reparation for that.
- Sanctions may be required when restorative approaches do not achieve the desired outcomes.

> ## QUESTIONS FOR DISCUSSION
>
> 1. Given what we know about the causes of bullying, what kinds of strategies are most likely to be effective in reducing it?
> 2. What arguments can be advanced in the debate between sanctions-based, restorative and non-punitive approaches to bullying incidents?

References

Anderson, B., Beinart, S., Farrington, D., Longman, J., Sturgis, P. and Utting, D. (2001) *Risk and Protective Factors Associated with Youth Crime and Effective Interventions to Prevent It.* London: Youth Justice Board.

Baginsky, W. (2004) *Peer Mediation in the UK: A guide for schools.* London: NSPCC.

Blatchford, P. (1998) *Social Life in School: Pupils' experiences of breaktime and recess from 6 to 16.* London: Routledge.

Boulton, M. (1994) 'Understanding and preventing bullying in the junior school playground', in P.K. Smith and S. Sharp (eds), *School Bullying: Insights and perspectives.* London. Routledge.

Braithwaite, J. (2002) *Restorative Justice & Responsive Regulation.* New York: Oxford University Press.

Cowie, H. and Smith, P.K. (2006) 'Peer support as a means of improving school safety and reducing bullying and violence', in B. Doll, J. Charvat, J. Baker and G. Stoner (eds), *Handbook of Prevention Research.* New Jersey: Lawrence Erlbaum.

Cowie, H. and Wallace, P. (2000) *Peer Support in Action: From bystanding to standing by.* London: Sage.

Cunningham, C.E., Cunningham, L.J., Martorelli, V., Tran, A., Young, J. and Zacharias, R. (1998) 'The effects of primary division, student-mediated conflict resolution programs on playground aggression', *Journal of Child Psychology and Psychiatry*, 39: 653–62.

Daniels, A. and Williams, H. (2000) 'Reducing the need for exclusions and statements for behaviour', *Educational Psychology in Practice*, 15: 221–7.

DCSF (2007) *Safe to Learn: Embedding anti-bullying work in schools.* London: DCSF.

Edgar, K., Bitel, M., Thurlow, J. and Bowen, G. (2002) *The Evaluation of the Lambeth Restorative Justice Conference Pilot Project in Schools.* London: Youth Justice Board.

Espelage, D.L., Bosworth, K. and Simon, T.R. (2000) 'Examining the social context of bullying behaviors in early adolescence', *Journal of Counseling and Development*, 78: 326–33.

Frankham, J., Edwards-Kerr, D., Humphrey, N. and Roberts, L. (2007) *School Exclusions: Learning partnerships outside mainstream education.* York: Joseph Rowntree Foundation.

Hallam, S., Rhamie, J. and Shaw, J. (2006) *Evaluation of the Primary Behaviour and Attendance Pilot.* London: DCSF.

Kane, J., Lloyd, G., McCluskey, G., Riddell, S., Stead, J. and Weedon, E. (2007) *Restorative Practices in Three Scottish Councils: Final report of the evaluation of the first two years of the pilot projects, 2004–2006.* Edinburgh: Scottish Executive.

Lambert, P., Scourfield, J., Smalley, N. and Jones, R. (2008) 'The social context of school bullying: evidence from a survey of children in South Wales', *Research Papers in Education*, 23: 269–91.

Learning through Landscapes (2003) 'National school grounds survey'. Winchester: Learning through Landscapes. Available online at: www.ltl.org.uk/schools_and_ settings/research/research-downloads.htm

McGrath, H. and Noble, T. (eds) (2006) *Bullying Solutions: Evidence-based approaches to bullying in Australian schools*. Frenchs Forest, NSW: Pearson.

OFSTED (2003) *Bullying: Effective action in secondary schools*. London: OFSTED.

Olweus, D. (1991) 'Bully/victim problems among school children: Basic facts and effects of a school-based intervention program', in D.J. Pepler and K. Rubin (eds), *The Development and Treatment of Childhood Aggression*. Hillside, NJ: Erlbaum.

Pikas, A. (1989) 'A pure concept of mobbing gives the best results for treatment', *School Psychology International*, 10: 95–104.

Pikas, A. (2002) 'New developments of the shared concern method', *School Psychology International*, 23: 307–26.

Rigby, K. and Johnson, B. (2006) 'Expressed readiness of Australian schoolchildren to act as bystanders in support of children who are being bullied', *Educational Psychology*, 26: 425–40.

Robinson, G. and Maines, B. (2007) *Bullying: A complete guide to the support group method*. Bristol: Lucky Duck Publishing.

Schwartz, D., Dodge, K.A., Pettit, G.S. and Bates, J.E. (2000) 'Friendship as a moderating factor in the pathway between early harsh home environment and later victimization in the peer group', *Developmental Psychology*, 36: 646–62.

Sharp, S. and Smith, P.K. (eds) (1994) *Tackling Bullying in Your School: A practical handbook for teachers*. London: Routledge.

Shields, A. and Cicchetti, D. (2001) 'Parental maltreatment and emotion dysregulation as risk factors for bullying and victimization in middle childhood', *Journal of Clinical Child Psychology*, 30: 349–63.

Smith, P.K., Cowie, H. and Sharp, S. (1994) 'Working directly with pupils involved in bullying situations', in P.K. Smith and S. Sharp (eds), *School Bullying: Insights and perspectives*. London: Routledge.

Smith, P.K., Howard, S. and Thompson, F. (2007) 'Use of the support group method to tackle bullying, and evaluation from schools and local authorities in England', *Pastoral Care in Education*, 25: 4–13.

Smith, P.K., Mahdavi, J., Carvalho, M., Fisher, S., Russell, S. and Tippett, N. (2008a) 'Cyberbullying: its nature and impact in secondary school pupils', *Journal of Child Psychology and Psychiatry*, 49: 376–85.

Smith, P.K. and Myron-Wilson, R. (1998) 'Parenting and school bullying', *Clinical Child Psychology and Psychiatry*, 3: 405–17.

Smith, P.K. and Sharp, S. (eds) (1994) *School Bullying: Insights and perspectives*. London: Routledge.

Smith, P.K., Smith, C., Osborn, R. and Samara, M. (2008b) 'A content analysis of school anti-bullying policies: progress and limitations', *Educational Psychology in Practice*, 24: 1–12.

Smith, P.K. and Watson, D. (2004) 'Evaluation of the CHIPS (ChildLine in Partnership with Schools) programme', research report RR570, DfES.

Taylor, M.J. (2003) *Going Round in Circles: Implementing and learning from circle time*. Slough: NFER.

Tinker, R. (2002) *The Evaluation of the Nottingham Restorative Conferencing Project*. Nottingham: Nottingham City Anti-Bullying Support Team.

Utting, D., Monteiro, H. and Ghate, D. (2007) *Interventions for Children at risk of Developing Antisocial Personality Disorder: Report to the Department of Health and Prime Minister's Strategy Unit*. London: Policy Research Bureau.

Woods, S. and Wolke, D. (2003) 'Does the content of anti-bullying policies inform us about the prevalence of direct and relational bullying behaviour in primary schools?', *Educational Psychologist*, 23: 381–402.

Young, S. (1998) 'The support group approach to bullying in schools', *Educational Psychology in Practice*, 14: 32–9.

Youth Justice Board (2004) *National Evaluation of the Restorative Justice in Schools Programme* (Youth Justice Board Publication, Number D61). London: Youth Justice Board.

9

Intervening with Youth who Engage in Fire-setting

Daryl L. Sharp, Robert E. Cole, Carolyn E. Kourofsky and Susan W. Blaakman

Introduction

Fires set by children and young people pose a significant public health concern. Whether begun intentionally or unintentionally as a result of juveniles playing with fire (the term fire-setting encompasses both), youth-initiated fires result in considerable injuries, deaths and property damage each year (Hall, 2005a). Estimates from the National Fire Protection Association (NFPA) indicate that, every day, seven people are killed or injured in fires set by juveniles (Hall, 2005a).

Children are at high risk for injury and death due to fires. In a study of unintentional injuries, researchers with the Home Safety Council found that fire and burns were the leading cause of death for children aged 1 to 14 (Runyan and Castell, 2004). Although the incidence of arson is declining in the USA and Canada, it is growing in some other parts of the world, including the United Kingdom and Japan (Hall, 2005b).

The context of fire-setting: cognitive development

The nature and meaning of children's involvement with fire is, in part, a function of their level of cognitive development. Preschool, or preoperational (Piaget and Inhelder, 1969), children have little capacity to understand cause and effect (Coppens, 1986) and transformations. Consequently, they have little ability to appreciate the danger inherent in even the smallest flame or understand how a small candle, match or lighter flame might become a large fire. In addition, parents often overestimate their children's ability to understand this risk (Garling and Garling, 1995). Indeed, many common family practices – giving children candles to hold in church and blowing out birthday candles, for example – might actually support the preschool child's notion that the small candle, match and lighter flames they are so familiar with are not particularly dangerous (Cole et al., 2006).

Primary school, or concrete operational, children *do* understand cause and effect and transformations, but many overestimate their own ability to control a small fire (Grolnick et al., 1990). This overestimation is enhanced by the concrete operational child's failure to appreciate the full range of possible outcomes of a small fire suddenly getting out of control (Piaget and Inhelder, 1969). They cannot easily anticipate an outcome that they have not experienced. Grolnick et al. (1990) found that children who felt that they could extinguish a small fire were three times more likely than those who felt unable to extinguish a fire to self-report at least one instance of fire play. This sense of self-control was, in turn, related to greater exposure to household activities involving fire, more supervised experiences with fire, such as building campfires, more responsibility for chores involving fire (such as cooking) and greater access to ignition materials.

The young person, in the stage of formal operations, like the adult, does appreciate the full range of possible outcomes. There are no developmental limitations to the young person's understanding of the risk of being involved with a fire. The misuse of fire or deliberate fire-setting in this age group is likely to be linked to risktaking or individual or family pathology.

The context of fire-setting: individual and family pathology

The studies examining the correlates of fire-setting typically categorize children into two groups based on this single behaviour. Given the high prevalence of self-reported involvement with fire, the various manifestations and definitions of fire involvement, the various methods of obtaining information from children and families (anonymous surveys, in-depth clinical studies) and the nature of the sample (representative community samples, clinic outpatients, inpatients or juvenile offenders), one must be cautious of drawing firm conclusions about what such fire involvement represents. In studies limited to clinic samples or juvenile offenders, the fire-setting occurred in the context of pathology and the question being addressed is whether or not it is associated with a higher level of pathology. Conclusions drawn from such studies may not be relevant to, nor usefully guide interventions for, community samples of young children. Rather, the studies reviewed suggest areas for inclusion in a comprehensive assessment, not a known pathway for intervention.

The available data, at first glance, seem to provide a consistent picture of juvenile involvement with fire – impulsive, aggressive children with poor social skills and parents who are either abusive or uninvolved. The data, however, represent only associations – a possible increase in the likelihood of pathology – not the certain presence.

The nature of an intervention should be based on a comprehensive examination of an individual child and their family. Brett (2004) comments that fire-setters are a heterogeneous group and studies of recidivism do not support the notion that, as a group, they are inherently dangerous. Dadds and Fraser (2006) add 'not all fire-setting is attributable to antisocial youth and being able to identify youths with abnormal patterns of fire interest and behaviour regardless of their other problems would be advantageous.'

Nonetheless, the available evidence suggests areas of concern linked to fire-setting. Children involved in doing this, especially older children, are more likely to exhibit:

- externalizing behaviour, aggression and conduct disorder (Del Bove et al., 2008)
- poor social skills and poor peer relationships (Sakheim et al., 1991)
- impulsivity, hyperactivity and symptoms of attention deficit hyperactivity disorder (Dadds and Fraser, 2006)
- depression, hopelessness, low self-esteem and anxiety (Dadds and Fraser, 2006)
- lying, stealing, vandalism and delinquency (Del Bove et al., 2008).

Children involved in fire-setting are also more likely to have experienced:

- stressful life events, such as the death of a family member or close friend, parental separation or divorce, family illness, frequent moves and family unemployment (Dadds and Fraser, 2006)
- physical abuse, sexual abuse, neglect or domestic violence (Becker et al., 2004)
- parental mental illness, including depression, hostility and criminal history (Becker et al., 2004)
- harsh or lax parental discipline, a lack of parental involvement and poor monitoring or supervision (Dadds and Fraser, 2006).

Primary interventions to reduce the incidence of the problem

Systematic clinical assessment of an interest in fire and associated behaviour

Although fire-setting is relatively common among young people (Simonson and Bullis, 2001), practitioners often fail to assess such behaviour when gathering mental/behavioural health data in clinical settings. MacKay and colleagues (2006) argue that many tools exist to guide clinicians when assessing antisocial behaviour, which is positively correlated with fire-setting in young people, yet there is a paucity of valid and reliable instruments to assess fire-specific behaviour (such as an interest in fire). Moreover, despite the presence of psychological morbidity among many young people who set fires, most evaluations of juvenile fire-setters in the USA are conducted by fire service professionals, who are not trained in how to assess or intervene regarding such morbidity.

Primary care and mental health clinicians generally have not systematically included a fire history, including an interest in fire and related behaviours, as an essential component of a comprehensive assessment of the children and young people entrusted to their care. Many erroneously assume that an effective intervention with children who set fires requires highly specialized skills over and above their expertise. The treatment of fire-setting behaviour, however, is best approached by intervening regarding the underlying issues motivating the behaviour, such as knowledge deficits, maltreatment, depression, suicidality, substance abuse, parental stress and inadequate supervision (Root et al., 2008).

Primary care clinicians can routinely assess for an interest in fire and related behaviours and refer young people to the appropriate mental health services as needed. Most mental health professionals are specifically trained to address the underlying issues that motivate fire-setting behaviour. It is likely, therefore, that the incidence of fire-setting can be reduced if clinicians proactively take a fire history, including an assessment of factors known to put young people at higher risk for fire-setting, so that targeted interventions can be employed as early as possible to ameliorate the underlying issues that motivate such behaviour (Root et al., 2008). Such systematic assessment could also identify those young people who primarily need educational interventions, so that appropriate referrals to fire service and other professionals who provide such education can be made before they engage in further fire-setting.

Developmentally informed preventative education

The specific content of fire safety education is highly dependent on each young person's developmental level. The approach appropriate for preschoolers is exemplified by the *play safe! be safe!* programme (see the Resources section at the end of this chapter). Based on our understanding of preschool children's inability to understand cause and effect and transformations, no attempt is made to show or explain how fire spreads or the possible consequences. Rather, *play safe! be safe!* offers children a simple and familiar classification of fire and ignition materials as adult tools that must be used carefully and stored safely. The children are then involved in the enterprise of family fire safety by asking them to ensure that the adults in the family 'put matches and lighters away.' The programme teaches and rewards behaviour that is incompatible with children misusing fire. This same approach can be extended, involving preschool children in the testing and maintenance of smoke alarms, the development and practice of exit drills and so on.

A similar approach is used with primary school children. While children of this age will understand cause and effect and the transformation of the small match or lighter flame into the large, destructive fire, their inability to anticipate and prepare for unexpected outcomes supports taking the same basic approach that is used with younger children. The fundamental educational message must be that ignition materials are adult tools, to be used only by adults. Children of this age might benefit from video presentations that demonstrate how quickly fire can escape our control. These should be presented in a way that supports the fundamental message, not as a means of instruction regarding how to use or manage fire.

Young people (like adults) have achieved the stage of formal operations and will be able to anticipate a wide range of potential problematic outcomes. Like many adults, however, they will underestimate the likelihood that these outcomes will occur and overestimate their ability to respond. Education for young people should therefore include proper instruction in how to handle and use ignition materials safely. Video or other demonstrations of the power of fire and the speed with which it moves might be appropriate as a way to address young people's underestimation of the risks of all uses of fire, and particularly its misuse.

Interventions to address the problem

Intervention approaches to working with young people who set fires are guided by collaborative models in which mental health, social service, police and fire service professionals come together to address the underlying issues motivating the fire-setting behaviour. Several programmes are described in the literature. Three of them are highlighted below and the common intervention components identified.

The Arson Prevention Program for Children (TAPP-C)

The most comprehensive clinical guide available is the Arson Prevention Program for Children (TAPP-C) (MacKay et al., 2004).

The programme began in the early 1990s as a joint venture by the Centre for Addiction and Mental Health, Office of the Fire Marshal of Ontario and Toronto Fire Services. It had been designed to target fire-setting as well as other inappropriate uses of fire by children and young people and includes a component for parents and carers as well as a component for children and young people. The specific intervention strategies used are based on the scientific principles of parent management training and cognitive behavioural therapy for children and young people and are discussed in the manualized clinical programme (MacKay et al., 2004).

The programme is founded on the premise that clinicians, parents or carers and children should work collaboratively to develop individualized solutions to fire-setting behaviour. The children learn fire-safe behaviours, which their parents or carers reinforce. The children are also coached in how to develop strategies designed to help them recognize and control fire-related impulses and behaviours. Parental supervision is also emphasized.

As the efficacy of the programme is enhanced when clients actively participate in their treatment (Bloomquist and Schnell, 2002), it emphasizes participants' interaction and active involvement. The treatment component of the programme consists of five 90-minute sessions for parents or carers and the children respectively, with some content overlap (MacKay et al., 2004).

TAPP-C also includes a fire education component that is conducted by a specially trained fire service professional and begins with a home visit that is designed to target fire safety. Additional education sessions are usually conducted at the local fire station.

Results from evaluations of the programme to date indicate that approximately three-quarters of parents or carers participating in TAPP-C report no return to fire-setting among their children (MacKay et al., 2004).

Depending on the results of the children's fire-setting risk assessment, TAPP-C can either be used alone (for those presenting a low fire-setting risk) or as a complement to other mental health treatments (for young people at higher risk of doing so; MacKay et al., 2004). Those who return to fire-setting tend to require more intensive treatment – they are likely to be older, struggle with aggression (which they can express through fire-setting) and exhibit covert antisocial behaviours (such as lying and being secretive; Kennedy et al., 1991). Additionally, in comparison to young people with behaviour problems who don't set fires, fire-setting young people have been associated with higher levels of family dysfunction (poor parental supervision and discipline; Walsh et al., 2004). This suggests that merely targeting the fire-setting behaviour will be inadequate in successfully treating such young people because they and their families will require more comprehensive clinical interventions, such as family therapy, that targets such dysfunctional family interaction patterns, day or residential treatment and/or the use of medication.

The Bradley Hospital FireSafe Families Program

Another example of a comprehensive programme is the Bradley FireSafe Families Program, which is a community-based interdisciplinary form of treatment for fire-setting young people (Barreto et al., 2004).

The programme is designed to address fire safety knowledge, which is delivered by members of the fire service, along with parent and family functioning. This latter content is delivered by mental health professionals who focus on helping families to build healthy communication and problem-solving skills, as well as strengthening parental supervision, including parent–child boundary maintenance.

Skill-based communication exchanges are first practised among groups of children and then refined and reinforced by including parents in multiple family intervention groups. Parents first learn how to make such exchanges through group education and then are linked to outpatient providers if needed.

The programme's developers describe the model as being founded on an ecological framework that underscores the importance of the ability to regulate emotions to treating fire appropriately in the context of how the families function and their community support networks. The full programme is delivered over four consecutive weekly sessions, amounting to a total of 18 hours of education and intervention. The fire safety component for the young people and the companion educational module for the parent group comprise six of those 18 hours (Barreto et al., 2004).

The Trauma Burn Outreach Prevention Program

The Trauma Burn Outreach Prevention Program (TBOPP) is another multidisciplinary approach to working with young fire-setters, but it is less comprehensive than the programmes described above (Franklin et al., 2002). It is distinct because it focuses on the medical, financial, legal and societal impacts of fire-setting behaviour, with an emphasis on individual responsibility and accountability.

Young people (aged from 4 to 17 years) who have a history of at least one fire-setting or arson incident (without ill intent) are referred to this day-long programme by the court system, schools, fire departments and parents. It is conducted at the University of Michigan Burn Trauma Center, where participants experience didactic presentations and interactive opportunities with nurse educators, trauma surgeons, social workers and firefighters. Peer counsellors (graduates of the programme and fire victims) interact with the participants and there are opportunities for the young people to spend time in the intensive care unit, skin bank, morgue and injury prevention centre. The participants also observe a moulage burn patient in a tub room experiencing burn wound debridement to simulate the experience of an 'actual' victim.

The outcomes of the programme are reportedly quite favourable, with essentially no return to fire-setting among participants (Franklin et al., 2002). It is important to be mindful, however, that these results have not been replicated. Moreover, such a programme could traumatize young people if the potentially threatening and anxiety-provoking experiences described are not skilfully processed with them. Although threats can induce short-term behavioural compliance, sustained change typically occurs over time when the motivation to engage in prosocial, healthy behaviours has been internalized and replacement behaviours have been learned (Grolnick et al., 1997; Sharp et al., 2005).

Common intervention components

In summary, the following components of interventions are commonly found in the available intervention programmes for young people who set fires.

- *Fire safety education for children and parents*

    - The nature of fire.
    - Personal safety strategies, such as notifying adults if matches and lighters are found.
    - Appropriate responses in the event of fire – stop, drop and roll, crawl low under smoke and so on.

- *Cognitive behavioural therapy and/or strategies*

    - Recognizing the purposes fire-setting behaviour serves:
        - expressing emotions
        - gaining attention
        - communicating
        - problem-solving.
    - Assisting children and young people to recognize the urge to start a fire.
    - Interrupting behaviour before it starts.
    - Identifying and practising socially appropriate substitution behaviours to self-express or elicit functional communication.

- *Parenting*

    - Understanding the developmental capacities of children and young people.
    - Improving supervision and monitoring.

- *Collaboration between fire service and mental health professionals*

    - Understanding and respecting each discipline's scope of practice.
    - Open communication between professionals and/or securing appropriate releases to facilitate the exchange of information.

Resources

Further reading

Cole, R., Crandall, R., Kourofsky, C., Sharp, D., Blaakman, S. and Cole, E. (2006) *Juvenile Firesetting: A community guide to prevention and intervention.* Pittsford, NY: Fireproof Children/Prevention First. This handbook summarizes more than twenty-five years of research, training and hands-on experience by fire investigators and experts in child development. It is intended for social workers, mental health professionals, the fire service, teachers and nursery workers.

Kourofsky, C. (2004) *Mikey Makes a Mess.* Pittsford, NY: Fireproof Children/Prevention First. This storybook, in English and Spanish, was developed to provide key fire safety messages in an engaging way via a story with colourful illustrations.

Websites

Arson Prevention Bureau www.arsonpreventionbureau.org.uk
Provides advice and information to help tackle the problem of arson nationally. On this site you will find statistics on arson trends, measures you can take to protect yourself, information about arson and arson prevention and more detailed research reports.

The award-winning *play safe! be safe!* multimedia classroom kit is available via this site. Designed for children aged three to five, *play safe! be safe!* includes a 20-minute DVD, activity boards, 'Keep Away!'/Aléjate card game and a teacher's manual. The kit is available in English (with an English and Spanish DVD and activities) and French.

The website also lists a wide variety of resources, organized for ease of use for several audiences, including early childhood teachers, parents and fire service and mental health professionals.

Bradley Hospital FireSafe Families www.lifespan.org/services/childhealth/research/interests/firesafe/about.htm
Provides information about Bradley Hospital's FireSafe Families Program.

Centre for Addiction and Mental Health www.camh.net
This site for Canada's leading addiction and mental health teaching hospital includes, on its 'Resources for professionals' page, ordering information for the TAPP-C Clinician's Manual for Preventing and Treating Juvenile Fire Involvement.

Fire Marshal's Public Fire Safety Council www.firesafetycouncil.com
In English and French, this Ontario website provides fire safety information, including brochures, pamphlets, public service announcements and a 'Teacher's corner'.

Fireproof Children/Prevention First www.fireproofchildren.com
David J. Kolko www.pitt.edu/~kolko
Information on D.J. Kolko's *Handbook on Firesetting in Children and Youth* (Academic Press, 2002), including assessment tools and other fire-related studies.

National Fire Protection Association (NFPA) www.nfpa.org
The NFPA's website contains the latest information about the Association, including its research findings and publications. Resources include RiskWatch®, a school-based curriculum divided into five age-appropriate teaching modules (for ages 4 to 14), including fire and other safety topics, and Sparky the Dog® games, activities and materials.

Safe Kids Worldwide www.safekids.org
The Safe Kids website offers safety tips and checklists, activities for children and resources for teachers and parents. It includes links to programmes in 16 countries.

SOS Fires Youth Intervention Programs www.sosfires.com
The website posts information that may be useful for professionals who work with young people who set fires or are in intervention programmes, as well as parents, teachers and others.

Tito Lorito www.iahff.org
Created by the International Association of Hispanic Firefighters, this site in Spanish has games and songs for children, a guide for parents and links to other sites with information in Spanish.

Trauma Burn Center's Straight Talk Program www.traumaburn.org
Click on 'injury prevention & education' and in the 'Straight talk' section, you will find additional information about this programme.

KEY POINTS

- Children's involvement with fire is, in part, a function of their level of cognitive development.
- Fire-setters are a heterogeneous group and research does not support the notion that they are inherently dangerous.
- Treating fire-setting is best approached by intervening with regard to the underlying issues motivating the behaviour.
- Common intervention components include education for young people and parents, cognitive behavioural therapy, appropriate parenting and collaboration between fire service and mental health professionals

QUESTIONS FOR DISCUSSION

1. Discuss ways in which underlying issues in conjunction with environmental and systemic factors might contribute to a young person's fire-setting behaviour.
2. Imagine a 13-year-old boy who is setting fires and lives in a troubled family environment. Describe how you would manage his case to enable appropriate interventions to be put into effect. Predict any problems that you might encounter when implementing your plan and explain how you might deal with them.

References

Barreto, S., Boekamp, J., Armstrong, L. and Gillen, P. (2004) 'Community-based interventions for juvenile firestarters: a brief family-centered model', *Psychological Services,* 1: 158–68.

Becker, K.D., Stuewig, J., Herrera, V.M. and McCloskey, L.A. (2004) 'A study of fire-setting and animal cruelty in children: family influences and adolescent outcomes', *Journal of the American Academy of Child & Adolescent Psychiatry,* 43 (7): 905–12.

Bloomquist, M. and Schnell, S. (2002) *Helping Children with Aggression and Conduct Problems: Best practices for interventions.* New York: Guilford Press.

Brett, A. (2004) '"Kindling theory" in arson: how dangerous are firesetters?', *Australian and New Zealand Journal of Psychiatry*, 38 (6): 419–25.

Cole, R., Crandall, R., Kourofsky, C., Sharp, D., Blaakman, S. and Cole, E. (2006) *Juvenile Firesetting: A community guide to prevention and intervention*. Pittsford, NY: Fireproof Children/Prevention First.

Coppens, N.M. (1986) 'Cognitive characteristics as predictors of children's understanding of safety and prevention', *Journal of Pediatric Psychology*, 11 (2): 189–202.

Dadds, M.R. and Fraser, J.A. (2006) 'Fire interest, fire-setting and psychopathology in Australian children: a normative study', *Australian & New Zealand Journal of Psychiatry*, 40 (6–7): 581–6.

Del Bove, G., Caprara, G., Pastorelli, C. and Paciello, M. (2008) 'Juvenile firesetting in Italy: relationship to aggression, psychopathology, personality, self-efficacy, and school functioning', *European Child & Adolescent Psychiatry*, 17 (4): 235–44.

Franklin, G., Pucci, P., Arbabi, S., Brandt, M., Wahl, W. and Taheri, P. (2002) 'Decreased juvenile arson and firesetting recidivism after implementation of a multidisciplinary prevention program', *The Journal of Trauma Injury, Infection, and Critical Care*, 53: 260–6.

Garling, A. and Garling, T. (1995) 'Mothers' anticipation and prevention of unintentional injury to young children in the home', *Journal of Pediatric Psychology*, 20 (1): 23–36.

Grolnick, W.S., Cole, R.E., Laurenitis, L. and Schwartzman, P. (1990) 'Playing with fire: a developmental assessment of children's fire understanding and experience', *Journal of Clinical Child Psychology*, 19 (2): 128–35.

Grolnick, W.S., Deci, E.L. and Ryan, R.M. (1997) 'Internalization within the family: the self-determination theory perspective', in J.E. Grusec and L. Kuczynski (eds), *Parenting and Children's Internalization of Values: A handbook of contemporary theory*. New York: John Wiley pp. 135–61.

Hall, J. (2005a) *Children Playing with Fire*. Quincy, MA: National Fire Protection Association.

Hall, J. (2005b) *Intentional Fires and Arson*. Qunicy, MA: National Fire Protection Association.

Kennedy, P., Vale, E., Khan, S. and McAnaney, A. (2006) 'Factors predicting recidivism in child and adolescent fire-setters: a systematic review of the literature', *The Journal of Forensic Psychiatry and Psychology*, 17: 151–64.

Kolko, D.J. (ed.) (2002) *Handbook on Firesetting in Children and Youth*. San Diego, CA: Academic Press.

Kolko, D.J. and Kazdin, A.E. (1991) 'Aggression and psychopathology in matchplaying and firesetting children: a replication and extension', *Journal of Clinical Child Psychology*, 20 (2): 191–201.

MacKay, S., Henderson, J., Del Bove, G., Marton, P., Warling, D. and Root, C. (2006) 'Fire interest and antisociality as risk factors in the severity and persistence of juvenile firesetting', *Journal of the American Academy of Child & Adolescent Psychiatry*, 45 (9): 1077–84.

MacKay, S., Henderson, J., Root, C., Warling, D., Gilbert, K. and Johnstone, J. (2004) *Clinician's Manual for Preventing and Treating Juvenile Fire Involvment*. Toronto, Canada: Center for Addiction and Mental Health and the Office of the Fire Marshal of Ontario.

Piaget, J. and Inhelder, B. (1969) *The Psychology of the Child*. New York: Basic Books.

Root, C., MacKay, S., Henderson, J., Del Bove, G. and Warling, D. (2008) 'The link between maltreatment and juvenile firesetting: correlates and underlying mechanisms', *Child Abuse and Neglect*, 32 (2): 161–76.

Runyan, C. and Castell, C. (eds) (2004) *The State of Home Safety in America: Facts about unintentional injuries in the home* (2nd edn). Washington, DC: Home Safety Council.

Sakheim, G.A., Osborn, E. and Abrams, D. (1991) 'Toward a clearer differentiation of high-risk from low-risk fire-setters', *Child Welfare Journal,* 70 (4): 489–503.

Sharp, D.L., Blaakman, S.W., Cole, E.C. and Cole, R.E. (2005) 'Evidence-based multi-disciplinary strategies for working with children who set fires', *Journal of the American Psychiatric Nurses Association,* 11 (6): 329–37.

Simonson, B. and Bullis, M. (2001) *Fire Interest Survey: Final report.* Unpublished manuscript.

Walsh, D., Lamble, I. and Stewart, M. (2004) 'Sparking up: family, behavioral and empathy factors in adolescent firesetters', *American Journal of Forensic Psychology,* 22: 5–32.

Part V

Substance Abuse

10

Alcohol and Young People

Brad Levingston and Jenny Melrose

Introduction

From a young person's point of view, drinking may be seen as an essential rite of passage – a rebellion against adult restrictions by participating in a popular adult pastime. The search for fun, confidence and identity can seem more achievable and more enjoyable when intoxicated. For many, intoxication creates opportunities to form relationships, take risks or escape the pain of self-consciousness, loneliness or sadness. Most Western societies proudly promote alcohol consumption as part of adult life, so young people aspiring to join adult ranks are likely to believe that it is essential for them to drink alcohol.

In this chapter, we provide a framework that will guide workers in understanding and responding to problematic alcohol use by young people and young adults. The age range covered is broadly the teen years up to the early twenties. We have focused on clinical issues rather than health promotion and prevention as this summary is primarily a practical guide to working with troubled individuals. Clearly, health promotion and prevention are essential and we urge readers to become familiar with the fundamental principles of these programmes and support their implementation.

An Assessment with Understanding

Establishing trust and achieving engagement are fundamental to all therapeutic or helping relationships. To build trust and respect, it is important not to underestimate the value of a sensitive assessment of the young person's circumstances, emotional experiences and substance use. Such an assessment may help to build a platform for personal change. It may give a sense of hope sufficient to get them through the day even if nothing else changes.

A sensitive assessment may be conducted over a couple of sessions and involve not only talking but also drawing, listening to music, walking in the park – using modalities that are comfortable for the client, not just the modalities that the service providers demand or impose (Monti et al., 2001).

Workers who wish to gain the trust of a young person need to explore that young person's reasons for seeking help and find out whether they are doing so voluntarily or under pressure. Issues related to confidentiality and/or the need for reporting should be considered and discussed with them. Failure to address such issues will render a meeting useless or destructive and the young person may decide that youth workers 'can't be trusted', the system 'sucks' or 'there is no one who genuinely wants to help'.

The Assessment Format

We believe that all agencies should develop a comprehensive assessment proce-dure based on the following guidelines.

- *Establish the young person's primary concerns*
  Young people are not necessarily concerned about the quantity and frequency of their drinking. The physical, legal, financial, social and/or psychological problems that occur in conjunction with alcohol use are more likely to bother them. To establish our credibility and relevance, it is essential that we make our starting point the concerns that the young person has, and use that as a springboard to discussing underlying factors, including what, when, how and why they drink.
- *Obtain an outline of their current circumstances*
  We need to establish where the client lives, who supports them and how they finance their life. Clients who have chaotic living arrangements are rarely able to make substantial changes in their alcohol use until they experience more stability.
- *Enquire about what experiences they have had with other helping services*
  Previous experience with helping services as well as legal, educational and med-ical agencies may have been positive or negative. Establishing what has worked and what hasn't can guide your work with clients. It will indicate what they expect, what they reject and what they appreciate.
- *Explain why it is important to know about a person's use of alcohol and other drugs*
  Subject to an agreement about confidentiality and reporting obligations, it is important to obtain an agreement that you and the client will talk about their drug use. You can then discuss alcohol use in a routine, matter-of-fact way and minimize the appearance of being judgemental or accusatory.
- *Develop a list of the substances taken over the past 12 months and discuss the pattern of use*
  The worker does not have to be an expert on all substances in order to follow this basic routine. Be confident and comfortable and ask about all drugs that have been used. The review should include alcohol, tobacco, prescribed medications, medica-tions purchased from pharmacies and illicit drugs, such as cannabis, amphetamines, ecstasy, heroin, steroids, solvents and any other substances known to be used locally. For each substance, get an estimate of the *quantity* consumed in a typical session, the *frequency* of sessions and the approximate date when it was last used. Don't expect this information to be exact – estimates are OK.
- *Identify the function or purpose that alcohol consumption serves for the client*
  This is most important. It takes time and has to be done in collaboration with your client. An alcohol problem is not just one of it resulting in occasional arguments or hangovers. Problematic drinking often occurs as a way of coping with low

self-esteem and a desire to be accepted by the peer group. It often masks these concerns, but it is a poor strategy as it can interfere with judgement and emotional regulation, resulting in 'incidents' that perpetuate the cycle of despair or self-consciousness that drinking was supposed to eliminate. Getting drunk is a short-term solution to a long-term problem for a young person who is socially anxious or struggling with a problematic family history. These are matters that a sensitive assessment will begin to identify with the result that the young person feels understood.

- *Recognize and acknowledge mental health problems*
An underlying mental health problem, such as anxiety, depression, unresolved grief or a post-traumatic disorder, is a significant complicating factor that always requires sustained investigation and treatment (Lopatko et al., 2002; Melrose, 2007; Sellman and Deering, 2002; Szirom et al., 2004). Focusing on the young person's drinking behaviour is insufficient in these situations as it fails to address the emotional pain that is part of the mental health problem. The potential for self-harm, recurrent suicidal ideation, suicide attempts and completed suicide is high in the context of alcohol abuse, so workers must be vigilant and have contingency plans to deal with emergencies if they arise. It is important to ask clients whether or not there have been times in the past month when they have felt depressed, worried, anxious, self-harmed or thought about suicide. Checking whether or not they still have any of these feelings will not cause a problem – it may open the door to some very important discussions.

- *Enquire about other issues*
Effective intervention deals with many topics other than substance use (Spooner et al., 1999). Some of the problems that young people may disclose include:

    - legal problems
    - use of negative personal labels
    - influence of socio-economic status
    - peer influence
    - relationship breakdown
    - cultural issues, such as being a member of a minority group
      boredom
    - lack of information with regard to rights, behaviours and opportunities
    - academic, language and literacy problems
    - effects of trauma
    - family problems
    - financial security and employment prospects.

- *Ask the young person what they would like to do about their alcohol use*
Many well-intentioned workers assume that their clients recognize there is a connection between their alcohol use and the problems they have. Workers, further, assume that the young person will *want* to change their drinking behaviour and *now*. Both assumptions are likely to be wrong. Clients often believe that the way they currently live is the best they can do under the circumstances. They may want the *circumstances* to change or want *other people* to change, but they may have no intention of making enduring *personal* changes. In seeing a worker, they may be complying with the wishes of a friend, parent or court order. Unfortunately, this can reinforce their belief that they are not really in charge of their life. Drinking to the point of being oblivious to life's pain may be seen by such young people as one way to exercise control and direction. To give up drinking therefore, is, to give up this form of control. It is

unlikely that real progress will be made in helping a young person if they do not believe that they can exercise some choice and control over their future.

The process of change described by Prochaska, et al. (1992) has become a popular description of the steps or stages that a person may move through in the process of making a personal change. We recommend that workers think carefully about how they prepare clients to make change and tailor their interventions to the clients' priorities and readiness. The six stages of the process of change model are as follows.

- *Precontemplation* These young drinkers are 'happy' in their use – that is, they enjoy the fun and put up with the fights, hangovers and other costs associated with drinking. They have not considered making any change in their behaviour so their motivation to participate in treatment is negligible.
- *Contemplation* The young drinker recognizes that some problems are linked to their current drinking pattern. They occasionally think about making some changes, but take no action.
- *Determination/preparation* At this stage, the drinker recognizes that the costs of drinking outweigh the benefits and a change in their pattern of use is called for. There may still be some ambivalence about giving up the benefits, but they are ready to make personal changes.
- *Action* The young drinker is engaged in monitoring and changing their drinking habits in order to achieve a specified goal.
- *Maintenance* Changes made by the young drinker have been sustained and there is a resolve to maintain this recently acquired pattern of drinking or abstinence.
- *Relapse* Relapse is the alternative to maintenance and is also a feature of the change process (Werch and DiClemente, 1994). It may involve a return to previous drinking patterns, but it does not have to be seen as a sign of failure. Many interventions focus on relapse prevention and how to manage 'lapses' constructively.

- *Use motivational interviewing techniques to help the young person to explore their choices about alcohol use*
  Motivational interviewing builds on the change process and recognizes that individuals are usually ambivalent about changing a behaviour that has been an enjoyable and central part of their social life. With the emphasis on ambivalence rather than resistance, workers casually but systematically assist their clients to consider what it is they like and don't like about drinking (Miller and Rollnick, 2002). Motivational interviewing challenges the common myth that clients must be motivated before they can be helped and places responsibility on the helping agent to promote the motivation for change. There are five basic features of motivational interviewing and, like any skill, they have to be practised if they are to be performed well. Effective workers have the ability to do the following.

  - *Express empathy* Reflective, empathic listening will reassure the client that the worker is able to understand both the facts and the feelings that are being expressed. When ambivalence about change is high, empathy – not coercion – is most important.
  - *Develop discrepancy* Gentle but persistent highlighting of any discrepancy between continuing the present behaviour and achieving other important goals can create a desire for change. For example, the worker may say, 'You see yourself as being reliable and honest with your mates, but you just hocked their

sound system and you can't pay your share of the rent. What does that feel like for you?' Here the worker is helping the client to recognize the discrepancy between what they believe about themselves and how they behave. The aim is to enable the client to produce arguments for making a change. It is not a time to make them feel guilty or see themselves as a failure.

- *Avoid arguments* Arguing with the client is counterproductive, as it breeds defensiveness and reduces rapport. Using confrontational methods will cause further defensiveness.
- *Roll with resistance* Client 'resistance' is often an indication that the worker needs to change strategies. Working through resistance can produce new perspectives or possibilities that will enable the worker to have a fuller understanding of their client.
- *Support self-efficacy* Clients often feel quite powerless when it comes to dealing with life's problems. If they feel more relaxed and confident when they have been drinking, giving up alcohol may feel like giving up a lifejacket when they think that they can't swim. Self-efficacy is the belief that you have the capacity to learn to swim and survive. Starting small and working up to bigger things is a good way to go at the beginning of any intervention. For example, self-efficacy is promoted by pointing out that 'You decided to come and see me today even though you could have been out with your mates. It seems as if you are in charge of what you do when you make up your mind.' Overall, motivational interviewing is a matter of 'interpersonal style' – not just a technique to be used in an attempt to manipulate clients. It is an empathic enquiry designed to help clients to think carefully about their situations and then consider the options while feeling empowered as well as understood.

• *Provide feedback and a menu of options for the young person to consider*
After all this discussion, the information has to be put together in a concise, practical way that maximizes the chances that the young person will take some action. This can be done effectively by following the framework known as FRAMES (Bien et al., 1993). Using this short, verbal summary (see Figure 10.1) a worker can pull the story together in a sensitive way that demonstrates to the young person that they have been understood as well as listened to. It provides a chance to capture the essence of what has been happening and challenges the young person to seize the opportunity to make a decision about what to do and when to do it.

Workers will find it useful to follow this outline in order to summarize, challenge and focus the attention of those they hope to assist. It can be used in relation to any topic, not just alcohol or other drugs. The collaboration that is required in designing the menu is a crucial part of this activity. Like all skills, it is essential to practise in order to be able to deliver FRAMES in a calm, warm and convincing way.

Implementing an Intervention

When implementing an intervention, it is important to recognize our expectations. For instance, it is unlikely that 'responsible' drinking or abstinence will be achieved quickly or that young people will be keen to understand the things that provoked or still maintain their drinking.

Implementation requires a trusting relationship with a therapist and support workers who are credible, persistent and patient. Develop a simple game plan in

F R A M E S stands for:

- *feedback* a sensitive, factual summary of the pros and cons of the drinking or any other issue that a young person is prepared to consider
- *responsibility* making it clear that the young person has a personal choice and responsibility for what happens next
- *advice* a recommendation that is carefully crafted to challenge the young person to make some decisions, noting the risks if nothing changes
- *menu* a balanced list of practical actions that can be implemented and have a good chance of being beneficial in the short-term
- *empathy* all the above are delivered with a sensitivity that demonstrates a clear respect for the young person
- *self-efficacy* a message that affirms the capacity of this person to take decisions and make things happen.

FIGURE 10.1   *The FRAMES process.*

Source: Adapted from Bien et al. (1993)

collaboration with the young person so that you both know what you are currently focusing on.

If the client continues to engage in high-risk behaviours, it will be tempting to say that nothing has worked. That is not true if the relationship is playing a role in helping the young person to change their belief that 'everyone lets me down'. Equally, the relationship has to able to handle honest challenges. It is important to anticipate problems and have an agreement as to what to do if a lapse (a drinking binge, for example) occurs. When this happens, it is a time to review the goals or consider using some different strategies. The review should discuss such questions as

- 'What is your drinking goal?'
- 'How were you feeling before you started drinking?'
- 'Who were you with?'
- 'What were you thinking about when you gave yourself permission to get drunk?'
- 'What would you need to do to avoid this happening again?'

Specific interventions

Provide information and practise ways to reduce the risks associated with alcohol use

Many young clients will continue to drink alcohol, so workers need to be able to suggest ways to reduce the risk of harm from alcohol consumption. More detailed information may be found by visiting the websites listed in the resource section. Harm-reduction interventions include making suggestions such as:

- drink within the limits recommended by the health authorities
- plan in advance where you are going and who you will be with
- spread your drinking over the week – don't save up for one big session
- go to new places – don't hang out with people who only want to get drunk
- do not drink before driving, swimming, boating and so on
- do not mix alcohol with prescribed medication or other drugs

- do not drink to become intoxicated
- alternate alcoholic and non-alcoholic drinks
- before you start, decide how many drinks will be your limit and choose low-alcohol drinks so that your blood alcohol level does not rise quickly
- eat when you are drinking
- plan how you will get home – do not accept lifts from someone who has been drinking
- drink slowly – don't gulp and put your glass down between sips
- watch your drinks to protect yourself against them being spiked
- intoxication can make you more willing to take risks, including the likelihood of having sex – unplanned, unprotected sex is unsafe, so plan ahead and always use a condom and water-based lubricant.

Working with parents and families

A young person may refuse to participate in treatment, but the parents or carers may be desperate to help or be helped. Telling a parent that nothing can be done until the young person wants help is destructive and untrue. Such a message fails to recognize the gradual approach to change that is needed and that parental suffering is real and deserving of attention. When parents' concerns are validated and attended to, they may change their approach to the young person's behaviour and reduce family conflict (Davis, 2003; Lawrence and Melrose, 2002).

Internet help

Internet-based assistance is attractive to young people who prefer the anonymity and safety of a computer screen. The Internet provides access to peer support, factual information and therapy. It is also a source of misinformation and extreme points of view. Workers who explore Internet resources with their clients will find this is a valuable way to stimulate conversation and guide the young person in their evaluation and interpretation of the sites they visit.

Summary

A multilayered approach to education, prevention, early intervention and treatment is essential. Youth and community workers as well as health and education professionals have an obligation to be well informed and equipped to handle alcohol use and abuse rather than think that it is a job just for substance abuse experts. It is a job for everyone.

Resources

Websites

Alcoholics Anonymous (AA) and *Alateen*
These are well-known, well-established programmes. The AA encourages complete abstinence as well as participation in a 12-step programme. These can be

potent options for those who accept the disease model of alcoholism. Details of your nearest group can be found in your local phone directory or on the Internet.

Australian Government's alcohol website www.alcohol.gov.au
A useful source of resources and information, including a free booklet to download entitled *Drinking Decisions: Young people and drinking*.

DrugScope and D-World www.drugscope.org.uk
DrugScope is the UK's leading independent centre of expertise on drugs. It website provides information about various drugs, including alcohol. D-World is its website for 11–14 year olds and can be accessed via the DrugScope website.

National Institute on Drug Abuse (NIDA) www.nida.nih.gov
This organization is based in the USA and provides information and resources to health professionals, parents, teachers and young people.

Substance Abuse and Mental Health Services Administration http://www.samhsa.gov/

The website of the United States Department of Health and Human Services that provides publications, statistics and information about programmes from the USA.

Talk to Frank http://www.talktofrank.com/

This UK website provides useful information about drugs and alcohol, including a section where questions can be posted and will be answered.

The Drinker's Guide to Cutting Down or Cutting Out http://www.dasc.sa.gov.au

This is a 45 page booklet from the Drug and Alcohol Services Council of South Australia (DASC) that can be downloaded free of charge its from website.

Youth Beyond Blue http://www2.youthbeyondblue.com/ybblue

An extension of the Australian Depression Initiative providing information about depression and suicide to young people.

Youth Drug Support Australia http://www.yds.org.au

A website with fact sheets and interactive sections where young people can ask questions about AOD, sex and sexuality.

Youth Information http://www.youthinformation.com/

An information toolkit for young people from the National Youth Agency of the UK. This website covers a broad range of issues relevant to young people.

KEY POINTS

- making an assessment with understanding is essential to building trust and a platform for change
- the process of change includes precontemplation, contemplation, determination/ preparation, action, maintenance and relapse

- the FRAMES process can encourage a young person to make a decision about what to do and when to do it
- motivational interviewing builds on the change process while recognizing that young people are usually ambivalent about changing their drinking behaviour.

QUESTIONS FOR DISCUSSION

1. Discuss how you would use an assessment process to determine the stage that a young person had reached with regard to their motivation to change.
2. Discuss the relevance of parental and family beliefs, peer influence and cultural issues with regard to a young person's drinking behaviour.

References

Bien, T., Miller, W. and Tonigan, J. (1993) 'Brief interventions for alcohol problems: a review', *Addiction*, 88 (3): 315–55.

Davis, C. (2003) *Caught in the Gap: Dual diagnosis and young people*. New South Wales: New South Wales Association for Adolescent Health (NAAH).

Lawrence, K. and Melrose, J. (2002) *The Do-it-yourself Guide to Peer Education with Parents*. Sydney: Manly Drug Education and Counselling Centre (MDECC).

Lopatko, O., McLean, S., Saunders, J., Young, R., Robinson, G. and Conigrave, K. (2002) 'Alcohol', in G. Hulse, J. White and G. Cape (eds), *Management of Alcohol and Drug Problems*. South Melbourne: Oxford University Press.

Melrose, J. (2007) *Mental Health Reference Resource for Drug and Alcohol Workers*. North Sydney: NSW Health.

Miller, W. and Rollnick, S. (2002) *Motivational Interviewing: Preparing people to change addictive behaviour*. New York: Guilford Press.

Monti, P.M., Colby, S.M. and O'Leary, T. (eds) (2001) *Adolescents, Alcohol and Substance Abuse: Reaching teens through brief interventions*. New York: Guilford Press.

Prochaska, J.O., DiClemente, C.C. and Norcross, J.C. (1992) 'In search of how people change: applications to addictive behaviors', *American Psychologist*, 47 (9): 1102–14.

Sellman, D. and Deering, D. (2002) 'Adolescence', in G. Hulse, J. White and G. Cape (eds), *Management of Alcohol and Drug Problems*. South Melbourne: Oxford University Press.

Spooner, C., Mattick, R.P. and Noffs, W. (1999) *The Nature and Treatment of Adolescent Substance Use: Supplement to Monograph 26: Final report of the adolescent treatment project*. Sydney: National Drug and Alcohol Research Centre (NDARC).

Szirom, T., King, D. and Desmond, K. (2004) *Barriers to Service Provision for Young People with Presenting Substance Misuse and Mental Health Problems*. Canberra: Department of Family and Community Services.

Werch, C.E. and DiClemente, C.C. (1994) 'A multi-component stage model for matching drug prevention strategies and messages to youth stage of use', *Health Education Research: Theory and Practice*, 9: 37–46

11

Tackling the Misuse of Volatile Substances

Richard Ives

Introduction

Volatile substance abuse (VSA), inhalant abuse or solvent abuse are all terms used to describe the deliberate inhalation of any of a range of products, including some types of glues, aerosols and fuels, to achieve intoxication. Because so-called 'poppers' (amyl (pentyl) and isobutyl nitrites) have different patterns of misuse, they are not discussed here. For information on these, see Haverkos and Dougherty (1988).

Inhaling such volatile substances as ether and nitrous oxide (laughing gas) has a long history. In the USA during the 1950s and 1960s, publicity about glue sniffing helped to increase awareness of the possibilities of glue as an intoxicant (Brecher, 1972). In the UK, public anxiety about VSA reached a peak in 1983, when there were more press cuttings on the subject than on all other drugs (Ives, 1986). Although public concern has waned, the problem has not gone away. Table 11.1 shows some products that can be used as inhalants.

VSA is a worldwide problem (see WHO, 1999; NIDA report, Kozel et al., 1995). Data from 35 European countries show that lifetime experience of VSA (that is, whether they had *ever tried* VSA) among 15 to 16 year olds ranged from 2 per cent in Romania to 22 per cent in Greenland. There was little difference between boys' and girls' lifetime prevalence (the 2003 ESPAD results, reported by Ives, 2006).

Although young people from all socio-economic groups experiment with volatile substances, for some of those who are poor or dispossessed, VSA is the drug of choice (Beauvais et al., 2004). Chronic VSA is associated with poor socio-economic conditions, delinquency and illegal drug use (NSDUH, 2005), disrupted families and other social and psychological problems. It is also common among some people living on the street.

Volatile substances intoxicate swiftly, and small doses rapidly lead to 'drunken' behaviour, similar to the effects of alcohol, although users may also experience delusions and hallucinations. Volatile substances are readily available and, along with

Table 11.1   *Some products that can be abused by inhailing them*

Product	Major volatile components
Adhesives	
Balsa wood cement	Ethyl acetate
Contact adhesives	Butanone, hexane, toluene and esters
Cycle tyre repair cement	Toluene and xylenes
Woodworking adhesives	Xylenes
Polyvinylchloride(PVC) cement	Acetone, butanone, cyclohexanone, trichloro-ethylene
Aerosols	
Air freshener	LPG, DME and/or fluorocarbons
Deodorant, antiperspirant	LPG, DME and/or fluorocarbons
Fly spray	LPG, DME and/or fluorocarbons
Hair lacquer	LPG, DME and/or fluorocarbons
Paint sprayer	LPG, DME and/or fluorocarbons and esters
Anaesthetics/analgesics	
Inhalational	Nitrous oxide, cyclopropane diethyl ether, halothane, enflurane, isoflurane
Topical	FC 11, FC 12, monochloroethane
Dust removers ('air brushes')	DME, FC 22
Commercial dry cleaning and degreasing agents	Dichloromethane, FC 113, methanol, 1,1,1-tri-chloroethane, tetrachloroethylene, toluene, trichloroethylene (now rarely carbon tetrachloride, 1,2-dichloropropane)
Domestic spot removers and dry cleaners	Dichloromethane, 1,1,1-Trichloroethane, tetrachloroethylene, trichloroethylene
Fire extinguishers	Bromochlorodifluoromethane, FC 11, FC 12
Fuel gases	
Cigarette lighter refills	LPG
'Butane'	LPG
'Propane'	Propane and butanes
Nail varnish/nail varnish remover	Acetone and esters
Paints/paint thinners	Acetone, butanone, esters, hexane, toluene, trichloroethylene, xylenes
Paint stripper	Dichloromethane, methanol, toluene

Source: Adapted from B. Flanagan and R. Ives (1994) 'Volatile substance abuse', *Bulletin on Narcotics* XLVI, 2: 49–78.

alcohol and tobacco, are therefore the first intoxicating substances that some children and young people try. Most experimenters with volatile substances do not continue to use it and VSA does not lead to the use of other psychoactive substances.

Those among the small proportion who continue to misuse volatile substances, however, can develop serious problems and often have other difficulties in their lives. Some heavy misusers inhale large quantities. There was one report of a weekly intake of six litres of adhesive.

For every 'sniffer', death is always a possibility. It may follow convulsions and coma, inhalation of vomit or direct cardiac or central nervous system toxicity. VSA-related deaths may be more common than the statistics show, as post-mortem examinations do not always reveal much – only, in some cases, acute lung congestion and, perhaps, cold-induced burns to the mouth and throat (Flanagan et al., 1997).

In the UK, an ongoing annual survey has identified 2,198 VSA-related deaths between 1971 and 2005 (Field-Smith et al., 2007). The death rate peaked in 1990, with 152 deaths, declining since, with 45 deaths being recorded in 2005 (Field-Smith et al., 2007). Most of those who die are male, but the proportion of female deaths has increased. Although deaths do occur across the social classes in the UK, Esmail et al. (1993) found that there was a marked difference in mortality across social classes with nearly four times as many deaths occurring in the lowest social class grouping compared with the highest.

Apart from death, intoxication itself has potential dangers. Intoxicated people may be more reckless and may do bizarre things in response to hallucinations. They may become unconscious and choke on vomit. Volatile substances are often misused along with other drugs and poly-drug use can potentiate the drugs' effects and increase risks unpredictably (Ives and Ghelani, 2006). The effects of combining volatile substances with alcohol or/and other drugs are poorly understood.

Deleterious health effects directly related to the products have been observed, but, for most sniffers, are fortunately relatively rare. These include:

- sensitization of the heart – cardiac arrhythmia may occur if exertion or fright follows sniffing
- spraying substances such as butane gas directly into the mouth cools the throat tissues, which may cause swelling, leading to suffocation
- many products are inflammable, so there is a risk of fire, especially when sniffing is combined with smoking
- some sniffers use large plastic bags, so suffocation is therefore a risk
- most products are chemical mixtures and formulas may change, and as the products are not intended for ingestion, manufacturers will not list the constituents.

There are specific risks attached to particular products. For example, some contain poisonous substances, such as lead in some petrol and n-hexane in some glues. Chronic abuse of toluene-containing products and chlorinated solvents, such as 1,1,1-trichloroethane, can cause liver and kidney damage. Damage to the lungs, bone marrow and nervous system is uncommon and generally reversible. Some people are more vulnerable (perhaps genetically) to some of the harmful effects than others. The actual morbidity from VSA is unknown as reports of chronic toxicity are nearly all single case studies.

Although there have been reports of brain damage, a review did not find conclusive evidence of this (Ron, 1986). While it is difficult to identify specific causes of fetal damage, misusing volatile substances during pregnancy can lead to increased maternal and fetal morbidity. Paternal exposure to volatile substances may also have deleterious effects.

Regular sniffers develop tolerance, so need larger quantities to achieve intoxication. While there does not seem to be a dependence syndrome, some people are compulsive and habitual misusers: 'There are ... pharmacological reasons for suspecting that persistent exposure to volatile substances might be able to induce a dependence of the so-called depressant type' (Advisory Council on the Misuse of Drugs, 1995: paragraph 3.11).

Interventions

Immediate intervention

When a sniffer is intoxicated, a calm and firm approach is best as exertion or high emotion may raise adrenaline levels dangerously high for an oversensitized heart. Therefore, keep an intoxicated person calm and:

*   remove the product, unless this will cause conflict – never fight with or chase a sniffer
*   remember it will not be possible to have a serious conversation with an intoxicated person, so just be calm and reassuring
*   once inhalation stops, the sniffer will 'sober up' in a few minutes (unless, of course, alcohol or other drugs have also been taken)
*   later, a check-up may identify if there are any particular health problems.

Medical help might be needed, so keep monitoring the situation and, if the person collapses, place them in the recovery position and call an ambulance. Williams et al. (2007) suggest the following medical interventions:

> Most acutely intoxicated inhalant abusers do not seek medical attention, and only when intoxication is life-threatening or has led to serious injury will an abuser present to the emergency department. Acute medical management of inhalant abuse starts with ... assess[ing] and stabiliz[ing] the patient and address[ing] any specific acute injury or toxicity. ... Myocardial sensitization by inhalants necessitates a calm and supportive environment. ... No medications reverse acute inhalant intoxication or have been found to be helpful with dependence or withdrawal symptoms.

Dealing with experimental misuse

Young people try volatile substances from curiosity or as part of their peer group's activities. For most people, it is merely an experiment not to be continued, so appropriate intervention can be limited to a warning of the dangers and (maybe) increased supervision. Specialist treatment is not required – it may even be counterproductive as it could entrench an activity that would otherwise be transient.

Dealing with dependent misuse

Biology may predispose some young people to dependent use, but chronic VSA is connected with other problems. Persistent misuse of volatile substances is a complex behaviour, often associated with low self-esteem, family problems, isolation and psychological difficulties. These factors may also be associated with the problematic use of legal and illegal drugs – indeed, a large proportion of people who misuse volatile substances also misuse other drugs.

Because chronic VSA is intertwined with social and psychological problems and the misuse of illegal drugs, support services for young misusers should not be narrowly focused on volatile substances, but, rather, should be able to deal with VSA in the context of a range of problematic behaviours. Moreover, these other problems may need attention first, because they are often more important for sniffer than problems associated with their misuse of volatile substances.

Services for young people

Services for young people must be specifically designed for their needs and effectively address key issues such as confidentiality and consent. Generic youth services deal more effectively with broader social and psychological problems, so they should take the lead, with support from specialist substance abuse agencies. For example, mental health services will have an important role to play in the treatment of psychiatric comorbidity.

Female volatile substance misusers may suffer additional stigmatization and they often do not present for treatment.

Social and cultural contexts

Treatment should take account of social and cultural contexts. Members of some groups (such as people living on the street and indigenous peoples) have special problems with substance use that require different approaches. Some indigenous peoples have identified that their cultures have useful perspectives and approaches that can be utilized in the treatment of people with drug and volatile substance problems (Brady, 1992). Treatment should work 'with the grain' of the culture, rather than impose inappropriate treatment models.

It is important for practitioners to remember that VSA is not simply a problem of individual pathology but also occurs partly because of the failure of social structures. Thus, in the broadest sense, treatment involves healing the family and the community, as well as making changes in society.

Follow-up

Follow-up is a crucial part of the treatment process. After-care, long-term rehabilitation, social reinsertion, relapse management and following up discharged patients are all important. Group activities for ex-users may be useful to help them maintain abstinence and utilize the group's support. Relapse is common, as with other drugs, but it should be treated non-judgmentally – it is an opportunity for learning rather than being seen as 'failure'.

Harm minimization

VSA has unpredictable dangers, so harm minimization advice should not be routinely given. Some misusers, however, are not able to quit the habit, so they may benefit from individual guidance – carefully given – on minimizing the risks. This would include avoiding certain particularly harmful products (such as leaded fuel), not using large plastic bags and avoiding spraying gases directly into the mouth.

When stopping sniffing, no clearly defined withdrawal syndrome has been identified, so special detoxification regimes are not necessary. The chemicals (being lipid–soluble) can be detected in body tissues for some weeks after misuse has stopped, but they do not have psychoactive effects. As part of treatment pro-grammes, however, rest, sleep and good food may aid recovery.

Summary of treatment issues

Williams et al. (2007) provide a concise summary of the treatment issues:

> Little research exists concerning treatment needs and successful treatment modalities specific to inhalant users, so clinicians rely on applying methods that are used to treat other addictive disorders, such as cognitive behavioral therapy, multisystem and family therapy, 12-step facilitation, and motivational enhancement techniques. ... Increasing personal and ethnic self-identity through role-modelling has been suggested as helpful in treating some groups of inhalant abusers, and positive cultural identification has been shown to be important in American Indian/Alaska Native populations. Treatment challenges are posed by the diversity of abused inhalants and user populations, comorbid psychopathology, psychosocial problems, poly-drug use, and the physiologic and neurologic effects of inhalant abuse. Treatment of longer-term inhalant users is hindered by the fact that there are few programmes designed specifically for inhalant abuse treatment, access to care may be limited, providers generally have a pessimistic view about users' neurologic damage and chance for recovery, and providers often lack sufficient knowledge and training about inhalant abuse, inhalant users, and their treatment needs. Although the principles of effective substance abuse treatment in general apply to inhalant abuse treatment, any treatment regi-men must address the many clinical, emotional, social, academic, pharma-cologic, neurocognitive, cultural, and demographic factors that make this type of substance abuse unique.

Prevention

Prevention is an important but difficult task. As with other substances, there are two areas of prevention to address: controlling the supply and reducing the demand.

Controlling supply

Controlling the supply of these readily available and socially useful substances is tricky. Sniffable products are legion and many different chemicals are involved. Users will substitute one product for another and information about the relative harm of various products and practices is lacking.

There are several possibilities regarding prevention on the supply side.

- *Eliminating the product* Some products are particularly dangerous and have satisfactory substitutes. In the UK, there have been calls for butane lighter refill cans to be banned because smokers can use disposable cigarette lighters.

- *Reformulating the product to remove the intoxicating substance* The substitution of petrol with unsniffable 'Opal' – an unleaded fuel with low levels of aromatics – has been a success in Australian indigenous communities (Wilson, 2007).
- *Modifying the product* Adding a chemical to make the product unpalatable, but experiments with the bittering agent Bitrex have been inconclusive.
- *Modifying the container* To make misuse difficult.
- *Warning labels on the product container* These can be helpful to adults as they alert them to the dangerous possibilities of products, but young people will probably be aware of which products are sniffable. Many sniffable products in the UK carry the 'SACKI' warning: 'Solvent Abuse Can Kill Instantly'. In Germany, however, such warning labels are banned because of fears that such labelling may draw children's and young people's attention to a product's potential for misuse.
- *Supplier education* Retailers need information and advice about a product's potential for misuse. This is difficult, because of the wide range of products and the many retail outlets.
- *Legal controls* On the sale and supply of misusable products. These do exist in many countries, but are difficult to enforce.
- *Making sniffing illegal* VSA is an offence in Japan, Singapore and the Republic of Korea, but, in most countries, the criminalization of misusers of volatile substances is considered counterproductive.

Reducing demand

The focus for tackling the demand for VSA is on information and education. Information is given by public advertising, booklets and leaflets, websites, helplines, as well as in schools and informal education. Many parents do not know about the potential for misuse of some household products, so they, too, may need information and help in talking to their children about the issues involved.

While most sniffers are young, the age of people dying from sniffing in the UK has increased. In 2005, the median age of death was 26 years, whereas for the period 1971–2004, it was 18 years (Field-Smith et al., 2007). It may be that the average age of misusers has increased and interventions are urgently needed for older people, as well as teenagers.

Although there are doubts about the effectiveness of substance misuse education, VSA education should be part of school drug education and integrated into health education or personal and social education. Because sniffable products are in most people's homes and can be obtained by young children, this education needs to start early.

Education cannot just be about providing information – research and professional experience shows that young people need to be helped to develop skills to deal with substance-related situations and given a chance to explore their attitudes towards substance use and misuse.

Education is not a cure-all, however. Addressing the underlying causes of substance misuse is also important. Behind some substance misuse are problems not only experienced by the individual but also by communities and societies: for example, the stresses that some young people experience – a lack of employment opportunities and fulfilling leisure activities.

Summary

A study of VSA highlights many issues that are common to tackling all forms of substance misuse. It demonstrates that controls on supply can have only limited effects because users are able to substitute similar substances if their preferred intoxicant is unavailable. It identifies the difficulties of pinning down the effects of intoxicants as they are used in different ways by genetically different people in different social contexts. It shows, too, how complex treatment is, requiring an holistic and open-minded approach, as well as a long-term commitment of time and resources if successful outcomes are to be achieved.

Resources

Further reading

Advisory Council on the Misuse of Drugs (1995) *Volatile Substance Abuse*. London: HMSO.

Department of Health *Out of sight? ... Not out of Mind: Children, young people and volatile substance abuse (VSA): A Framework for VSA*. London: Department of Health. Also available online at: www.dh.gov.uk/assetRoot/04/11/56/05/ 04115605.pdf – the UK government's strategy for tackling VSA.

Field-Smith, M.E., Butland, B.K., Ramsey, J.D. and Anderson, H.R. (2007) *Trends in Deaths Associated with Abuse of Volatile Substances: 1971–2005*. London: St George's, University of London. Also available online at: www.vsareport.org, Report 20.

Flanagan, R.J., Streete, P.J. and Ramsey, J.D. (1997) *Volatile Substance Abuse: Practical guidelines for the analytical investigation of suspected cases and interpretation of results*. Vienna: United Nations Drug Control Programme.

Ron, M. (1986) 'Volatile substance abuse: a review of possible long-term neurological, intellectual and psychiatric sequelae', *British Journal of Psychiatry*, 148: 235–46.

Skellington Orr, K. and Shewan, D. (2006) *Review of Evidence Relating to Volatile Substance Abuse in Scotland*. Edinburgh: Scottish Executive Substance Misuse Research. Also available online at: www.scotland.gov.uk/Resource/Doc/147377/0038818.pdf – this document has a very comprehensive references list.

Williams, J., Storck, M. and the Committee on Substance Abuse and Committee on Native American Child Health (2007): 'Inhalant abuse', *Pediatrics,* 119 (5): 1009–17. Also available online at: http://pediatrics.aappublications.org/cgi/content/full/119/ 5/1009

Websites

A useful reading list from the UK's Drug Scope is available at: www. drugscope.org. uk
Information on UK VSA related deaths: www.vsareport.org
National UK charity Re-Solv solely dedicated to VSA: www.re-solv.org
National Inhalant Prevention Coalition (in USA): www.inhalants.org
National Institute on Drug Abuse (NIDA in USA): http://inhalants. drugabuse. gov

KEY POINTS

- Volatile substances intoxicate swiftly and small doses rapidly lead to drunken behaviour, similar to the effects of alcohol, although users may also experience delusions and hallucinations.
- Most experimenters with volatile substances do not continue and VSA does not lead to the use of other psychoactive substances.
- For every sniffer, death is always a possibility. It may follow convulsions and coma, inhalation of vomit or direct cardiac or central nervous system toxicity.
- Because chronic VSA is intertwined with social and psychological problems and the misuse of illegal drugs, support services for young misusers should not be narrowly focused on volatile substances alone but should also be able to deal with VSA in the context of a range of such problematic behaviours.

QUESTIONS FOR DISCUSSION

1. Carol shared her college room with Betsy. One day she came in to find Betsy giggling to herself. A bag and two cans of hairspray were on the floor. What could Carol do?
2. You are working as a prison education officer in a young person's jail. You want to inform the inmates about VSA. Devise a strategy for doing this.

References

Advisory Council on the Misuse of Drugs (1995) *Volatile Substance Abuse*. London: HMSO.

Beauvais, F., Wayman, J.C., Jumper-Thurman, P., Plested, B. and Helm, H. (2004) 'Inhalant abuse among American Indian, Mexican American, and non-Latino white adolescents', *The American Journal of Drug and Alcohol Abuse*, 28 (1): 2171–87.

Brady, M. (1992) *Heavy Metal: The social meaning of petrol sniffing in Australia*. Canberra: Aboriginal Studies Press.

Brecher, E. (1972) 'How to launch a nationwide drug menace', in E. Brecher and the Editors of *Consumer Reports* Magazine, *Licit and Illicit Drugs: The Consumers Union report on narcotic stimulants, depressants, inhalants, and marijuana – including caffeine*. Boston, MA: Little, Brown. pp. 321–34.

Esmail, A., Meyer, L., Pottier, A. and Wright, S. (1993) 'Deaths from volatile substance abuse in those under 18 years: results from a national epidemiological study', *Archives of Disease in Childhood*, 69: 356–60.

Field-Smith, M.E., Butland, B.K., Ramsey, J.D. and Anderson, H.R. (2007) *Trends in Deaths Associated with Abuse of Volatile Substances: 1971–2005*. London: St George's, University of London. Also available online at: www.vsareport.org, Report 20.

Flanagan, R.J., Streete, P.J. and Ramsey, J.D. (1997) *Volatile Substance Abuse: Practical guidelines for the analytical investigation of suspected cases and interpretation of results*. Vienna: United Nations Drug Control Programme.

Haverkos, H. and Dougherty, J. (ed.) (1988) *Health Hazards of Nitrite Inhalants: NIDA Research Monograph 83*. Rockville, MD: National Institute on Drug Abuse.

Ives, R. (1986) 'The rise and fall of the solvents panic', *Druglink*, 1 (4): 10–12.

Ives, R. (2006) 'Volatile substance abuse: a review of findings in ESPAD 2003', *Drugs: Education, Prevention and Policy*, 13 (5): 441–9.

Ives, R., and Ghelani, P. (2006) 'Polydrug use (the use of drugs in combination): a brief review', *Drugs: Education, Prevention and Policy*, 13 (3): 225–32.

Kozel, N., Sloboda, Z. and De La Rosa, M. (eds) (1995) *Epidemiology of Inhalant Abuse: An international perspective: NIDA Research Monograph series No. 148*. Washington, DC: NIDA.

NSDUH (2005) *Inhalant Use and Delinquent Behaviors among Young Adolescents*. Rockville, MD: NSDUH. Also available online at: www.oas.samhsa.gov/2k5/inhale/inhale.htm

Ron, M. (1986) 'Volatile substance abuse: a review of possible long-term neurological, intellectual and psychiatric sequelae', *British Journal of Psychiatry*, 148: 235–46.

Skellington Orr, K. and Shewan, D. (2006) *Review of Evidence Relating to Volatile Substance Abuse in Scotland*. Edinburgh: Scottish Executive Substance Misuse Research Programme. Also available online at: www.scotland.gov.uk/Resource/Doc/147377/0038818.pdf

WHO Programme on Substance Abuse (1999) *Volatile Substance Abuse: A global overview*. Geneva: WHO.

Williams, J. and Storck, M. (2007) The Committee on Substance Abuse and the Committee on Native American Child Health 2007, 'Inhalant abuse', *Pediatrics*, 119 (5): 1009–17.

Wilson, A. (2007) 'Petrol sniffing scourge defeated', *The Australian*, 17 March.

12

Responding to the Use of Illicit Drugs

Cindy M. Schaeffer, Rocio Chang and
Scott W. Henggeler

Introduction

This chapter provides an overview of factors that are important to consider when
working with young people who use illicit substances. It also describes key features
of interventions that have empirical support for their effectiveness.

Causes and Correlates of Illicit Drug Use

Illicit drug use by young people is multiply determined, with no single cause being
either necessary (that is, present in every case) or sufficient (enough in and of itself)
to result in use. Although the effects of some risk factors may be simple and direct
(such as being offered a drug), most effects tend to be cumulative (that is, experiencing the risk factor for a longer period of time is worse) and synergistic in their interactions with other risk factors (low parental monitoring contributed to the young
person's truancy, which, in turn, led to being offered drugs during school hours, for
example). Risk factors and their effects also interact over time to exacerbate problematic substance use by young people (for instance, trying the drug gives the young
person a reputation of being a drug user and, thus, they receive more offers to use).

Individual risk factors

Behavioural genetic studies have indicated that substance use is, in part, genetically
determined (for example, Lynskey et al., 2002; True et al., 1999). Personality characteristics such as high sensation/novelty seeking, disinhibition and antisocial traits
also increase the risk of substance use (See Comeau et al., 2001, for example). In
addition, although determining which problem occurs first is difficult, the percentage of young people with substance use disorders who have a co-occurring mental health problem is extremely high in the community (60 per cent; Armstrong

and Costello, 2002), outpatient (61–88 per cent; Couwenbergh et al., 2006) and inpatient (68–82 per cent; Stowell and Estroff, 1992) samples. Similarly, a high percentage of substance-abusing young people also have experienced traumatic events. Thus, co-occurring mental health problems should be considered when treating substance abuse in young people.

Family risk factors

A broad range of family problems has been shown to increase the risk of substance use in young people, including parental substance abuse, domestic violence, negative family communication patterns, inconsistent discipline and harsh or permissive parenting (Wills and Yaeger, 2003). In addition, tolerant parental attitudes towards drug use and low educational aspirations for their children also place youth at risk (Molina et al., 1994). Low parental involvement, especially a lack of monitoring of a young person's friends and whereabouts, is one of the strongest predictors of drug use in this age group (Chilcoat and Anthony, 1996; Williams and Hine, 2002).

Peer risk factors

Associating with peers who use substances is perhaps the single greatest risk factor for substance abuse among young people (Friedman and Glassman, 2000). Peers provide access to drugs, reinforce positive attitudes to and expectancies of drug use and foster negative attitudes towards competing non-using behaviours, such as sport or clubs. Substance-abusing peers also model maladaptive coping strategies (such as using drugs to feel less anxious) and contribute to the young person's reputation in the broader social network (as a 'burn-out' or 'pothead', for example), further limiting opportunities for encounters with non-using, conventional peers.

Less contact with conventional peers promotes misperceptions regarding peer norms (that is, believing that 'everyone uses drugs'), another risk factor for drug use (Johnston et al., 2007).

School and community risk factors

Young people who have poor levels of academic achievement, low engagement with school and/or behavioural problems at school are at high risk for substance abuse (Friedman et al., 1994). Although individual (poor impulse control, for instance) and parent (for example, low educational aspirations) risk factors impede young people's success in school, school-level factors also contribute to risk. For example, well-organized schools with high levels of parent and teacher involvement in decision making, structures for responding to discipline problems and support for the prosocial activities of young people have lower rates of substance use, even after controlling for socio-economic status, neighbourhood deprivation and family substance use (Feinberg et al., 2007).

At the community level, young people are at greater risk when they live in neighbourhoods where drugs are accessible and strong norms against drug use are not in place (Newcomb, 1995).

Protective factors

Determining whether or not unique factors bolster young people against illicit substance use is difficult. The presence of such factors might simply represent the absence of other, more well-established risk factors. Nevertheless, research suggests that young people with positive or 'easy' temperaments, high levels of intelligence, good decision making abilities, a strong sense of self-efficacy, a low tendency towards taking risks, high levels of social support and involvement in conventional activities are less likely to engage in problematic levels of substance use than those who do not have these attributes (Brown et al., 2001).

Reducing the Incidence of Illicit Drug Use: Primary Prevention

The most effective prevention programmes are those that attempt to ameliorate the empirically established risk factors that lead to the problem occurring. Fortunately, several risk factor-based prevention programmes for substance use by young people have been developed, empirically tested using rigorous research designs and made available for dissemination. Two such programmes are briefly summarized here. For a broader review of empirically validated programmes, see the National Institute on Drug Abuse's (2003) book, listed in the References section.

LifeSkills® training programme (LST)

LST (Botvin et al., 2000; 2001) is a classroom-based programme that provides drug education (such as accurate use rates), drug resistance skills, personal self-management skills (problem-solving, stress reduction and so on) and general social skills (for instance, assertiveness and conflict resolution).

This programme can be administered by teachers, health professionals or peer leaders in schools or other classroom-type settings (such as church youth programmes), with three versions tailored to different age groups (from 9 to 16 year olds). Depending on the version, LST requires 10 to 30 class sessions of approximately an hour each.

Randomized controlled trials (Botvin et al., 2000, 2001) have confirmed the efficacy of the programme. Implementation support and LST materials are available at www.lifeskillstraining.com

Strengthening Families Program for Parents, and Youth aged 10–14 (SFP)

The SFP (Molgaard and Spoth, 2001) is a family-based intervention that targets coping and peer refusal skills, future orientation and the decision making abilities of the young person, and parenting skills for their parents or carers.

The programme is administered with groups of eight to 13 families, who participate together in two-hour sessions once a week for seven weeks, held at times and locations convenient to the families. The sessions are divided into one-hour segments that involve separate parent and youth groups, followed by family sessions in which the parents and young people practise skills together. All the group and family sessions involve group discussions, role playing, behavioural skills activities and the use of videotapes to model positive and negative parent–child interactions.

Results from a large-scale randomized trial of the SFP have confirmed the efficacy of the programme (Spoth et al., 2004). For more information about the SFP, visit www.extension.iastate.edu/sfp/inside/implement.php

Interventions to Address Illicit Substance Abuse Among Young People

Voluntary versus mandated treatment

Young people typically do not enter substance abuse treatment voluntarily. The most common referral pattern is that they and their parents or carers have been urged to obtain treatment in response to problems that they are having related to use, such as criminal arrests or truancy. Accordingly, the young people (and sometimes their parents or carers) tend not to view their use as a problem and do not want to stop using drugs.

Fortunately, research indicates that mandated substance abuse treatment is just as effective as voluntary treatment and, in fact, stricter mandates result in better attendance and longer treatment retention (Kelly et al., 2005).

Community-based versus residential treatment

Another common misconception regarding substance abuse treatment is that lengthy stays at residential programmes are necessary to alter drug use. Research does not support the effectiveness of such treatment programmes.

First, no rigorous research has found residential substance abuse treatment to be more effective than community-based services.

Second, considerable rigorous research has supported the effectiveness of several well-specified outpatient and home-based treatments for young people (for a review, see Waldron and Turner, 2008).

Third, and this is important, clustering young people with serious substance abuse problems in residential facilities puts them at risk for peer contagion – a process by which they receive positive reinforcement for deviant attitudes and behaviours from peers with problems similar to their own, thereby exacerbating them (Dodge et al., 2006). Research suggests that the risk for peer contagion in group-based interventions is greatest when young people spend large amounts of unstructured time together and when contact with peers who do *not* have the target problem is low (Dishion et al., 2006). Both of these exacerbating conditions are widespread in residential facilities.

Two additional reasons to prefer community-based over residential treatments are the greater ability to involve parents or carers in treatment and the potential for an enhanced generalizability and sustainability of treatment effects.

As noted, multiple family contextual factors influence drug use among young people and residential programmes are not well equipped to address those risk factors. In addition, parents or carers can themselves be key intervention agents and have the ability to provide contingencies (punishments and rewards) for use and non-use. When parents or carers are also involved in addressing other youth risk factors (such as limiting access to drug-using peers, or providing incentives for school attendance), the likelihood that the young people concerned will be able to achieve and sustain abstinence in the real world is enhanced.

With these contextual factors in mind, we provide brief overviews of two community-based intervention approaches that have been identified as being among the most effective substance abuse treatments available for young people in a meta-analysis (Waldron and Turner, 2008).

Cognitive Behavioural Therapy with Motivational Enhancement Therapy (CBT-MET/12)

Recently a manualized CBT approach for young people was tested across different research groups and made available in the public domain (Sampl and Kadden, 2001; Waldron et al., 2001). Here, we describe the most extensive version examined in these studies – CBT-MET/12 – which involves two sessions of MET, followed by ten sessions of CBT. It can be administered using either an individual or group format.

In the MET component, the therapist provides the young person with feedback regarding their substance use, related problems and possible reasons for quitting. The therapist discusses with the young person how their drug use compares to national norms, in an effort to shift their frame of reference. The young person also participates with the therapist in a functional assessment of drug use that identifies the reasons for (stress reduction or social facilitation, for example) triggers and the outcomes of their use and identifies personal life goals. The intention of this phase is to increase their motivation to change.

The ten-session CBT component teaches skills for:

- refusing offers to use drugs
- expanding the young person's networks of non-drug using peers
- avoiding high-risk drug use situations
- solving social problems
- managing anger
- communicating with parents and peers
- dealing with depressed mood
- coping with cravings.

Each session involves brief didactic presentations by the therapist, followed by modelling, role playing and homework assignments. Throughout, the therapist guides the young person so that they come to notice and modify negative automatic thoughts (for example, pertaining to low self-confidence or drug cravings) and practise replacing them with more positive, efficacious thoughts (such as 'the urge to use will pass if I use my relaxation skills').

CBT-MET has been evaluated primarily in cases of young people abusing marijuana. Although various versions of CBT-MET exist (CBT alone or with MET, individual *v.* group formats and so on), 10 out of 12 randomized clinical trials have supported the effectiveness of the approach, with the effects persisting for as long as 30 months after treatment (Waldron and Turner, 2008). CBT-MET treatment manuals are available online at: http://ncadi. samhsa.gov (search for 'CYT' or 'cannabis youth treatment') and a DVD for training therapists can be ordered at: www.mid-attc.org/metcbt5page.html

Multisystemic Therapy with Contingency Management (MST-CM)

MST (Henggeler et al., 1998) is an intensive home-based treatment for serious anti-social behaviour and substance abuse by young people. MST has been rigorously evaluated over the past thirty years and has been identified as an effective treatment for youth substance abuse by several federal organizations (see NIDA, 1999; US Public Health Service, 2001; www.modelprograms.samhsa.gov).

In one randomized clinical trial (Henggeler et al., 2006), standard MST, which had already demonstrated success with young people abusing substances, was enhanced by integrating a behaviourally-based treatment, contingency management (CM) (Donahue and Azrin, 2001). This enhanced model – MST-CM – is described here.

MST is a highly individualized, family-based treatment intended for young people exhibiting very serious antisocial behaviour and at high risk for out-of-home placement. To facilitate access to services, clinical services are delivered in home, school and/or neighbourhood settings at times that are convenient to the family. Also, therapists are available to respond to clinical problems 24 hours a day, seven days a week. In addition, therapists carry small caseloads of four to five families to allow for intensive services to be delivered to each family (on average, 2–15 hours per week, depending on clinical need). Families receive services for a period of four to six months, with greater intensity at the beginning and a tapering off of contact as treatment goals are achieved.

MST clinical procedures are operationalized through nine core principles (see Henggeler et al., 1998) that guide assessment practices, treatment planning, and the integration of evidence-based interventions. These principles are applied within a standardized analytical/decision making process that structures the treatment plan, its implementation and effectiveness. To enhance the fidelity of MST implementation, extensive quality assurance procedures (such as, weekly consultation with an MST expert and quarterly booster trainings) are used.

Because substance abuse by young people is multiply determined, MST targets a comprehensive set of risk factors across all domains of the young person's natural ecology (that is, family, school, peer and neighbourhood). For each case, an analysis is conducted of the individualized 'fit factors', or, characteristics of the young person's ecology that are maintaining the substance use. For one young person, their substance abuse might be being maintained primarily by the fact that they have been expelled from school and, because of their parents' work schedule, are unmonitored during the day. For some girls, drug use might be being maintained primarily by the enhanced status they have in their peer group as a result of going out with an older boy in college who uses drugs.

In devising treatment plans, MST prioritizes the more proximal fit factors (such as unstructured time during the day) that are linked to the problem over the more distal fit factors (anger over their parents' divorce, for example), where the link to the problem is less clear.

After determining the fit for the particular young person and family, strengths in the natural ecology (such as parents who are well motivated) are leveraged to effect changes in the young person's behaviour. Interventions focus on promoting behavioural changes in the ecology by empowering caregivers with skills and resources that they can use to address the difficulties that arise in bringing up a young person and on empowering the young person to cope with and respond prosocially to problems.

Specific MST interventions incorporate empirically-based clinical techniques (such as from cognitive behavioural, behavioural or family systems-based therapies) and integrate them using an ecologically focused framework that addresses the fit of identified problems in each system as well as at the interfaces between those systems (conflicts between parents and school staff, for example).

In addition to broader ecological interventions that target the young person's substance use (such as having parents enroll the young person in a GED programme), this problem is more immediately addressed by the integration of CM. Specifically, a detailed functional analysis of their drug use behaviour is conducted with the young person, from which an individualized self-management plan for dealing with the desire to use is developed. Parents of carers are brought in at the design stage of the plan and taught to monitor and provide rewards for the young person's successful implementation of it. In addition, the parents or carers administer drug-screening tests (urine and breathalyser tests) randomly and at times when use is suspected (such as when they violate their curfew). They then reward them when the test results are clean with vouchers for money and other desired privileges, but provide negative consequences (such as the loss of privileges or personal possessions – a television, say) for dirty screens.

Four clinical trials (for a review, see Sheidow and Henggeler, 2008) and two meta-analyses (Curtis et al., 2004; Waldron and Turner, 2008) support the effectiveness of MST with substance-abusing juvenile offenders (to learn more about implementing MST, contact www.mstservices.com).

Summary and Conclusions

The most effective interventions target the range of risk factors that has been empirically associated with substance use by young people. At the same time, interventions should be tailored to the unique set of factors that are operative in a given case and treatments should address the specific functions (such as anxiety reduction or social connection) that drug use serves for the individual. Treatment is unlikely to be effective if the benefits that a young person receive from their drug use (relaxation, status among peers and so on) are not provided to them through other, more prosocial means.

A non-confrontational therapeutic stance facilitates the young person's honest disclosure about the benefits of use and factors that maintain use (for example, triggers such as specific people or places) so that accurate, individualized self-management plans can be created.

Interventions for substance abuse by young people should involve cognitive, behavioural, and motivational components. In terms of cognitive interventions, young people should receive accurate information about norms pertaining to drug use to counteract the misperception that 'everyone does it' and should be taught specific coping skills to use when they experience cravings or other cognitions that lead to use. With regard to behavioural interventions, young people need to practise new skills for refusing offers of drugs, ways to relax that do not involve drugs and how to avoid high-risk situations. In addition, rewards for abstinence and punishments for use should be administered contingently and consistently, based on accurate and timely information obtained through urine toxicology and breathalyser tests. Finally, non-confrontational techniques designed to enhance motivation can facilitate the engagement of the young person in interventions, illustrate that continued use is inconsistent with the young person's other life goals and foster an intrinsic desire to remain abstinent.

Parental involvement in interventions is essential for success. In addition to making it possible to intervene to deal with family-level risk factors directly, parental involvement allows for risk factors in other domains of the youth's ecology to be addressed. For example, parents can be empowered to attenuate school problems, instil a motivation towards academic achievement and facilitate the young person's access to prosocial activities and peers. Parents should also be enlisted to clarify the family's values and beliefs about drug use, monitor the young person's drug use and provide sanctions for continued use and rewards for abstinence. When parents are engaged in treatment, substance use by a young person can be greatly reduced or eliminated, regardless of the young person's initial intrinsic motivation to be drug-free.

Resources

Further reading

Dodge, K.A., Dishion, T.J. and Lansford, J.E. (eds) (2006) *Deviant Peer Influences in Programs for Youth: Problems and solutions*. New York: Guilford Press.

National Institute on Drug Abuse (NIDA) (1999) *Principles of Drug Addiction Treatment: A research-based guide* (NIH Publication No. 99-4180). Washington, DC: NIDA. Available online at: www.drugabuse.gov/PDF/PODAT/PODAT.pdf

National Institute on Drug Abuse (2003) *Preventing Drug Abuse Among Children and Adolescents: A research-based guide for parents, educators, and community leaders* (2nd edn). Washington, DC: NIDA. Also available online at: www.drugabuse.gov/Prevention/prevopen.html

Websites

LifeSkills® Training www.lifeskillstraining.com

Mid-Atlantic Addiction Technology Transfer Center www.mid-attc.org/metc bt5page.html

MST Services www.mstservices.com

Strengthening Families Program for Parents and Youth 10–14 www.extension. iastate.edu/sfp/inside/implement.php

Substance Abuse and Mental Health Services Administration (SAMHSA)'s national cleaning house for alcohol and drug information http://ncadi. samhsa.gov

KEY POINTS

- Interventions need to target a broad set of risk factors in a way that is tailored to the unique factors that are operative in a particular case.
- Mandated treatment programmes are just as effective as voluntary programmes.
- Community-based treatment programmes are to be preferred over residential programmes.
- Useful community-based interventions include the CBT-MET/12 and MST-CM programmes.

QUESTIONS FOR DISCUSSION

1. Why might a school be reluctant to implement a drug use prevention programme? Why might parents be reluctant to allow their children to participate in such a programme? Assuming that you wanted to implement a programme, what would you say to school administrators and parents to address their concerns?
2. Under what circumstances would you recommend that young people who use illicit drugs receive an outpatient treatment such as CBT-MET versus a more intensive inhouse treatment such as MST-CM?

References

Armstrong, T.D. and Costello, E.J. (2002) 'Community studies on adolescent substance use, abuse, or dependence and psychiatric comorbidity', *Journal of Consulting and Clinical Psychology,* 70: 1224–39.

Botvin, G.J., Griffin, K.W., Diaz, T. and Ifill-Williams, M. (2001) 'Drug abuse prevention among minority adolescents: Post-test and one-year follow-up of a school-based preventive intervention', *Prevention Science,* 2: 1–13.

Botvin, G.J., Griffin, K.W., Diaz, T., Scheier, L.M., Williams, C. and Epstein, J.A. (2000) 'Preventing illicit drug use in adolescents: long-term follow-up date from a randomized control trial of a school population', *Addictive Behaviors,* 25: 769–74.

Brown, T.N., Shulenberg, J., Bachman, J.G., O'Malley, P.M. and Johnston, L.D. (2001) 'Are risk and protective factors for substance use consistent across historical time?: National data from the high school classes of 1976 through 1997', *Prevention Science,* 2: 29–43.

Chilcoat, H. and Anthony, J.C. (1996) 'Impact of parent monitoring on initiation of drug use through later childhood', *Journal of the American Academy of Child and Adolescent Psychiatry,* 35: 91–100.

Comeau, N., Stewart, S.H. and Loba, P. (2001) 'The relations of trait anxiety, anxiety sensitivity, and sensation seeking to adolescents' motivations for alcohol, cigarette, and marijuana use', *Addictive Behaviors,* 26: 803–25.

Couwenbergh, C., van den Brink, W., Zwart, K., Vreugdenhill, C., van Wijngaarden-Cremers, P. and van der Gaag, R.J. (2006) 'Comorbid psychopathology in adolescents and young adults treated for substance use disorders: a review', *European Child and Adolescent Psychiatry*, 15: 319–28.

Curtis, N.M., Ronan, K.R. and Borduin, C.M. (2004) 'Multisystemic treatment: a meta-analysis of outcome studies', *Journal of Family Psychology*, 18: 411–19.

Dishion, T.J., Dodge, K.A. and Lansford, J.E. (2006) 'Findings and recommendations: a blueprint to minimize deviant peer influence in youth interventions and programs', in K.A. Dodge, T.J. Dishion and J.E. Lansford (eds), *Deviant Peer Influences in Programs for Youth: Problems and solutions*. New York: Guilford Press. pp. 366–46.

Dodge, K.A., Dishion, T.J. and Lansford, J.E. (eds) (2006) *Deviant Peer Influences in Programs for Youth: Problems and Solutions*. New York: Guilford Press.

Dodge, K.A., Lansford, J.E. and Dishion, T.J. (2006) 'The problem of deviant peer influences in intervention programs', in K.A. Dodge, T.J. Dishion and J.E. Lansford (eds), *Deviant Peer Influences in Programs for Youth: Problems and solutions*. New York: Guilford Press. pp. 3–13.

Donohue, B. and Azrin, N. (2001) 'Family behavior therapy', in E.F. Wagner and H.B. Waldron (eds), *Innovations in Adolescent Substance Abuse Interventions*. Amsterdam: Pergamon/Elseview Science Inc. pp. 205–27.

Feinberg, M.E., Ridenour, T.A. and Greenberg, M.T. (2007) 'Aggregating indices of risk and protection for adolescent behavior problems: the communities that care youth survey', *Journal of Adolescent Health*, 40: 506–13.

Friedman, A.S., Bransfield, S. and Kreisher, C. (1994) 'Early teenage substance use as a predictor of educational–vocational failure', *The American Journal of Addictions*, 3: 325–36.

Friedman, A.S. and Glassman, K. (2000) 'Family risk factors versus peer risk factors for drug abuse: a longitudinal study of an African American urban community sample', *Journal of Substance Abuse Treatment*, 18: 267–75.

Henggeler, S.W., Halliday-Boykins, C.A., Cunningham, P.B., Randall, J., Shapiro, S.B. and Chapman, J.E. (2006) 'Juvenile drug court: enhancing outcomes by integrating evidence-based treatments', *Journal of Consulting and Clinical Psychology*, 34: 658–70.

Henggeler, S.W., Schoenwald, S.K., Borduin, C.M., Rowland, M.D. and Cunningham, P.B. (1998) *Multisystemic Treatment of Antisocial Behavior in Children and Adolescents*. New York: Guilford Press.

Johnston, L.D., O'Malley, P.M., Bachman, J.G. and Schulenberg, J.E. (2007) *Monitoring the Future National Survey Results on Drug Use, 1975–2006: Volume I: Secondary school students* (NIH Publication No. 07-6205). Bethesda, MD: National Institute on Drug Abuse.

Kelly, J.F., Finney, J.W. and Moos, R. (2005) 'Substance use disorder patients who are mandated to treatment: characteristics, treatment process, and 1- and 5-year outcomes', *Journal of Substance Abuse Treatment*, 28: 213–23.

Lynskey, M., Heath, A.C., Nelson, E.C., Bucholz, K., Madden, P.A.F., Slutske, W.S., Statham, D. and Martin, N. (2002) 'Genetic and environmental contributions to cannabis dependence in a national twin sample', *Psychological Medicine*, 32: 195–207.

Molgaard, V. and Spoth, R. (2001) 'Strengthening Families Program for young adolescents: overview and outcomes', in S. Pfeiffer and L. Reddy (eds), *Innovative Mental Health Programs for Children*. Binghamton, NY: Haworth Press. pp. 15–29.

Molina, B.S.B., Chassin, L. and Curran, P.J. (1994) 'A comparison of mechanisms underlying substance use for early adolescent children of alcoholics and controls', *Journal of the Study of Alcoholism*, 55: 269–75.

National Institute on Drug Abuse (NIDA) (1999) *Principles of Drug Addiction Treatment: A research-based guide* (NIH Publication No. 99-4180). Washington, DC: NIDA. Also available online at: www.drugabuse.gov/PDF/PODAT/PODAT.pdf

National Institute on Drug Abuse (2003) *Preventing Drug Abuse Among Children and Adolescents: A research-based guide for parents, educators, and community leaders* (2nd edn). Washington, DC: NIDA. Also available online at: www.drugabuse.gov/Prevention/prevopen.html

Newcomb, M.D. (1995) 'Identifying high-risk youth: prevalence and patterns of adolescent drug abuse', in E. Rahdert and D. Czechowicz (eds), *Adolescent Drug Abuse: Clinical assessment and therapeutic interventions: Volume 156.* Washington, DC: NIDA Research Monographs. pp. 7–38.

Sampl, S. and Kadden, R. (2001) *Motivational Enhancement Therapy and Cognitive Behavioral Therapy for Adolescent Cannabis Users: Cannabis Youth Treatment (CYT) Series: Volume 1.* Rockville, MD: US Department of Health and Human Services, Substance Abuse and Mental Health Services Administration and Center for Substance Abuse Treatment. Also available online at: www.chestnut.org/li/cyt/products/mcb5_cyt_v1.pdf

Sheidow, A.J. and Henggeler, S.W. (2008) 'Multisystemic therapy for alcohol and other drug abuse in delinquent adolescents', *Alcoholism Treatment Quarterly,* 26: 125–45.

Spoth, R.L., Redmond, C., Shin, C. and Azavedo, K. (2004) 'Brief family intervention effects on adolescent substance initiation: school-level curvilinear growth curve analyses six years following baseline', *Journal of Consulting and Clinical Psychology,* 72: 535–42.

Stowell, R.J. and Estroff, T.W. (1992) 'Psychiatric disorders in substance-abusing adolescent inpatients: a pilot study', *Journal of the American Academy of Child and Adolescent Psychiatry,* 31: 1036–40.

True, W.R., Heath, A.C., Scherrer, J.F., Waterman, B., Goldberg, J., Lin, Nong, Eisen, S.A., Lyons, M.J. and Tsuang, M.F. (1999) 'Genetic and environmental contributions to smoking', *Addiction,* 92 (10): 1277–88.

US Public Health Service (2001) *Youth Violence: A report of the Surgeon General.* Washington, DC: US Public Health Service.

Waldron, H.B., Slesnick, N., Brody, J.L., Turner, C.W. and Peterson, T.R. (2001) 'Treatment outcomes for adolescent substance abuse at 4- and 7-month assessments', *Journal of Consulting and Clinical Psychology,* 69: 802–13.

Waldron, H.B. and Turner, C.W. (2008) 'Evidence-based psychosocial treatments for adolescent substance abuse', *Journal of Clinical Child and Adolescent Psychology,* 37: 238–61.

Williams, P.S. and Hine, D.W. (2002) 'Parental behaviour and alcohol misuse among adolescents: a path analysis of mediational influences', *Australian Journal of Psychology,* 54: 17–24.

Wills, T.A. and Yaeger, A.M. (2003) 'Family factors and adolescent substance use: models and mechanisms', *Current Directions in Psychological Science,* 12: 222–6.

Part VI
Sexual Behaviour

13

Sexual Health-related Interventions

Susan Moore

Young people, in the flower of their youth, beauty and energy, are very much sexual beings. They are likely to be physically, although not necessarily emotionally, ready for sex. In the cognitive domain, recent brain research suggests that their decision making capacities are often still 'a work in progress' and, in situations of high arousal, those capacities are likely to be even less reliable. Additionally, sexual behaviour among teenagers may well occur in contexts that are risky, ill-advised or downright dangerous – for example, when under the influence of drugs or alcohol, in situations of strong peer or partner pressure and among groups where there are high rates of sexually transmitted infections (STIs).

Avoidable negative outcomes of young people's sexual activity include sexually transmitted infections (STIs) and unwanted or unplanned pregnancies. There are also emotional and social risks associated with sexual activity that is violent, forced or regretted and/or does not live up to expectations with respect to relationship outcomes. Interventions targeting the reduction of these negative outcomes are the focus of this chapter.

Despite the risks associated with the sexual behaviour of young people we should not overlook the fact that some expression of sexuality in this age group is both normative and normal. Studies in Western nations such as the USA, Britain and Australia suggest that 40–50 per cent of those aged 13 to 17 have had sex at least once, 80 per cent of males and 70 per cent of females are sexually active by the time they transition to adulthood and the median age of first intercourse is about 16 years in these countries (Moore and Rosenthal, 2006). It is well to keep in mind that sexual behaviour is a normal aspect of mature adulthood and what is learned in teenage years about relationships and sexual expression will doubtless influence sexual health at later ages. A further issue is that economic and social forces in Western nations have led to the average age for marriage/partnering being much later than in previous eras. Along with this change, norms have developed that allow young people more freedom to express their sexuality. In some cases/areas/groups this freedom is interpreted as a pressure or licence for early first intercourse and multiple partnering, while in other situations it has enabled a healthier approach to sexual behaviour when viewed within a lifespan context. Most health professionals would probably acknowledge that, while it is important to teach caution, restraint and responsibility in sexual matters, sex education that is punitive, arouses fear and presents sex as dirty and dangerous is unlikely to add to the sum of human happiness or ensure satisfying relationships. So, the question arises, what forms should interventions that aim to alter the sexual behaviours of young people take?

Part of the answer to this question involves making decisions as to what the appropriate goals and outcome variables for such interventions are and it on this point that much debate has ensued.

Types of Interventions

Interventions regarding the reproductive health of young people can be targeted at the school, community agency or clinic level. Disseminating information and making attempts to change attitudes and beliefs can be achieved through various widely available media, such as websites, advertising and television programmes. Although discussion of these latter interventions is beyond the scope of this chapter, several websites are listed in the Resources section at the end of this chapter.

School-based interventions

These have the advantages of there being a captive audience, the potential to present a series of age-appropriate interventions to different years and the resource-base for high-quality service delivery. A more difficult challenge for schools, however, is that of targeting the needs of specific groups within the one classroom, for example young gays, young mothers and those with markedly different degrees of vulnerability and/or sexual experience. Additionally, school-based programmes can still miss some at-risk groups, including dropouts, non-attendees, and those 'excused' from sex education because of parental sensibilities.

Parents' concerns can often be addressed by keeping them in the picture with respect to a programme's aims and goals. For example, some interventions have included parent education sessions not only about the programme that will be experienced by their sons or daughters but also about their development in puberty, the challenges of becoming a teenager and ways to communicate with children about sex (see O'Donnell et al., 2005, for example).

Kirby and Miller (2002) suggest that the most effective programmes for parents increase their knowledge of the sexual behaviours of young people and help them to understand that talking about sex to teenagers is difficult but likely to be beneficial. Good programmes also help parents to improve their skills in talking about sexuality by enabling them to feel more comfortable with the material, improving their listening skills and their capacity to initiate discussions.

An Australian school-based sex education programme based on best practice principles (Kirby, 2001, 2002) is Talking Sexual Health, produced under the auspices of the Australian National Framework for Education about HIV/AIDS, STIs and Blood-borne Viruses in Secondary Schools (Mitchell et al., 2000).

The programme acknowledges that young people are sexual beings and attempts to facilitate them in making informed decisions when faced with sexual choices. It is built on research indicating that comprehensive sex education tends to delay (rather than encourage) the early onset of sexual activity and increase safe sex behaviours among those who are already sexually active (DiCenso et al., 2002; Grunseit et al., 1997).

A whole-school approach is promoted, as are partnerships with community organizations concerned with youth well-being. An important aspect of the programme is that the sex education curriculum and its delivery are not marginalized within the school, but supported by school policies and backed up with student welfare and pastoral care provisions. For example, if issues relating to sexual forcing are raised in class, appropriate support must be in place for those who seek counselling or assistance after such discussions. Tolerance of diversity in views and behaviours is promoted within the curriculum and through school policies, such as those attempting to tackle bullying and teasing in the playground.

The curriculum is based on young people's developmental needs and abilities, uses a range of teaching methods that engage children and requires skilled teachers who are comfortable with the material and can provide a classroom climate of safety and trust. Professional development and training of teachers for the programme is therefore considered essential and both parents and relevant community organizations are kept informed of the goals and directions so that they can support what is happening at the school level. Indeed, the specifics of this and similar programmes are developed through wide community consultation.

Finally, a range of materials is available to assist with the delivery of the programme, including information and resource booklets for parents and students.

Community-based reproductive health interventions

Such interventions can build on what is available in schools or fill gaps not covered by a broad sex education curriculum. Community organizations can effectively target specific, highly vulnerable groups of young people and deliver tailor-made programmes, in context, to meet their needs. Such vulnerable groups may include particular ethnic subpopulations of known high risk for unwanted pregnancies and STIs (for example, poor urban Afro-Americans in US cities, Aboriginal populations in rural Australia), young people with substance abuse issues, homeless young people, teenage sex workers and those young people who are incarcerated in detention centres. Also included may be young people who are already dealing with sexual health problems and/or issues, such as pregnancy, gay and lesbian young people, and those living with STIs, including HIV. With these groups, the major problem seems to be getting the target population 'through the door' and, once in, keeping them coming so as to deliver the message.

One of the most successful programmes, mentioned in several major evaluation reviews (Alford, 2003), is the Carerra Program, under the auspices of the Children's Aid Society in New York (www.childrensaidsociety.org). This is an after-school sex education, pregnancy prevention and youth development programme for 13 to 15 year olds who are urban socio-economically disadvantaged and considered to be at high risk. Particular risk groups targeted include Afro-American and Hispanic young people. Activities run five days per week for the whole school year and there are summer programmes as well.

The Carerra Program is a comprehensive whole-of-life intervention that has several basic principles. Staff treat young participants 'as family' and 'as pure potential'. Holistic services and comprehensive case management are available for each young person in the programme.

Participants sign a long-term contract relating to their goals and how they expect to achieve them. The services and interventions are all offered under one roof in a relatively casual and non-punitive environment. Parents and family are included in the programme, if they can be accessed. As well as comprehensive sex education (including information about contraception and abstinence/delay of sexual involvement), the programme offers academic tutoring and assistance, career exploration opportunities, arts and sporting activities, interpersonal development workshops, healthcare (primary, mental, dental and reproductive) and access to social services. Thus, there are many enticements for the young people to get them through the door and then keep them there.

Evaluations of the programme have occurred in seven community-based service agencies in New York City (Philliber et al., 2002). These followed a best practice methodology, in that they included control groups, long-term follow-ups of participants (up to six years) and good sample sizes (600 at baseline and 484 after three years).

Their major sexual health-related findings included, that for females following the programme (compared to a control group), there was delayed initiation of sexual intercourse, increased reported resistance to sexual pressure, increased use of dual methods of contraception and, in the long term, reduced rates of teenage pregnancy. Also, both males and females in the programme had significantly increased odds of receiving good healthcare.

The researchers speculated that the effects of the programme may have been weaker among young men in part because they were already sexually experienced on entering the programme and in part because the strong social norms among inner-city males stressed the benefits of early intercourse. They suggest that lowering the age of entry of young men to the programme may strengthen outcomes for this difficult to treat group.

It is clearly a challenge to change the sexual behaviour of at risk young men, even when a great deal of money and good will are committed to the problem and best practice guidelines are adhered to, such as in this instance with the Carerra Program.

Clinic-based programmes

Such programmes relating to young people's reproductive and sexual health are usually designed for those who have already sought assistance because of concerns about STIs, symptoms of STIs, pregnancy or abortion. The clients have already come through the door, so motivating them to make that first visit is not an issue. Young people may only want medical interventions, however, and be more or less resistant to psychological and educational services, even though such interventions may, in the long run, prevent further problems.

Clinics are in the position to offer one-to-one or group counselling, but, for young people to accept these services, they must perceive the health professionals who run them as trustworthy and non-judgemental and the interventions as worthwhile. Bradford and Russell (2006) suggest a series of strategies that health professionals can use to facilitate discussion of sexual issues with clients. They advocate the use of direct and open-ended questions about sexual behaviour, using generalizing invitations to discuss issues (for example, 'It's often difficult for young women to ask a partner to use a condom. Is this an issue for you?') and a non-judgemental approach based on trust and confidentiality. They caution health professionals to make no assumptions about their patients' relationships, sexuality, intimacy or knowledge and to give simple answers, avoid medical jargon and provide concrete directions or instructions.

The PLISSIT model for talking to clients about sex (Annon, 1974) is one of several recommended approaches for health professionals who see value in clients of any age exploring sexual issues further. It is readily adaptable to shaping how health professionals might talk to young people about sex, with the goal of encouraging them to learn and practise safer and more healthy behaviours.

PLISSIT is an acronym for the stages of the model.

- **P** stands for giving the client permission to talk about sex. For example, using statements such as, 'I know that sex is a bit hard to talk about at first, but sex is pretty important in our lives and sometimes can lead to problems that can make us ill or unhappy. How do you feel about that?'
- **LI** stands for limited information and/or feedback. Once the client has taken up the offer to discuss sex, the health professional has the opportunity to provide feedback and information. The 'limited' is there because it should not end up being a lecture, but, rather, an interactive discussion. The purposes of providing information are, first, to ensure that basic facts are known by the client, second, to acknowledge the client's worth and demonstrate concern/listening and, third, to promote further discussion.
- **SS** stands for specific suggestions. In the case of young people, the suggestions might relate to using condoms and/or other forms of contraception, sexual abstinence, and ways to refuse unwanted sex and the like, depending on the goal of the intervention and the experiences of the client. These suggestions can be followed up as homework and discussed at the next visit.
- **IT** is the intensive therapy component of the model. Such therapy may occur in a one-to-one situation or involve group sessions or referral.

General Principles for Reproductive Health Interventions

In general, there are some established criteria for a good sexual health intervention. First, it is important to decide what outcome measures are appropriate – not only to guide the nature of the intervention but also to enable the intervention to be evaluated. Possible outcomes for interventions of this kind might include increasing access to services, improving levels of knowledge, sensitizing and involving community members (teachers, religious leaders and so on, for example) to the needs and issues of young people with respect to their reproductive health, delaying their first experience of intercourse, increasing the use of contraception, including condoms, and increasing communication with parents and other adults about sexual health or greater sexual self-efficacy. Most evaluative literature about sexual health interventions for young people focuses on very practical and observable outcome variables, including a reduction in rates of pregnancy among young people and STIs and/or delaying when they first have intercourse.

Kirby (2001, 2002) conducted extensive reviews of research into the effectiveness of sex education/community interventions in the USA, using what he described as minimum standards of scientific evidence. His conclusions were that the most effective sex and HIV education programmes for young people shared ten characteristics, as follows:

- the programmes were behaviourally based
- one or more theoretical frameworks of demonstrated effectiveness guided the intervention in terms of identifying both the sexual antecedents to be targeted and the means for implementing change
- the messages presented were clear, unambiguous and frequently reinforced
- the information provided was accurate and did not make unwarranted assumptions about young people's current levels of knowledge
- the programmes addressed issues of social and peer pressure that influence sexual behaviour and profitably included activities designed to assist young people in standing up to those pressures
- communication, negotiation and refusal skills were demonstrated and young people given the opportunity to practise those skills
- teaching methods were employed to encourage young people to personalize the information they received and the efficacy of the teaching was enhanced by utilizing good resources such as booklets and websites
- the programmes' goals, teaching methods and materials were tailored to the age, sexual experience and culture of the students
- the programmes were sustained over a period of time
- the teachers or peer leaders received appropriate and adequate training and were in tune with the direction and philosophy of the programmes.

For further, detailed information regarding the above findings see Kirby (2001).

Controversy in Sexual Health Interventions for Young People

Several hot issues arise when sexual health programmes for young people are discussed, regarding what should be the key goals and how they should be focused. These issues are heavily value laden and consideration of them is vital if the programme is to be accepted by the community in general and young people specifically.

Difficulties arise for sex education programmes and related interventions when educators, workers and health professionals must consider many different sets of values and beliefs, such as are evidenced in multicultural societies. Bartz (2007) describes the system in Norway where rates of STIs and teenage pregnancy are very low. She points out that sex education is compulsory, even though some of the information and activities might be offensive to some cultural groups. The rationale she provides is that the skills and knowledge being taught are important in a civilized and health-promoting society. To cater for different viewpoints, schools have held information sessions for parents and encourage them to talk to their children about sexual issues. There is recognition of the need to be sensitive to and inclusive of a range of cultural values, but also an important aim is to not compromise a system that has worked effectively to date.

This is an issue for which there are no simple answers and one that poses an ongoing challenge to those implementing sex education.

Summary

Young people have unacceptable rates of STIs, unwanted pregnancies and abortions, even in Western societies where sexual information appears, on the surface, to be readily obtainable. Sex education and community and clinic/individually based interventions for young people at risk, however, face problems because patterns of sexual behaviour are difficult to change, sex is a sensitive subject and there is a good deal of debate regarding what the appropriate values and ideals are underlying these interventions.

Not surprisingly, programmes that target behaviour change and focus on both delaying the first experience of intercourse and using contraception appear more effective in achieving their goals than those focusing less on behavioural goals. Programmes that adequately prepare young people for their adult sexual lives, however, may need to be more broader in their content and consider attitudes and values as well as behaviours.

Resources

Websites

Advocates for Youth www.advocatesforyouth.org/about/index.htm
This American website 'is dedicated to creating programs and advocating for policies that help young people make informed and responsible decisions about their reproductive and sexual health. Advocates provides information, training, and strategic assistance to youth-serving organizations, policy makers, youth activists, and the media in the United States and the developing world.' The site addresses a large range of issues and presents many resources on the topic of sexual health.

Brook Advisory Centres www.brook.org.uk/content
This is a UK-based website providing free and confidential sexual health advice and services for young people under 25. It includes sections such as 'the facts' (on contraception, pregnancy, STIs, abortion, the body), 'your rights' (UK laws on sexual issues), position statements and research summaries.

Guttmacher Institute www.guttmacher.org
The Guttmacher Institute is a US-based, non-profit making organization focused on sexual and reproductive health research, policy analysis and public education. It presents regularly updated research summaries, analyses and policy documents on sexual health and sex education.

The Hormone Factory www.thehormonefactory.com
This website, designed by Australian researchers, offers sex education and reproductive health information for 10 to 12 year olds in a format that is fun and age-appropriate. There is a section for parents and teachers, as well as quizzes and cartoons for young people.

The National Campaign to Prevent Teen and Unplanned Pregnancy
www.thenationalcampaign.org
This is an American website that houses extensive research reports, policy documents and other resources concerning unplanned pregnancy. It tends to take a conservative line on sex education. The wealth of information it provides makes it worth a visit for anyone researching youth sexuality.

Your Sex Health www.yoursexhealth.org
This award-winning, Australian-developed website is designed for middle to older young people and young adults. It provides information about reproductive and sexual health, including that on emotional, practical and relationship issues, exploring real-life dilemmas in a 'True stories' section, and is likely to have a great appeal for young people. One aim of the site is to help young people assess the potential impacts of their sexual health decisions. The contacts page leads to many further websites of interest in the field of the sexual health of young people.

KEY POINTS

- Avoidable negative outcomes of sexual activity in young people include sexually transmitted infections, unwanted or unplanned pregnancies and open to emotional and social risks.
- School-based interventions have the potential to present age-appropriate interventions.
- Community-based interventions can effectively target specific, highly vulnerable groups of young people and deliver tailor-made programmes to meet their needs.
- Clinic-based programmes can offer counselling and psychological and educational services in addition to medical interventions.

QUESTIONS FOR DISCUSSION

1. What evidence exists regarding the health and social implications of teenage pregnancy? How might social conditions modify those effects?
2. What is meant by 'sex-positive' sex education? What are the arguments for and against a sex-positive educational curriculum?

References

Alford, S. (2003) *Science and Success: Sex education and other programs that work to prevent teen pregnancy, HIV and sexually transmitted infections* (2nd edn). Washington, DC: Advocates for Youth. Also available online at: www.advocatesforyouth.org/programs thatwork/toc.htm

Annon, J.S. (1974) *The Behavioural Treatment of Sexual Problems: Vol. 1: Brief therapy enabling systems.* Honolulu: Enabling Systems.

Bartz, T. (2007) 'Sex education in multicultural Norway', *Sex Education*, 7: 17–33.

Bradford, D. and Russell, D. (2006) *Talking with Clients About Sex: A health professional's guide.* Melbourne, Australia: IP Communications.

DiCenso, A., Guyatt, G., Willan, A. and Griffith, L. (2002) 'Interventions to reduce unintended pregnancies among adolescents: systematic review of randomized control trials', *British Medical Journal*, 324: 1426.

Grunseit, A., Kippax, S., Aggleton, P., Baldo, M. and Slutkin, G. (1997) 'Sexuality education and young people's sexual behaviour: a review of studies', *Journal of Adolescent Research*, 12: 421–53.

Kirby, D. (2001) *Emerging Answers: Research findings on programs to reduce teen pregnancy.* Washington, DC: National Campaign to Prevent Teen Pregnancy.

Kirby, D. (2002) *Do abstinence-only programs delay the initiation of sex among young people and reduce teen pregnancy?* Washington, DC: National Campaign to Prevent Teen Pregnancy.

Kirby, D. and Miller, B.C. (2002) 'Interventions designed to promote parent–teen communications about sexuality', in S.S. Feldman and D.A. Rosenthal (eds), *Talking Sexuality: Parent–adolescent communication.* San Francisco, CA: Jossey-Bass. pp. 93–110.

Mitchell, A., Ollis, D. and Watson, J. (2000) 'Talking sexual health: what goes into a national framework for AIDS education in secondary schools?', *Youth Studies Australia*, 19: 22–7.

Moore, S. and Rosenthal, D. (2006) *Sexuality in Adolescence: Current trends.* London: Taylor & Francis.

O'Donnell, L., Agronick, A., Wilson-Simmons, R., Duran, R. and Jeanbaptiste, V. (2005) 'Saving sex for later: an evaluation of a parent education intervention', *Perspectives on Sexual and Reproductive Health*, 37: 166–73.

Philliber, S., Kaye, J.W., Herrling, S. and West, E. (2002) 'Preventing pregnancy and improving health care access among teenagers: an evaluation of the Children's Aid Society-Carrera Program', *Perspectives on Sexual Reproductive Health*, 34: 244–51.

14

Young People with Sexual Behaviour Problems: Towards Positive and Healthy Relationships

Ian Lambie

Introduction

Sexual abuse perpetrated by young people is of significant concern. In the United States, the Federal Bureau of Investigation (FBI) Uniform Crime Report noted that, in 2002, young people made up 16.7 per cent of arrests for rape and 20.6 per cent of arrests for other sex crimes (FBI, 2003). Statistics in other countries are of similar concern, so the development of effective interventions for this age group is clearly warranted.

Despite the available statistics, due to under-reporting by victims, we are unable to accurately ascertain the true number of young people who engage in sexually inappropriate behaviour.

With the public awareness of the damage caused by high-profile adult sexual offender cases, there is now a call in some countries, such as the United States, for the lifelong registration of young people who are sexually abusive. Others, however, argue for more community-based interventions and strength-based interventions (see Chaffin, 2008, for example). Regardless of the position taken, the recognition that sexual abuse of children by young people results in considerable emotional and financial cost to society has led to this group becoming the target for specialized treatment programmes, and the subject of research efforts to increase our understanding of the factors that contribute to the causes of and predictors for sexual offending.

Characteristics of Sexually Abusive Young People

When considering treatment options, it is important to consider the range of factors found to be evident in young people who are sexually abusive. In doing so, this information can be used to guide treatment and services for them and their families. A significant body of research has focused on previous victimization as a causal factor in sexual offending (Burton, 2000, 2003).

Non-sexual offending

We now know that many young people who engage in sexually abusive behaviour are also likely to have committed non-sexual offences, including aggressive acts and other antisocial behaviour, predating or as part of their sexual offending (Fehrenbach et al., 1986).

Comorbid mental health issues and educational needs

Young people who sexually abuse often have coexisting mental health issues, such as depression (Morenz and Becker, 1995) and learning difficulties. These include learning problems, truancy and non-specific but chronic academic and behavioural problems (Bourke and Donohue, 1996; Davis and Leitenberg, 1987; Morenz and Becker, 1995). Ferrara and McDonald (1996) also found it to be common for young sex offenders to have difficulties with executive functioning and expressive and receptive language.

Family issues

While not all young people who are sexually abusive come from multi problem families, many do come from families that are characterised by instability, frequent violence and high rates of disorganization (Morenz and Becker, 1995).

Marshall et al., (1993) note the importance of attachment styles in the development of sexual offending by young people. They argue that poor attachment styles, combined with parental abuse, were more likely to increase a child's likelihood of sexually offending.

Typologies of sexually abusive young people

While much of the early treatment and research efforts appeared to regard young sexual offenders as a single, homogeneous group, more recently typologies have emerged that have significance for both the understanding and treatment of offenders. These typologies have clearly identified that they are a heterogeneous group of young people with diverse developmental and treatment needs (Worling, 2001).

What was once thought of as a 'typical' clinical presentation is now challenged by the research findings. For example, early characterizations of young sex offenders described them as a socially isolated group with low self-esteem (Becker et al., 1986). In contrast, other studies have found no significant deficits in their social skills (Ford and Linney, 1995). Indeed, many young people who sexually abuse have *good* social skills, but use them inappropriately to groom their victims. Some individuals use these skills to become part of a larger group of antisocial peers, with whom they commit other crimes.

Using a developmental framework, Seto and Barbaree (1997) used Moffitt's (1993) distinction between 'life-course persistent' and 'adolescent-limited delinquents'. Seto and Barbaree proposed that life-course persistent offenders have an extensive history of conduct problems from a young age, with a persistent presentation of anger and hostility. The second type of offender – adolescent-limited – however, has few anti-social behaviours and is more similar behaviourally to non-offenders than life-course offenders.

One weakness of this theory, however, is that most young people do not go on to sexually offend in adulthood, suggesting that, as a population, they differ not only in associated characteristics, such as those described above, but also in their offending behaviour trajectories (Caldwell, 2007).

Smith et al., (1987) used a Minnesota Multiphasic Personality Inventory (MMPI)-based typology and identified four groups:

- immature
- personality disorders
- socialized delinquents
- conduct-disordered adolescent.

Worling (2001) administered the California Psychological Inventory (Gough, 1987) to develop a personality-based typology. He distinguished four personality-based typologies:

- antisocial/impulsive
- unusual/isolated
- overcontrolled/reserved
- confident/aggressive.

Richardson et al's (1997) study used the Millon Adolescent Clinical Inventory (Millon et al., 1993), to identify five subgroups from an outpatient sample:

- normal
- antisocial
- submissive
- dysthymic/inhibited
- dysthymic/negativistic.

It appears that there may be at least three main group typologies:

- those young people who come from relatively stable and functional families and do not have significant comorbid disorders and/or other non-sexual offending behaviours
- those who have high levels of conduct disorder and antisocial behaviour and are likely to come from dysfunctional and problematic families
- those who are socially withdrawn and introverted – they have few friends, low self-esteem, act alone, befriend and offend against younger children for fear of rejection by same-aged peers.

Although the work on typologies is still in its infancy, it offers clinicians a useful framework from which to plan and undertake treatment. Reliable typologies can be used to predict the level of risk, guide what is appropriate treatment for clients and predict the outcome of that treatment.

Given the role of families in young people's lives, however, consideration also needs to be given to the level of support the family of a young person can provide when assessing risk and planning treatment. In St Amand et al's (2008) meta-analysis, looking at practice elements within treatment programmes, they found evidence for the important role of family-based treatments that are multisystemic therapy- and community-based. Clearly, in order to achieve good clinical outcomes with children, family involvement is crucial and the more complex and younger the children, the more involvement from parents and other carers is needed.

Assessment and Treatment

Risk assessment

An important element in interventions with young people who sexually abuse is the assessment of risk to the community. Typically, the question is, how likely it is that they will re-offend?

The answer is important when addressing issues of safety. For example, lack of safety may determine whether treatment can proceed with the young person living at home or whether they must be moved to a controlled living environment.

An assessment should also address what treatment is needed for other problems that exist in addition to their sexual offending.

Two risk assessment measures that have been developed to use with young people who sexually abuse are the Juvenile Sex Offender Assessment Protocol (JSOAP) (Prentky et al., 2000) and the Estimate of Risk of Adolescent Sex Offender Recidivism (ERASOR) (Worling and Curwen, 2000).

Interventions

Traditionally, the treatment of young people has mirrored approaches used for adult offenders, despite there being significant differences in their treatment needs. Yet there is a need for programmes to take a more developmental focus and not utilize techniques and strategies from the adult sexual offender field. For example, young people are likely to be sexually aroused by a range of sexual stimuli and have fewer deviant sexual fantasies than older people (Chaffin, 2008). Young people are also likely to be living within, and be dependent on, their families. Also, as previously stated, both clinical experience and evidence clearly point to the fact that family involvement is very effective in producing positive changes (Letourneau et al., 2008). Furthermore, by involving the young person's family and providing ongoing support, the clinicians further sets the scene for assisting them towards making the necessary changes to reduce their level of risk.

So, with an increasing emphasis on changing the focus and way in which young sexual offender treatment is implemented, there is now a shift to learning and understanding from the field of oppositional defiant and conduct disorder. Given the significant number of such young people who have both sexual and non-sexual behaviour problems, it has invited close consideration of the treatment approaches that have been found to be effective with that group. Such interventions include behavioural parent training, functional family therapy, multisystemic therapy (MST) and treatment foster care (for reviews, see Eyberg et al., 2008; Kazdin, 1997).

An example of treatment methods from conduct disorder treatment being applied to this group is seen in the only randomized studies undertaken in the field of sexually abusive youth to date that have utilized multisystemic therapy (Borduin et al., 1990; Borduin et al., 2000). The results provide some indication of what some future services for treating sexually abusive youths may look like.

For those young people with complex needs and at high risk of reoffending, it is now recognized that treatment requires a continuum of care that meets clients' needs for appropriate treatment and also the community's need for safety. Programmes need to be structured and provide containment and safety for clients and staff. This continuum of treatment includes community treatment within the immediate or extended family, specialist one-on-one foster home placements, where one client is cared for by two house-parents, and small specialist homes where a number of young people live in secure residential treatment facilities.

One of the most important issues in the successful treatment of young people who sexually abuse is the provision of a stable and supportive placement, given their developmental stage, which, typically, includes an ongoing reliance on adults. The most important people to assist the young person in making change are the people with whom they live. Obviously, many parents may not be supportive, due to their past abuse of their children, or may not be capable of being involved in their care due to their own lack of motivation or own issues. Nevertheless, finding appropriate adult caregivers and adults who can support the young person in the change process is vital, because young people typically have limited motivation or the ability to change without support.

Stable carers and placements provide somewhere for young people to receive the support, nurturing and consistency they may not have experienced before. The therapeutic relationships that they have with clinicians who undertake their primary treatment is of equal importance.

The use of motivational interviewing techniques forms part of a 'toolkit' that allows clinicians to systematically work with these young people to move them towards increasing their motivation to engage in therapy, thereby improving the likelihood of them making sustained changes. To this end, it is important that clinicians have personal qualities that are warm and the ability to motivate and engage clients and that they work with young people in a way that does not alienate them and does not further shame them. This is something that young people often experience and provides a challenge for clinicians at the outset of therapy in getting them to disclose their offending behaviour. An evaluation of New Zealand treatment programmes (Geary and Lambie, 2006) found that strong client therapist relationships were identified as making a strong contribution to therapeutic success, along with culturally appropriate counselling. There was also a very strong preference for both young people and their families to have a therapist from their own culture. This was seen as particularly important in achieving their engagement in treatment.

Young people considered at high risk of reoffending and who are likely to be unresponsive to treatment may require specialist residential treatment programmes. Though there is little outcome research on the efficacy of residential placements, decisions to place young people in care are typically made on the basis of public safety. Where residential services are required, ensuring that there is follow-up of the young people in the community is vitally important so that the positive psychological and behavioural changes they have made in residence are maintained and their life skills are successfully developed.

Treatment in the community

There are often significant differences in the ways treatment is undertaken for sexually abusive youth in New Zealand and Australia and overseas – particularly in the USA. In New Zealand, the first treatments used for young sexual offenders were family-based community programmes. They were developed in the late 1980s to early 1990s in community child and adolescent mental health and family therapy centres (Lambie et al., 2000). As a result of public and political pressure in the mid-1990s, a specialist residential faculty was opened. Yet, even today, in contrast with other countries (such as the USA), there is little reliance on residential treatment and community programmes continue to provide interventions to over 95 per cent of sexually abusive youth each year. Only a very small number of young people are in the residential facility (there is a maximum capacity of 12), which has operated below capacity since opening in 1997. I know that some of the young people who would be in residential programmes in the USA are treated successfully in community programmes in New Zealand and Australia. I consider this to be a positive sign of how well community treatment services can cater for this group of young people. Putting it simply, I believe that treatment should ideally take place in the least restrictive setting that best matches and enhances the developmental, emotional and psychological needs of each young person. At such an important time in the young person's life it is crucial that they have as normal a life as possible and are not removed from their peers or family unless for matters of safety and treatment responsivity.

Family interventions

New Zealand and Australian treatment programmes have always been family/system-focused first. The family has a powerful role in influencing a young person's motivation to attend treatment and, ultimately, whether or not that treatment has a successful outcome. Clinical experience suggests that treatment is likely to be more successful when it includes a stable living placement, ideally with members of the immediate or extended family.

Attempts should be made to provide specialist one-to-one foster care for young people who cannot remain with their families and intensive specialist social work support attached to their homes. Though not developed specifically for young people who have sexual behaviour problems, therapeutic fostercare is an effective intervention for children diagnosed with conduct disorder (Dishion and Andrews, 1995) and common sense would suggest that it would also be useful for young people who are sexually abusive. Also, the development of post-foster care services that support the young person transitioning to independence may be required where this is unable to be provided for by the family.

One approach to engaging families initially in the treatment of young offenders is through the use of multi-family groups. At SAFE in Auckland the multi-family groups have been adapted from the model used at the Morrison Centre in Oregon. The groups receive six weeks' education on sexual abuse and offending and the sessions are adapted uniquely for the New Zealand context. For families, it is often the first time they have spoken to other families about their children's offending. This offers relief in the experience that they are not alone and assists in removing the stigma and blame.

The importance of culture

In a recent national evaluation of community treatment programmes in New Zealand, Maori young people and their families reported that having a Maori therapist was crucial (Geary and Lambie, 2006). In addition, when Maori staff incorporated cultural components into treatment, this was found to enhance outcomes for Maori clients. In recognition of this, most community-based treatment programmes for young people in New Zealand contain programmes for Maori sexual offenders, run by Maori staff.

Treating non-sexual offending problems

Despite methodological variations, most studies report relatively low rates of sexual recidivism, with non-sexual recidivism being nearly twice as great. In a review by Fortune and Lambie (2006), it was noted that there is a wide variation in reported rates for sexual reoffending (4 per cent for those who successfully completed treatment), while the recidivism rates for non-sexual offending were higher (39 per cent).

As noted already, the recognition that high numbers of young people have concurrent non-sexual offending behaviour and/or comorbid mental health problems has led to the adoption of intervention programmes that include a wide range of treatment goals and methods derived from interventions provided for children with conduct disorder.

The use of different treatment modalities

Despite the push internationally for evidence-based clinical practice, it is generally acknowledged that a wide range of treatment methods and modalities must be utilized in order to make treatment accessible and interesting to the young people concerned.

Geary and Lambie (2006) found widespread support in New Zealand for not only mainstream models of practice (such as cognitive behavioural therapy (CBT) and family therapy) but also cultural components, experiential and expressive therapies (see, for example, Bergman and Hewish, 2003), multisystemic approaches and multimodal interventions. Experiential methods such as psychodrama and drama therapy have also been found to be useful (Bergman and Hewish, 2003) in assisting with motivating clients and assessing fully their social skills and behaviour. These therapies are particularly useful as they make the very difficult and shameful topic of sexual offending more able to be discussed and worked with by young people.

Some programmes, such as the SAFE Adolescent programme, also run an adjunct wilderness component to treatment (Lambie et al., 2000). There is, too, a growing emphasis in the field on psychodynamic approaches to address attachment issues and intensive systems work utilizing specialist social workers from the treatment programmes.

Special populations

The need for specialized interventions and services for children with special learning needs is now recognized as a sub-speciality in the field. In New Zealand and Australia, the development of such programmes has been introduced due to the recognition that these groups cannot be catered for properly within mainstream programmes for young male sexual offenders. A strengths-based model that is being used increasingly throughout New Zealand is the Good Way model, developed by Lesley Ayland and Bill West (Ayland and West, 2006). It utilizes a dualistic approach (good way/bad way) and language that is accessible for people with a concrete thinking style. It has been found to be effective with young people with intellectual disability as they readily assimilate these concepts.

Conclusion

In the last decade, significant developments have taken place in the treatment of young people who sexually abuse. These changes have come about, at least in part, from an increase in the amount of research focusing on causal factors, an increase in the number of outcome studies and, more recently, research on risk factors and the use of specific risk factor scales.

It is time the field considered more carefully the clinical implications of the vast literature on the conduct disorder and oppositional defiant disorder populations. This research indicates that behavioural parent training, functional family therapy, multisystemic therapy and treatment foster care are the interventions of choice in cases of childhood conduct disorder. Due to the fact that studies of young people who sexually abuse show high rates of non-sexual reoffending, it is important that we work to address those issues that are likely to impact on their ability to live healthy and productive lives.

KEY POINTS

- Young sexual offenders are a heterogeneous group with diverse developmental and treatment needs.
- Decisions about the treatment modality will depend on an assessment of risk to the community.
- All but a very small minority of young sex offenders can be treated effectively in the community.
- A wide range of treatment modalities is required in order to make treatment accessible and interesting to the young person.

QUESTIONS FOR DISCUSSION

1. Discuss what you consider to be the differences between normal sexual interest and experimentation by young people and offending behaviour.
2. Discuss, with anecdotal examples if possible, the way that case management might be adjusted to suit young sexual offenders coming from two of the different typologies described in this chapter.

References

Ayland, L. and West, B. (2006) 'The Good Way model: a strengths-based approach for working with young people, especially those with intellectual difficulties, who have sexually abusive behaviour', *Journal of Sexual Aggression*, 12: 189–201.

Becker, J.V., Kaplan, M.S., Cunningham-Rathner, J. and Kavoussi, R.J. (1986) 'Characteristics of adolescent incest sexual perpetrators: preliminary findings', *Journal of Family Violence*, 1: 87–97.

Bergman, J. and Hewish, S. (2003) *Challenging Experience: An experiential approach to the treatment of serious offenders*. Oklahoma: Wood N. Barnes.

Borduin, C.M., Henggeler, S.W., Blaske, D.M. and Stein, R.J. (1990) 'Multisystemic treatment of adolescent sexual offenders', *International Journal of Offender Therapy and Comparative Criminology*, 34: 105–13.

Borduin, C.M., Schaeffer, C.M. and Heilbluma, N. (2000) 'Multi-systemic treatment of juvenile sexual offenders: a progress report', presentation at the 6th International Conference on the treatment of Sexual Offenders, Toronto, Canada.

Bourke, M.L. and Donohue, B. (1996) 'Assessment and treatment of juvenile sex offenders: an empirical review', *Journal of Child Sexual Abuse*, 5: 47–70.

Burton, D. (2000) 'Were adolescent sexual offenders children with sexual behavior problems?', *Sexual Abuse: A Journal of Research and Treatment*, 12: 37–48.

Burton, D. (2003) 'The relationship between the sexual victimisation of and the subsequent sexual abuse by male adolescents', *Child and Adolescent Social Work Journal*, 20: 277–96.

Caldwell, M. (2007) 'Sexual offense adjudication and sexual recidivism among juvenile sexual offenders', *Sexual Abuse: A Journal of Research and Treatment*, 19: 107–13.

Chaffin, M. (2008) 'Our minds are made up – don't confuse us with the facts', *Child Maltreatment*, 13: 110–21.

Davis, G.E. and Leitenberg, H. (1987) 'Adolescent sex offenders', *Psychological Bulletin*, 101: 417–27.

Dishion, T. and Andrews, D. (1995) 'Preventing escalation in problem behaviors with high-risk young adolescents: immediate and 1-year outcomes', *Journal of Consulting and Clinical Psychology*, 63: 538–48.

Eyberg, S., Nelson, M. and Boggs, S. (2008) 'Evidence-based psychosocial treatments for children and adolescents with disruptive behavior', *Journal of Clinical Child & Adolescent Psychology*, 37: 215–37.

FBI (US Department of Justice) (2003) *Crime in the United States 2002*. Washington, DC: US Government Printing Office.

Fehrenbach, P.A., Smith, W., Monastersky, C. and Deisher, R.W. (1986) 'Adolescent sexual offenders: offender and offense characteristics', *American Journal of Orthopsychiatry*, 56: 225–33.

Ferrara, M.L. and McDonald, S. (1996) *Treatment of the Juvenile Sex Offender: Neurological and psychiatric impairments*. Northvale, NJ: Jason Aronson.

Ford, M.E. and Linney, J.A. (1995) 'Comparative analysis of juvenile sexual offenders, violent nonsexual offenders, and status offenders', *Journal of Interpersonal Violence*, 10: 56–70.

Fortune, C. and Lambie, I.D. (2006) 'Sexually abusive youth: a review of recidivism studies and methodological issues for future research', *Clinical Psychology Review*, 26: 1078–95.

Geary, J. and Lambie, I. (2006) *Turning Lives Around: A process evaluation of community adolescent sexual offender treatment programmes in New Zealand*. Wellington: Department of Child, Youth and Family.

Gough, H.G. (1987) *California Psychological Inventory: Administrators' guide*. Palo Alto, CA: Consulting Psychologists Press.

Kazdin, A. (1997) 'Psychosocial treatments for conduct disorder in children', *Journal of Child Psychology and Psychiatry*, 38: 161–78.

Lambie, I., Hickling, L., Seymour, F., Simmonds, L., Robson, M. and Houlahan, C. (2000) 'Using wilderness therapy in training adolescent sexual offenders', *Journal of Sexual Aggression*, 5: 99–117.

Letourneau, E., Chapman, J. and Schoenwald, S. (2008) 'Treatment outcome and criminal offending by youth with sexual behavior problems', *Child Maltreatment*, 13: 133–44.

Marshall, W.L., Hudson, S.M. and Hodkinson, S. (1993) 'The importance of attachment bonds in the development of juvenile sex offending', in H.E. Barbaree, W.L. Marshall and S.M. Hudson (eds), *The Juvenile Sex Offender*. New York: Guilford Press. pp. 164–81.

Millon, T., Millon, C. and Davis, R. (1993) *Millon Adolescent Clinical Inventory Manual*. Minneapolis, MN: National Computer Systems.

Moffitt, T.E. (1993) 'Adolescence-limited and life-course-persistent antisocial behavior: a developmental taxonomy', *Psychological Review*, 100: 674–701.

Morenz, B. and Becker, J. (1995) 'The treatment of youthful sexual offenders', *Applied and Preventive Psychology*, 4: 247–56.

Prentky, R., Harris, B., Frizell, K. and Righthand, S. (2000) 'An actuarial procedure for assessing risk with juvenile sex offenders', *Sexual Abuse: A Journal of Research and Treatment*, 12: 71–93.

Richardson, G., Kelly, T. P. Bhate, S. R. and Graham, F. (1997) 'Group differences in abuser and abuse characteristics in a British sample of sexually abusive children', *Sexual Abuse: Journal of Research and Treatment*, 9: 239–57.

St Amand, A., Bard, D. and Silovsky, J. (2008) 'Meta-analysis of treatment of child sexual behavior problems: practice elements and outcomes', *Child Maltreatment*, 13: 145–66.

Seto, M. and Barbaree, H. (1997) 'Sexual aggression as antisocial behaviour: a developmental model', in D. Stoff, J. Breiling and J.D. Maser (eds), *Handbook of Antisocial Behavior*. New York: Wiley. pp. 524–33.

Smith, W.R., Monastersky, C. and Deisher, R.M. (1987) 'MMPI-based personality types among juvenile sexual offenders', *Journal of Clinical Psychology*, 43: 422–30.

Worling, J. (2001) 'Personality-based typology of adolescent male sexual offenders: diffferences in recidivism rates, victim selection characteristics, and personal victimization histories', *Sexual Abuse: A Journal of Research and Treatment*, 13: 149–66.

Worling, J.R. and Curwen, T. (2000) 'Adolescent sexual offender recidivism: success of specialised treatment and implications for risk prediction', *Child Abuse and Neglect*, 24: 965–82.

Part VII

Mental Health

15

Addressing Eating Problems

Renee Rienecke Hoste and Daniel le Grange

Introduction

Eating disorders are serious psychiatric illnesses that usually begin in young people and are associated with serious medical complications, high rates of psychiatric comorbidity and psychosocial impairment. Both anorexia nervosa (AN) and bulimia nervosa (BN) can lead to electrolyte imbalances, cardiac abnormalities, gastrointestinal complications, cognitive impairment, fertility problems and death, with AN having the highest mortality rate of any psychiatric disorder (Powers and Bannon, 2004). Individuals with eating disorders also have elevated rates of mood disorders, anxiety disorders and substance abuse disorders compared with the general population (Lilenfeld, 2004).

The lifetime prevalence rates of AN and BN are 0.5 to 1 per cent and 3 per cent, respectively (Hoek and van Hoeken, 2003), although subthreshold levels of eating disorders have been found to be as high as 39 per cent among female college students (Drewnowski et al., 1994). The majority of individuals with eating disorders are female, with a female-to-male ratio of 9–10:1.

Diagnostic Criteria

AN is characterized by restrictive eating and weight loss, whereas BN consists of regular binge eating and compensatory behaviours (such as self-induced vomiting and excessive exercising). The *Diagnostic and Statistical Manual of Mental Disorders* (4th edn) text revision – know as DSM-IV-TR (APA, 2000) – provides specific diagnostic criteria for both AN and BN.

A diagnosis of an eating disorder not otherwise specified (EDNOS) is reserved for those individuals who exhibit problematic behaviours or cognitions related to eating and whose symptoms are severe enough to cause distress or functional impairment but do not meet the full criteria for AN or BN. Binge eating disorder (BED), in which an individual engages in binge eating but does not engage in compensatory behaviours, is currently classified as EDNOS.

Risk Factors

A biopsychosocial model of disordered eating suggests that certain biological vulnerabilities, combined with exposure to a range of environmental stressors or circumstances (such as family interaction and societal pressures to be thin), lay the groundwork for the development of beliefs and behaviours that can lead to eating disorders. This confluence of biological, environmental, and sociocultural influences seems to reach a critical threshold during the life transition period of adolescence, suggesting that developmental factors also play an important role in the onset of disordered eating.

The majority of studies on the development of eating disorders are retrospective or cross-sectional in nature, which limits the conclusions we can make about the prospective development of these disorders. Nevertheless, their findings are important in furthering our understanding of a possible etiological and developmental trajectory for eating disorders.

Biological factors

Genetic influences may underlie vulnerability to developing an eating disorder. Compared to healthy controls, first-degree relatives of patients with AN or BN have increased rates of eating disorders (Strober et al., 2000). In addition, research suggests that certain eating disorder symptoms, such as binge eating, dietary restraint and body dissatisfaction, may also be heritable (Bulik et al., 1998). Studies of twins have found higher rates of eating disorders among monozygotic twins than dizygotic twins (Treasure and Holland, 1989), although the higher concordance rates for monozygotic twins may be due in part to the influence of shared environments.

Familial factors

Investigations into the role of family dynamics in the development of eating disorders has a long history. Early family theorists suggested that families of AN patients shared certain characteristics, including enmeshment, overprotectiveness, rigidity and a lack of conflict resolution (Minuchin et al., 1975). Families of BN patients were described as chaotic, conflicted and lacking boundaries (Root et al., 1986). Some research evidence has been found to support these hypotheses. For example, eating disorder patients have described their families as less cohesive, more rigid, and less communicative than those of healthy controls and BN patients have been found to report higher levels of family dysfunction than restricting AN patients (Vidovic et al., 2005).

Parental attitudes towards eating, weight and shape can also have a tremendous impact on children. Compared to mothers of girls without eating disorders, mothers of girls with eating disorders exhibit more eating disordered behaviours themselves, think their daughters should lose weight, believe that their daughters are less attractive and are less satisfied with the overall functioning of their families (Pike and Rodin, 1991).

Developmental factors

Most eating disordered thoughts and behaviours begin during the stage of transition from childhood to adulthood, suggesting that the onset of disordered eating may be related to the onset of puberty. A longitudinal prospective study of girls found that eating problems did, in fact, emerge in response to pubertal change (Attie and Brooks-Gunn, 1989).

For girls, puberty is associated with the development of secondary sex characteristics – the widening of hips and fat accumulation – taking them further away from the thin, prepubertal shape that characterizes the Western cultural ideal of beauty. Thus, it is not surprising that body dissatisfaction and unhealthy weight control behaviours would begin during this period of development.

Although the physical changes that boys experience during puberty – broadening of the shoulders, growing taller, increasing muscle mass – bring them closer to the Western cultural ideal of male beauty, boys are not immune from the sociocultural pressures that encourage conformity to a particular body type.

Research has found that male action figures, such as GI Joe and *Star Wars* characters, have grown increasingly muscular over the past thirty years. The male physiques that boys are now exposed to are often only attainable through artificial means, such as the use of anabolic steroids, and some exceed the limits of human possibility, which may be leading to increased body image concerns and disordered eating among men (Pope et al., 1999).

Interpersonal factors may further increase the likelihood of developing eating disorder symptoms during this life stage transition. The developmental task of individuation, along with the increased emphasis on social acceptance and physical attractiveness during this period of development, may lead some young people to experiment with weight loss strategies, such as dieting, in an attempt to emulate the cultural standard of beauty. Dieting, however, is a robust predictor of disordered eating (see Jacobi et al., 2004). Rates of dieting among females increase throughout adolescence (McCabe et al., 2002) and nearly 60 per cent of teenage girls engage in additional unhealthy weight control behaviors, such as skipping meals or smoking to control appetite (Neumark-Sztainer et al., 2002).

Other challenges common during adolescence may contribute to the development of disordered eating, including low self-esteem, discomfort about discussing problems with parents and increased exposure to sociocultural ideals of beauty.

Sociocultural factors

During adolescence, the influence of the media is increasingly salient (McCabe et al., 2002). Indeed, most young people are inundated with images of the thin ideal of the fashion world and many studies have found that viewing images of thin models increases girls' dissatisfaction with their bodies (Groesz et al., 2002). Such dissatisfaction among females has become so widespread that it is now considered 'normative' (Rodin et al., 1984).

Mere exposure to the media does not necessarily lead to disordered eating, however. Rather, internalizing society's thin ideal has been found to be associated with the onset of dieting and bulimic symptoms (Stice and Agras, 1998).

Prevention of Eating Disorders

The early onset of dissatisfaction with the body and weight control behaviours suggests that primary prevention efforts should target primary school children before they enter puberty. Unfortunately the few studies conducted with this age group have not used random assignment and most have not included a follow-up assessment, limiting the conclusions we can make regarding the efficacy of such prevention programmes.

In general, studies have found that prevention programmes increase students' knowledge but have little effect on eating attitudes and behaviours (Levine and Smolak, 2006).

A larger number of studies have targeted junior and secondary school students for primary prevention, but findings have been mixed and generally disappointing. Levine and Smolak (2006) provide an excellent review of prevention research into eating disorders.

Treatment for Young People with Eating Disorders

The potentially dangerous medical consequences of disordered eating necessitate a comprehensive and assertive approach to treatment. A team approach is generally recommended, to monitor the patient's physical health and medical stability, address their psychotherapeutic needs and manage any medications prescribed.

Until relatively recently, there were few clinical guidelines for the treatment of eating disorders. In 2004, the National Institute for Clinical Excellence in the United Kingdom summarized guidelines for eating disorders based on a comprehensive review of the treatment literature (Wilson and Shafran, 2005).

Treatment modalities were graded from A to C, with grade A reserved for those treatment approaches that have strong empirical support based on several well-conducted randomized controlled trials (RCTs) and grade C given to those treatment approaches where support was based on expert opinion without strong empirical data.

Over 100 recommendations were made, with the vast majority of treatment approaches receiving a grade C. For young people, the only exception was family-based treatment (FBT) for AN, which received a B recommendation. No specific recommendations were made for young people with BN because of the paucity of treatment studies on this population. Only two RCTs have been conducted with young people with BN and these will are described below.

Treatment for AN

Although FBT has been recognized as a promising treatment approach for young people with AN, ego-oriented individual therapy (Robin et al., 1999) has also received empirical support. Both treatment approaches are described below.

Family-based treatment (FBT)

Family-based treatment was developed at the Maudsley Hospital in London, so has come to be known as the 'Maudsley approach'. Several studies have found that FBT is more effective than individual therapy in helping young people with AN gain weight. Also, follow-up studies have found that those gains were maintained after five years (Eisler et al., 1997; Russell et al., 1987).

Family-based treatment takes an agnostic view of the etiology of eating disorders. The eating disorder is not viewed as an expression of family dysfunction or an attempt to exert control over chaotic surroundings. Instead, FBT views the family as a resource in the young persons' recovery and emphasizes the importance of a rapid return to health, particularly in the first phase of treatment (Lock et al., 2001). There is also a great deal of emphasis on separating the eating disorder from the patient. Parents are encouraged to view their son or daughter as being under the control of the eating disorder, which helps frustrated parents direct their anger towards the illness rather than towards their child.

The Maudsley approach is divided into three phases. In the first phase of treatment, parents are put in charge of their child's weight restoration. With the therapist's guidance, parents are encouraged to present a united front, directing their efforts towards refeeding, despite the patient's often considerable resistance. Parents are given the task of choosing what their child eats, when they eat, and how much they eat, and are encouraged to monitor all meals and snacks and prohibit physical activity.

The therapist explains that AN is a powerful illness that will not allow its victims to make appropriate decisions regarding food and exercise. Thus, the parents are required to temporarily take charge of this process. The therapist does not direct parents towards a particular course of action, but, instead, encourages them to refeed their child in the manner best suited to their particular family.

During this first phase of treatment, the focus is almost exclusively on weight restoration and the return of healthy eating patterns. The family is told that nothing is more important than reversing their child's self-starvation. Until this is accomplished, other topics are not addressed in therapy.

The second phase of treatment begins when the patient is steadily gaining weight and eating without much resistance. The parents are assisted in gradually returning responsibility for eating back to the young person to whatever extent is age-appropriate.

During this second phase of treatment, other topics that may have been put on hold can be explored, but only in so far as they relate to the young person's continued weight restoration.

The third and final phase of treatment begins when patients achieve a healthy weight at which they are able to menstruate (for females). At this point, therapy turns to more general issues of the young person's development and the ways in which they have been impacted by the eating disorder.

The Maudsley approach views the eating disorder as having 'derailed' the normal progression of the young person's development. Once they are back on track, treatment can then focus on upcoming developmental challenges and how parents can help their child to navigate those challenges.

Depending on the young person's stages of development, treatment during the third phase may focus on increased personal autonomy, relationships with peers or getting ready to leave home for the first time.

Although FBT seems to be helpful for the younger age group, there is some evidence that young people over the age of 18 may benefit from individual therapy (Russell et al., 1987). Perhaps this is because those over the age of 18 may be more able to utilize insight-orientated psychotherapy and have more of a need for privacy.

Ego-oriented individual therapy

Ego-oriented individual therapy (EOIT) has its origins in the psychodynamic tradition. It has been compared to behavioural family systems therapy (BFST) in a RCT of females (Robin et al., 1999). Although BFST resulted in greater weight gain at the end of treatment, there were no differences between the two groups on measures of eating attitudes, body and shape concerns and eating-related family conflicts. In addition, in a one-year follow-up, no differences were found between the two groups on any measures, suggesting that EOIT may be as effective as BFST, albeit slower, in achieving weight gain.

EOIT suggests that young people with AN have deficient ego-strength and are unable to manage the normal challenges faced by young people. In order to recover, patients must improve their sense of self-efficacy and successfully individuate from their family of origin.

Their eating disorder is viewed as a maladaptive attempt to cope with negative affect and an important component of therapy involves helping patients identify and tolerate their emotions. They are also encouraged to take responsibility for their recovery by increasing their caloric intake and refraining from physical activity.

EOIT consists of four phases. In the assessment phase, the therapist obtains information about the patient's functioning and motivation for treatment and begin to develop a formulation of the patient's psychological issues. The therapist also meets with the parents to assess parental functioning and family dynamics.

The next, early phase of treatment focuses on helping the patient to identify their emotions and bodily sensations, improve their negative self-image and increase assertiveness.

The middle phase focuses on helping the young person develop a better understanding of themselves and their needs and facilitate the process of separation and individuation from their family of origin.

The final, termination phase addresses relapse prevention and helps the patient to identify ways to continue to thrive without the help of their therapist.

The majority of EOIT sessions occur between the therapist and the young person on an individual basis, but the therapist meets periodically with the parents to discuss their child's progress and identify ways in which the parents can be involved in the recovery process.

Treatment for BN

Although over 100 studies have been conducted on *adults* with BN, only two RCTs have been conducted with young people, despite the fact that BN usually starts during adolescence.

Several effective treatments for adults with BN have been identified, including cognitive behavioural therapy (CBT), interpersonal psychotherapy (IPT) and selective serotonin reuptake inhibitors (SSRIs) (Agras et al., 2000). Unfortunately, these treatments have not been systematically studied with young people. To date, only CBT and FBT have received empirical support for the treatment of young people with BN.

Cognitive behavioural therapy (CBT)

The cognitive behavioural model of BN assumes that the disorder is maintained by an individual's overvaluation of the importance of body shape and weight. These beliefs lead to low self-esteem and body dissatisfaction, which, in turn, lead to dietary restriction in an attempt to lose weight or change their body shape. Dietary restriction inevitably leads to hunger, which then increases the likelihood of binge eating. Binge eating, in turn, leads to a fear of weight gain, which then compels these individuals to engage in inappropriate compensatory behaviours, such as self-induced vomiting or excessive exercise, to rid themselves of the calories consumed during the binge episode (Fairburn et al., 1993).

CBT consists of three phases. In the first phase, the focus of treatment is on helping patients to make behavioural changes. This includes eating meals and snacks at regular intervals throughout the day and reducing dietary restrictions, which then reduce intense feelings of hunger which can lead to binge eating and purging.

In the second phase, the focus turns towards the patient's dysfunctional cognitions about eating and weight. They are taught to realistically appraise their assumptions and come up with more balanced ways of thinking.

The third phase focuses on maintaining the changes the patients have made during treatment and addressing relapse prevention.

CBT as it is generally used with adults has not been tested with young people. Cognitive behavioural guided self-care (CBT-GSC), however, has been compared to family therapy in one of the two RCTs conducted with young people with BN (Schmidt et al., 2007).

In CBT-GSC, the young person and their parents use a workbook to reduce binge eating and purging while meeting regularly with their therapist. Schmidt et al. found no differences between the two treatment groups in terms of abstinence from binge eating and purging at the end of treatment. It should be noted, however, that the version of FBT used in this study differed in several respects from that described below.

Family-based treatment (FBT)

The second RCT conducted with young people with BN compared FBT and individual supportive psychotherapy (SPT) (Le Grange et al., 2007). The version of FBT used in this study is comparable to FBT for AN in that treatment progresses through three similar phases and emphasizes the importance of parental involvement in the treatment, but it was adapted for use with young people with BN and their families.

In FBT for BN, the focus of treatment is not on weight restoration but on regulating the patient's eating and on helping them reduce their binge eating and purging. Although the parents help their children through the recovery process, FBT for BN takes more of a collaborative approach to treatment than FBT for AN. This is possible, in part, because BN tends to be experienced by the young person as abnormal, so they are often motivated to improve.

Le Grange and colleagues found that FBT was more effective than SPT in reducing binge eating and purging. Although further research is needed, FBT seems to be a promising new form of treatment for young people with BN.

Conclusion

Eating disorders usually begin during adolescence and can easily keep their victims from meeting the normal tasks and challenges associated with this period of their development. Once an eating disorder has developed, research suggests that parental involvement in its treatment can be critical to young people's recovery.

Resources

Further reading

Brewerton, Timothy, D. (ed.) (2004) *Clinical Handbook of Eating Disorders: An integrated approach*. New York: Marcel Dekker.

Collins, Laura (2005) *Eating with Your Anorexic*. New York: McGraw-Hill.

Garner, D.M. and Garfinkel, Paul E. (eds) (1997) *Handbook of Treatment for Eating Disorders* (2nd edn). New York: Guilford Press.

Herzog, David B., Franko, Debra, L. and Cable, Pat (2008) *Unlocking the Mysteries of Eating Disorders: A life-saving guide to your child's treatment and recovery*. New York: McGraw-Hill.

Le Grange, Daniel and Lock, James (2007) *Treating Bulimia in Adolescents: A family-based approach*. New York: Guilford Press.

Lock, James and Le Grange, Daniel (2005) *Help Your Teenager Beat an Eating Disorder*. New York: Guilford Press.

Neumark-Sztainer, Dianne (2005) *I'm, Like, SO Fat!: Helping your teen make healthy choices about eating and exercise in a weight-obsessed world*. New York: Guilford Press.

Pope Jr, Harrison G., Phillips, Katharine A. and Olivardia, Roberto (2000) *The Adonis Complex: The secret crisis of male body obsession*. New York: The Free Press.

KEY POINTS

- Eating disorders are associated with serious medical complications and require a comprehensive and assertive treatment approach.
- Although parental attitudes towards eating and weight can contribute to the onset or maintenance of eating disorders, research suggests that a number of factors must be present for an eating disorder to develop. Rather than being blamed for causing an eating disorder, parents can be an important resource during treatment.
- Despite the fact that eating disorders generally begin during adolescence few randomized controlled trials have investigated treatment for young people's eating disorders and further research is greatly needed.

QUESTIONS FOR DISCUSSION

1. Describe the factors that increase a person's risk for developing an eating disorder and how those factors might influence treatment approaches.
2. Prevention programmes have been found to increase students' knowledge of eating disorders, but have had little impact on eating-related attitudes and behaviours. What are some possible reasons for that?

References

Agras, W.S., Walsh, B.T., Fairburn, C.G., Wilson, G.T. and Kraemer, H.C. (2000) 'A multicenter comparison of cognitive-behavioral therapy and interpersonal psychotherapy for bulimia nervosa', *Archives of General Psychiatry*, 57: 459–66.

American Psychiatric Association (APA) (2000) *Diagnostic and Statistical Manual of Mental Disorders* (4th edn). Washington, DC: APA.

Attie, I. and Brooks-Gunn, J. (1989) 'Development of eating problems in adolescent girls: a longitudinal study', *Developmental Psychology*, 25: 70–9.

Bulik, C.M., Sullivan, P.F. and Kendler, K.S. (1998) 'Heritability of binge eating and broadly defined bulimia nervosa', *Biological Psychiatry*, 44: 1210–18.

Drewnowski, A., Yee, D.K., Kurth, C.L. and Krahn, D.D. (1994) 'Eating pathology and DSM-III-R bulimia nervosa: a continuum of behavior', *American Journal of Psychiatry*, 151: 1217–19.

Eisler, I., Dare, C., Russell, G.F.M., Szmukler, G.I., Le Grange, D. and Dodge, E. (1997) 'Family and individual therapy in anorexia nervosa: a five-year follow-up', *Archives of General Psychiatry*, 54: 1025–30.

Fairburn, C.G., Marcus, M.D. and Wilson, G.T. (1993) 'Cognitive behavioral therapy for binge eating and bulimia nervosa: a comprehensive treatment manual', in C.G. Fairburn and G.T. Wilson (eds), *Binge Eating: Nature, assessment, and treatment*. New York: Guilford Press. pp. 361–404.

Groesz, L.M., Levine, M.P. and Murnen, S.K. (2002) 'The effect of experimental presentation of thin media images on body satisfaction: a meta-analytic review', *International Journal of Eating Disorders*, 31: 1–16.

Hoek, H.W. and van Hoeken, D. (2003) 'Review of the prevalence and incidence of eating disorders', *International Journal of Eating Disorders*, 34: 383–96.

Jacobi, C., Morris, L. and de Zwaan, M. (2004) 'An overview of risk factors for anorexia nervosa, bulimia nervosa, and binge eating disorder', in T.D. Brewerton (ed.), *Clinical Handbook of Eating Disorders: An integrated approach*. New York: Marcel Dekker. pp. 117–63.

Le Grange, D., Crosby, R.D., Rathouz, P.J. and Leventhal, B.L. (2007) 'A randomized controlled comparison of family-based treatment and supportive psychotherapy for adolescent bulimia nervosa', *Archives of General Psychiatry*, 64: 1049–56.

Levine, M.P. and Smolak, L. (2006) *The Prevention of Eating Problems and Eating Disorders: Theory, research, and practice*. New Jersey: Lawrence Erlbaum.

Lilenfeld, L.R.R. (2004) 'Psychiatric comorbidity associated with anorexia nervosa, bulimia nervosa, and binge eating disorder', in T.D. Brewerton (ed.), *Clinical Handbook of Eating Disorders: An integrated approach*. New York: Marcel Dekker. pp. 183–207.

Lock, J., Le Grange, D., Agras, W.S. and Dare, C. (2001) *Treatment Manual for Anorexia Nervosa: A family-based approach*. New York: Guilford Press.

McCabe, M., Ricciardelli, L. and Finemore, J. (2002) 'The role of puberty, media and popularity with peers on strategies to increase weight, decrease weight and increase muscle tone among adolescent boys and girls', *Journal of Psychosomatic Research*, 52: 145–53.

Minuchin, S., Baker, B.L., Rosman, B.L., Liebman, R., Milman, L. and Todd, T.C. (1975) 'A conceptual model of psychosomatic illness in children: family organization and family therapy', *Archives of General Psychiatry*, 32: 1031–8.

Neumark-Sztainer, D., Story, M., Hannan, P.J., Perry, C.L. and Irving, L.M. (2002) 'Weight-related concerns and behaviors among overweight and nonoverweight adolescents: implications for preventing weight-related disorders', *Archives of Pediatric and Adolescent Medicine*, 156: 171–8.

Pike, K.M. and Rodin, J. (1991) 'Mothers, daughters, and disordered eating', *Journal of Abnormal Psychology*, 100: 198–204.

Pope, H.G., Olivardia, R., Gruber, A. and Borowiecki, J. (1999) 'Evolving ideals of male body image as seen through action toys', *International Journal of Eating Disorders*, 26: 65–72.

Powers, P.S. and Bannon, Y. (2004) 'Medical comorbidity of anorexia nervosa, bulimia nervosa, and binge eating disorder', in T.D. Brewerton (ed.), *Clinical Handbook of Eating Disorders: An integrated approach*. New York: Marcel Dekker. pp. 231–55.

Robin, A.L., Siegel, P.T., Moye, A.W., Gilroy, M., Dennis, A.B. and Sikand, A. (1999) 'A controlled comparison of family versus individual therapy for adolescents with anorexia nervosa', *Journal of the American Academy of Child and Adolescent Psychiatry*, 38: 1482–9.

Rodin, J., Silberstein, L.R. and Striegel-Moore, R.H. (1984) 'Women and weight: a normative discontent', in T.B. Sonderegger (ed.), *Nebraska Symposium on Motivation: Vol. 32: Psychology and gender*. Lincoln, NE: University of Nebraska. pp. 267–307.

Root, M.P.P., Fallon, P. and Friedrich, W.N. (1986) *Bulimia: A systems approach to treatment*. New York: W.W. Norton & Co.

Russell, G.F., Szmukler, G.I., Dare, C. and Eisler, I. (1987) 'An evaluation of family therapy in anorexia nervosa and bulimia nervosa', *Archives of General Psychiatry*, 44: 1047–56.

Schmidt, U., Lee, S., Beecham, J., Perkins, S., Treasure, J., Yi, I., Winn, S., Robinson, P., Murphy, R., Keville, S., Johnson-Sabine, E., Jenkins, M., Frost, S., Dodge, L., Berelowitz, M. and Eisler, I. (2007) 'A randomized controlled trial of family therapy and cognitive behavior therapy guided self-care for adolescents with bulimia nervosa and related disorders', *American Journal of Psychiatry*, 164: 591–8.

Stice, E. and Agras, W. (1998) 'Predicting onset and cessation of bulimic behaviors during adolescence: a longitudinal grouping analysis', *Behavior Therapy*, 29: 257–76.

Strober, M., Freeman, R., Lampert, C., Diamond, J. and Kaye, W. (2000) 'Controlled family study of anorexia nervosa and bulimia nervosa: evidence of shared liability and transmission of partial syndromes', *American Journal of Psychiatry*, 157: 393–401.

Treasure, J. and Holland, A. (1989) 'Genetic vulnerability to eating disorders: evidence from twin and family studies', in H. Remschmidt and M. Schmidt (eds), *Child and Youth Psychiatry: European perspectives*. New York: Hogrefe & Huber. pp. 59–68.

Vidovic, V., Juresa, V., Begovac, I., Mahnik, M. and Tocilj, G. (2005) 'Perceived family cohesion, adaptability and communication in eating disorders', *European Eating Disorders Review*, 13: 19–28.

Wilson, G. and Shafran, R. (2005) 'Eating disorders guidelines from NICE', *The Lancet*, 365: 79–81.

16

Responding to Cult Group Membership

Lee Richmond and Carole Rayburn

Introduction

Law enforcement agencies and mental health professionals are concerned about the increasing numbers of young people who are attracted to cults. By one measure it is estimated that between 3000 and 5000 cults exist in the USA (Singer with Lalich, 1995) and, though no one knows the exact number of cults that exist in the world, approximately 5000 is the number currently assumed (Wikipedia, 2008).

There is abundant literature describing the seduction methods that cults use to recruit young people and the psychological methods used to retain them (Hassan, 1990; Singer with Lalich, 1995; Stoner and Park, 1977). Though this chapter touches on both of these topics, its primary objective is to delineate proactive interventions that can be used when working with communities, schools and parents to combat the entry and retention of teens in destructive cults.

It is noted, however, that not all cults are destructive and, among those that are, there are varying degrees of danger. According to Wikipedia (2008), the word, 'cult':

> typically refers to a social group devoted to beliefs or practices that the surrounding culture considers outside the mainstream.

Merriam-Webster's Collegiate Dictionary (1996) defines a 'cult' as:

> a system of religious beliefs that the majority culture considers unorthodox or spurious.

Another definition is that a cult is 'a system that gives great devotion to a person, a work and an object': one example that fits both definitions is early Christianity. A cult is also defined, however, as a small group that 'is regarded as strange or as imposing excessive mind control over members' (*Oxford Compact English Dictionary*, 2008).

The use of mind control is characteristic of destructive cults. Destructive cults are very different from pop cults, which are usually temporary and comprised of devotees to some form of fashion, music, fiction, film or even the latest method of psychotherapy. These less lethal groups, frequently designed to sell a product or programme (Singer with Lalich, 1995), are not the subject of this chapter, though even they may use mild forms of mind control (Richmond, 2004). Unfortunately, the English language has not been able to define cults in such a way that separates the two kinds of groups without prefixing them.

Destructive Cults

How, then, can one identify which groups are destructive and to what degree they are dangerous? Unfortunately, only by their actions can they be known.

Destructive groups often parade under names that are either, on the one hand, innocuous or, on the other, patriotic or religious. They are extremely difficult to recognize before any harm has been done! However, by whatever name they choose to call themselves, all destructive cults share some common characteristics that the public can use to recognize them. They use the same methods for recruitment and retention.

- A charismatic messianic-type leader whose message is never compromised leads each group. He, or she, sends a singular message that uses key words – words that are easily repeated by followers, thus having an hypnotic effect.
- Followers seek other followers and invite them to attend a succession of group meetings where neophytes are initially given unconditional acceptance. Called 'love bombardment' or 'love bombing' (Singer with Lalich, 1995: 114–15), high regard is given to recruits at the outset and continues through many encounters and group meetings.
- The meetings gradually grow lengthy and recruits are often offered meals and overnight stays. In such a social atmosphere, they learn of the group's mission, expressed by the leader in lofty terms that relate to solving both personal and world problems (Tully, 1995).
- In a relatively short time, new group members feel a sense of purpose in their lives and a real connection to the message that the cult puts forth.
- An intense feeling of loyalty to the group develops. It is at this point that members become 'hooked'. They begin to work for the unit, follow the path that the leader has set forth, take on a new identity and set aside old ways, often believing that they have found a special or 'secret' truth beyond that which is known by outsiders.
- Mind control deepens and the person who once began as a recruit engages in the work of recruiting others (Hassan, 1990; Hutchinson, 1994; Singer with Lalich, 1995).

Another common characteristic is that money is involved. This money does not go to the members, who will frequently live within the group in poverty, demonstrating commitment, self-sacrifice and devotion to the group. In the religious or civic name of the cult, members solicit money that is placed at the disposal of the group leadership. How and where the money is used and engagement in various nefarious activities gets cults in trouble with the law from time to time. According to Tully (1995) such activities supply the leader with a reason to further reject society and replace societal adherence with unconditional obedience to and by the group. Usually, when confrontations with the law and arrests of cult members occur, the happenings are generally carefully crafted for the purpose of gaining public attention.

Attraction to Cult Membership

It is a fact that teenagers like to belong to peer groups and it has been suggested that isolated young people, the ones left out, are the most susceptible to cult recruiters. There is no singular or simple portrait of teen cult members, however. Richmond (2004) cited five needs that provide the reasons for kids joining cults:

- the need to conform to a peer group
- the need to not conform to behaviours that seem contradictory
- the need to be led by a trusted leader
- the need to be devoted to a cause
- the need to replace a parent who is either absent or perceived to be distant from that which is cared about by the young person.

Singer with Lalich (1995) point out that cults thrive in periods of unrest. In 1970, Konrad Lorenz stated that tumultuous times, such as war, drug addiction and poverty, may be when cults seem most attractive, particularly to disconnected young people.

The confused and dissatisfied are the ones most likely to join a counter-culture group, whether because of personal disillusionment or ideological reasons. Some young people feel disconnected because they are idealistic and hold beliefs that do not conform to the seemingly contradictory and sometimes unethical behaviours of parents and governments. Frequently, superstitious adherence to doctrines occurs, which is indicative of increasingly destructive factors in the culture. Steven Hassan (2008) of the Freedom of Mind Center, a former cult member and now well-known exit family counsellor, told Rene Snyder, co-anchor of *The Early Show* the following:

> Any major life trauma, death of a loved one, divorce, break up of a relationship, moving to another state or county,[or] major illness can really disrupt a person's identity and sense of reality, especially with a young person.

Hassan believes that young people experiencing an identity crisis – and most young people do – can unwittingly be susceptible to the psychological suggestions given by recruiters from destructive cults.

People interested in both prevention and intervention need to find ways to help families to be alert, tell young people that there are no instant friends, seek prevention education and know that destructive cults are out there. Clearly, Hassan believes that there is much to be done.

Interventions to Help Prevent Young People from Joining Cults

In order to address the issue of intervention, one needs to know why people are attracted to cults and, specifically, why young people are attracted to cults.

There are ideas about why people generally join cults and then some very specific issues related directly to young people. Michael Langone (1996) identified three basic models for joining cults:

- the deliberative model
- the psychodynamic model
- the thought reform model.

That people join groups because of what they think about the group's purpose and its members constitutes the reason behind the deliberative model, according to Langone.

The psychodynamic model, as its name indicates, attracts people who have subconscious needs that cult membership purports to fulfil.

Last, the thought reform model suggests that people join because of the groups' influences through various forms of psychological manipulation. The latter two models have within them various factors that attract and retain young people.

Parental and Family Interventions

One of the best things that parents can do for their teenage children is bond with them. In its winter 2000 issue, *Adolescent and Family Health* published a study that noted children who feel closely attached to their families are less likely to get into trouble or behave violently. Measures of attachment that researchers used in the study were:

- how well the young people felt understood by their families
- how much attention they felt they received from their families
- how much fun time family members spent together.

The research also reported that regular attendance at religious services helped with attachment. Interestingly, three separate studies of faith in young people (Martin, et al., 2003; Pierce et al., 2003; Poll and Smith, 2003) found that spiritual movement is linear, parental influence in the teenage years is lasting, and religious belief mediates for depression and feelings of isolation. Religious institutions, the community, schools and parents all play a part in the development of young people.

During their teens, when young people acquire their identity, form their values and own their beliefs, happiness, heartbreak, tenderness and trouble all jumble together. The best, and perhaps the only way to truly bond with young people, is to actively listen to them. Active listening is a communication tool that can assist parents in understanding their teenagers and help them reach healthy adulthood.

According to Perkins and Fogarty (1999), to listen actively to young people means

- listening non-judgmentally
- asking good questions
- paraphrasing and empathizing.

Practitioners working with young people can help parents to understand that asking open-ended, non-judgmental questions helps to clarify meaning. Paraphrasing helps parents to make sure that they understand messages correctly and young people to know that they are understood.

To best help their teenage children, parents need first to be there for them. They can help prevent their children from becoming cult members by helping them to build their self-esteem and self-efficacy. They can help their children with the complexities of life by explaining that things are not black and white and easy answers are not always the best answers. Parents can further help by recognizing that their young people may be involved in a spiritual search and their quest should be taken seriously. Parents can also help by walking beside their children in their idealistic search for meaning and their explorations of various religious traditions. Assisting them to become involved in group activities within the community and providing just enough authority and structure to make them feel secure are also most useful.

Community Responses

Parents are aware that young people deserve a safe school, free of bullying and harassment, and have demanded, through community action, safe schools programmes. Preventative cult education programmes should also be mounted in schools that do not presently offer them.

Active parental attendance at their children's sports, drama and music productions, as well as participation in community efforts to raise funds and materials for their schools, helps to create an open, comfortable atmosphere between schools and families.

Parents have an obligation to educate themselves and make certain that the communities in which they live learn about cults. To do this, they need to know about organizations in their neighborhoods that are likely to attract young people. Knowing the purposes of the organizations and the personnel that staff them is essential.

The Young Person's Self-education

Young people have a duty to themselves. In a book entitled *Straight Talk about Cults,* Kay Marie Porterfield (1995) writes that they have a responsibility to educate themselves. She states that many critical issues occur in the bumpy journey from childhood to adulthood when young people try to get along with their families while, at the same time, attempt to gain independence from them. On the one hand, they want to fit in with the crowd, but, on the other, they do not want to be pushed around by their peers.

Porterfield sides with psychologists who study cults and believes that young people are most vulnerable to cult recruiters when their confidence is shaken by a crisis, they aren't sure about how they should act, find themselves in confusing situations where they are not sure of their own beliefs and values and feel that they need some answers fast. As leaving a cult is difficult, she asks young people, 'wouldn't you rather avoid joining one in the first place? Just because you may be a prime candidate for cult recruitment, doesn't mean you are defenceless.'

Porterfield (2008) offers young people the following advice.

1. Remind yourself that, even though you are smart, your intelligence doesn't make you immune from recruiters. Admitting your vulnerability helps you keep your emotional defences raised and your thinking critical.
2. Learn about spirituality and different religions. When you understand the terms a cult recruiter uses, you are less likely to accept the recruiter's explanations as correct.
3. Resist the social pressure to conform by remembering it is your right to say no. When a cult recruiter presents you with a false dilemma, forcing you to choose between two things like joining the group or going to hell, mentally add another alternative to the equation – none of the above.
4. Don't make life-changing decisions when you're hungry, tired, angry, feeling sorry for yourself, or stressed out. We all have our weak moments.
5. If a cult recruiter puts you on the spot, tell that person you'll get back to them later.
6. Look for hidden agendas. If you have a sneaking suspision that information about the true purpose of what's happening is being kept from you, pay attention to that feeling.
7. Ask sharp questions and don't settle for vague answers.
8. Recognize flattery and phony instant intimacy. If the cult recruiter seems too good to be true, beware.

Interventions to Address the Problem of Young People Who are Already in Cults

On 14 October 1998, an article headlined 'Australia getting tough on cults' appeared in *The Australian* (Bita, 1998). It spoke of a recent recommendation by a committee comprised of legal advisers from the federal, state and territory organizations that stated 'significant emotional harm' inflicted by religious groups be classified as a criminal offence (Bita, 1998). While the committee did not make charges against any religion or sect, it supported a ruling from the Supreme Court of California, which states that 'coercive persuasion' by any religious sect 'could cause serious physical and psychological disorders'. The text then explicitly enumerated the mind and physical control techniques that cults adopt to persuade, indoctrinate and use recruits, citing that the freedom of religion is no reason to harm or psychologically defraud anyone. It has previously been shown that many dangerous cults present themselves under a religious mantle.

The Cult Information Centre of the United Kingdom is a charity that provides information and advice for victims of cults, their families and friends. It uses the Internet to post answers to common questions about cults and, in this sense, is useful to researchers and the media. One of the questions that it addresses is whether or not cults are harmful. Speaking of destructive cults, the factsheet states that membership, even for only a short while, can result in the following:

- loss of choice and free will
- diminished intellectual activity
- reduced use of irony and metaphor
- reduced capacity to form flexible and intimate relationships
- poor judgment
- physical deterioration
- malnutrition
- hallucinations, panic, dissociation, guilt, identity diffusion and paranoia
- neurotic, psychotic or suicidal tendencies.

Following this list, there is a quote from Jeannie Mills, reportedly an ex-cult member:

> When you meet the friendliest people you have ever known, who introduce you to the most loving group of people you have ever encountered, and you find the leader to be the most inspired, caring, compassionate and understanding person you've ever met, and then you learn the cause of the group is something you never dared hope could be accomplished, and all of this sounds too good to be true – it probably is too good to be true. Don't give up your education, your hope and your dreams to follow a rainbow.

The Cult Information Centre (2008) reports that Jeannie Mills was later found murdered.

Exiting Cults and Exit Counselling

Leaving a cult or extricating someone from a cult is a serious matter. Hassan (1990), writing to cult members in the preface of his book, states that it takes a great amount of strength, courage and integrity to read *Combating Mind Control*. Hassan suggests that if one is merely thinking about questioning the practices of the group, it is not wise to speak of it to anyone in the group. Addressing family members, Hassan suggests that they avoid overreacting to *Combating Mind Control*, but, rather, regard its premises in a systematic and rational manner.

Singer with Lalich (1995) also writes about the difficulty of leaving. Because of member loyalty to the group and the guilt that occurs when one acts independently, leaving the cult becomes an almost impossible task. The authors tell the story of two long-term cult members who finally decided to leave. They were so used to reporting all of their actions to the cult's leadership that, when they arrived at the airport and were almost ready to catch their flight, they telephoned back to their 'cult parents' and told them where they were and what they were about to do. Singer reports that cult members immediately showed up at the airport, whisked the two out and took them back to the cult residence, just when they were about to board the airplane.

To long-term cult members who have been thoroughly indoctrinated, the home of their birth is alien and thought of as representing evil, while the cult 'home' represents what is right and good. 'Cult parents' replace birth parents and must be obeyed. Leaving one's cult home incurs tremendous guilt and anxiety. People who want to help them must realize this and act accordingly.

There may still be some fully indoctrinated members who are in need of the kind of rescue and deprogramming that was popular in the 1970s. Today, however, most cult education and exit counselling is not forced, but voluntary. Exit counselling is usually provided by volunteer ex-cult members who meet and conduct interventions with young people who have managed to extricate themselves.

Exit counsellors are experts in thought reform techniques. Frequently, they work in teams, teaching those who have left by giving them facts about their cult and its leadership – facts that were previously unavailable to these ex-cult members.

Exit counsellors who are former cult members also offer hope in the sense that, if *they* were able to return to society and be healthy, so can the newly exited person.

Exit counsellors live in communities throughout the world and cult awareness networks can help those who need to find them. Books by Singer with Lalich (1995) and Hassan (1990) reference these organizations and offer contact information. Additionally, current reliable sources for exit counselling can be found on the Internet and at the end of this chapter.

Summary

In conclusion, parents, school counsellors and community social workers can do much to help young people already involved in cults. Most who are still at school are at the dabbling stage, not yet deeply involved. Recognition of the early signs of cult involvement is a good start. These include:

- withdrawal from social groups and family
- aloofness or increased rebelliousness
- loss of interest in former religious activities.

Interested adults should also learn some additional signs (Richmond, 2004). Attention should be paid to young people who regularly dress in black and wear heavy silver chains. The clothing may well be meaningless, but mental health professionals should know that many young people who dress in the 'Goth' style are unaware that silver, an impure metal, is chosen over gold, a pure metal, by satanic worshippers. Thus, by dressing in this way, young people may seem available to cult recruiters.

Particular clothing, haircuts and ways of communicating may be part of an initiation and group identity stance. Such conformities to cult groups serve to solidify them and encourage bonding with other members regarding the group's differences from society at large.

Carrying a black notebook with drawings of daggers, swastikas or the numbers 666 are things that dabblers do. Counsellors should talk with young people – not in judgment, but for information – about what the symbols mean to them.

Parents and counsellors should know the music that their children listen to and the movies and TV shows that they watch. When talking to them about any of those things, the conversation should be gentle, not accusatory nor intimidating. In addressing young people about their group activities, one should be polite, perceptive, sympathetic, reassuring and informative (Hutchinson, 1994). When adults are knowledgeable about general and specific cult objects and symbols and want to talk to young people about them, the subject should be presented and discussed factually and without passion.

The proactive school counsellor provides information about cults to teachers, parents and students and is aware of when and how referrals to exit counsellors should take place. Referral by a trusted school counsellor should always occur when a student confides that they have been recruited, are currently involved in a cult and wish to leave, but do not do so. If mind-altering techniques are suspected, special exit counsellors who know them will use debriefing techniques.

People who leave cults must be reintegrated into society. This frequently involves a reorientation to religious institutions. Of help in this regard is a book entitled *Out of the Cults and into the Church* (Hutchinson, 1994), which provides a Christian approach to understanding and encouraging ex-cult members. Most of the major religions, Christian and non-Christian, sponsor groups that help ex-cultists reorientate themselves towards them. Websites sponsored by such groups are to be found on the Internet. One must be vigilant, however, and check out such Internet sources because some cults have infiltrated cyberspace and sometimes use sites to reattract members who have left.

Respectfully and attentively listening to ex-cult members or pre-cult members to discern where their true interests lie is a must if they are to be directed to healthy, appropriate, meaningfully valued groups and activities. Such direction is the only real solution to the deleterious problem of cults seducing young people, leading to their participation in dangerous groups.

Resources

Further reading

Langone, Michael (1993) 'Deprogramming, exit counseling and ethics: clarifying the confusion', *Cult Observer*, 10 (4), reprinted with permission from *The Christian Research Journal*, Winter 1993. Also available online at: www.icsahome.com/infoserv_articles_langone_Michael_deprogramming_clarify.htm

Websites

Steve Hassan www.freedomofmind.com/resourcecenter/contact
This is a link to Steve Hassan's website. His Freedom of Mind Centre offers many useful resources, including online, hard copy and video references.

Further information

Information related to recovery from cults can be found through the Cult Information Centre in the UK (www.cultinformation.org.uk) and the International Cultic Studies Association (www.icsahome.com). School counsellors may be particularly interested in reading the special issue on spirituality and school counselling by Richmond (2004), which contains an article about students in cults and what school counsellors can do to be of help.

KEY POINTS

- Destructive cults have certain characteristics in common, including a charismatic messianic leader, a singular message that includes key words, followers who seek other followers and, initially, give unconditional acceptance and money is involved.
- Young people join cults to conform to a peer group, because of their need to be liked by a trusted leader, to be devoted to a cause and to replace a parent who is either absent or distant from that which they care about.
- Interventions include parent and family interventions, community responses, self-education and interventions to address the problem of those already in cults.
- Leaving a cult involves serious emotional sequellae, which may be addressed by exit counseling.

QUESTIONS FOR DISCUSSION

1. What should one be wary of when talking to young people who have exited from cults?
2. How can school and mental health counsellors help parents and communities in areas of primary and secondary interventions?

References

Bita, N. (1998) 'Australia getting tough on cults', *The Australian,* 14 October. Also available online at: www.factnet.org/cults/anti–cult_activities/australia_001.html

Cult Information Centre (2008) see 'questions' section, 'Are cults harmful? at: www.cultinformation.org.uk/home.html

Hassan, S. (1990) *Combating Mind Control.* Rochester: Park Street Press.

Hassan, S. (2008) Steven Hasan's Freedom of Mind Center website at: www.freedomof mind.com/resourcecenter/help

Hutchinson, J. (1994) *Out of the Cults and Into the Church: Understanding and encouraging ex-cultists.* Grand Rapids, MI: Kregel Publications.

Langone, M. (1996) 'Clinical update on cults', *Psychiatric Times*, July. Also available online at: www.icsahome.com/infoserv_articles/langone_michael_clinical_update.htm

Lorenz, K. (1970) 'The enmity between generations and its probable etiological causes', *The Psychoanalytic Quarterly*, 57: 333–7.

Martin, T.F., White, J.M. and Perlman, D. (2003) 'Religious socialization: a test of the channeling hypothesis of parental influence on adolescent faith maturity', *Journal of Adolescent Research*, 18: 169–87.

Merriam-Webster's Collegiate Dictionary (10th edn) (1996) Springfield, MA: Merriam-Webster.

Oxford Compact English Dictionary. Available online at: www.askoxford.com.80/dictionaries/compact_oed?view=uk

Perkins, D.F. and Fogarty, K. (1999) 'Active listening: a communication tool', EDIS, Institute for Food and Agriculture Sevices, University of Florida. Available online at: www.edis.ifas.ufl.edu/HE361

Pierce, M.J., Little, T.D. and Parez, J.E. (2003) 'Religiousness and depressive symptoms among adolescents', *Journal of Clinical Child and Adolescent Psychology*, 32: 267–76.

Poll, J.B. and Smith, T.B. (2003) 'The spiritual self: towards a conceptualization of spiritual identity development', *Journal of Psychology and Theology*, 31: 129–42.

Porterfield, K.M. (1995) *Straight Talk about Cults*. New York: Facts on File.

Richmond, L.J. (2004) 'When spirituality goes awry: students in cults', *Professional School Counseling*, 75: 367–75.

Singer, M.T. with Lalich, J.L. (1995) *Cults in Our Midst: The hidden menace in our everyday lives*. San Francisco, CA: Jossey-Bass.

Stoner, C. and Parke, J.A. (1977) *All God's Children: The cult experience – salvation or slavery?* Radnor, PA: Chilton Books.

Tully, E.J. (1995) 'Extremists: cults, fangs and terrorism', Salt Lake City, UT: National Executive Institutes Associates, Major Cities Chiefs Association and Major County Sheriffs Association. www.neiassociates.org/cults.htm

Wikipedia (2008) www.wikipedia.org

Part VIII

Marginalized Young People

17

Understanding Young People in Care

Jan Foster

Introduction

For many of us, our life journies from birth to becoming young adults have included a safe and nurturing home environment that has, in one way or another, provided a space for our learning and growth into independent individuals. We may have finished our school years and perhaps gone to university, with family members giving us the support and encouragement that we needed along the way. Even so, we may have faced challenges as we navigated the journey to independence and individuation through the years of transition to adulthood.

For some young people, however, the taken-for-granted struggles during the turbulent years take on a different form. The things many of us take for granted – a safe home life, shelter, food and nurture – are not possible in their own families for a period of time or even permanently. Some young people face issues such as violence, family conflict, mental health problems and drug and alcohol abuse before they are ready to become independent individuals, capable of taking care of themselves. Those young people may find themselves in the care of people other than their own families.

This chapter provides an overview of the out-of-home care sector in modern Western contexts and draws on examples from Australia to illustrate the problems and possibilities for change. It outlines the care options available and some of the challenges presented by the current discourses and structures that are universal. It therefore considers the complexity of the world of young people in care beyond national borders and provides an overview of current thinking with regard to changes in intervention practices that are required to more constructively work towards the inclusion of marginalized young people in care.

Here, we also ask you to look at your own values, attitudes and assumptions and provide you with illustrations from Australia's experience to encourage you to reflect on the way you think about your practice when working with young people.

What is Out-of-home Care?

When young people need to live with people other than their own families, they can be provided with out-of-home care. Within Australia, the following options are available.

- Family group homes are for short-term care in houses owned by the various state governments responsible for the care and protection of young people. The young people live with approved carers in these houses and the carers receive small payments for looking after them.
- Home-based care is in private homes with approved carers. The first option is relative or kinship care, where the caregiver is a family member or someone who already has a relationship with the young person. The second is foster care, which may be provided in the home of a substitute family, the family, again, receiving a small payment intended to cover associated expenses. The third option is other home-based care that does not fit into the above categories. Home-based care is where over 90 per cent of young people in care reside (Cashmore et al., 2006).
- Independent living can be offered in the form of private boarding arrangements, such as lead tenant households.
- Residential care is provided in a building housing, generally, fewer than 10 young people and there are paid staff.

Another category is becoming more common as the strain on resources leads to stress on already overloaded child protection systems. Temporary commercial accommodation, most commonly hotels and motels, is reportedly being used to house young people for whom no other accommodation alternatives exist.

'At Risk' and Vulnerability – Young People on the Margins

Out-of-home care is provided for children and young people 'at risk'. Much of the literature in the 'at risk' arena does not clearly state what the risk is.

Young people can be 'at risk' if harm could come to them as a result of physical, sexual or emotional abuse or neglect at the hands of people such as parents, carers or others in authority. This understanding of 'at risk' is often used by state and federal authorities when determining whether or not it is feasible for a young person to live in the family home.

Young people can also be 'at risk' if their antisocial behaviour leads to poor educational outcomes, unemployment, an inability to maintain relationships and so on (Ainsworth, 2003).

Young people abusing drugs or alcohol are also 'at risk' as this behaviour can lead to health problems and, if associated with celebrating and driving, injury or even death (Elkington et al., 2006).

Young people can be 'at risk' of entering the criminal justice system, too, if antisocial behaviour escalates into criminal acts, such as vandalism, drug trafficking or assault (Vassallo et al., 2004).

An issue arising from the lack of clarity surrounding the term 'at risk' is the potential for privileging one construction of its meaning over another. Let's take a look at a newspaper report from around the time of writing this chapter (Gibson, 2008).

> An Australian newspaper in March 2008 outlined a new system for determining where young indigenous offenders are placed when removed from their families. Under the 'circle sentencing' programme community elders and a magistrate join caseworkers and parents to make relevant decisions, thus allowing the community greater input into the appropriateness of the placements. The article then goes on to mention that 'indigenous children make up 30 per cent of all children in out-of-home care in NSW, although they make up only 4 per cent of the general population'.

What message does this give about young indigenous people in out-of-home care? It may be that young indigenous people in care are criminals. In Australia, the reality does not reflect such a message. Of the 25,454 young people in out-of-home care across Australia in June 2006, 23,584 were on care and protection orders (AIHW, 2007: 52), meaning that over 92 per cent of young people in out-of-home care were there because they were in need of care and protection, not because they were criminals.

This is just one example of how particular ideas can be (re)created and how easy it is to make assumptions about 'others'. One challenge for human services professionals is to understand that dominant discourses about those with whom we work are not always accurate or helpful. An analogy may be that a rape victim might feel that she is being blamed for her rape when faced with an adversarial court system demanding to know intimate details of her sex life in an attempt to justify the violence. Sometimes those who are disadvantaged through no fault of their own can be constructed as being to blame for their circumstances. The challenge for human services workers is to critique such discourses in order to do what we can to reduce marginalization and exclusion for people who are already disadvantaged.

Issues Facing Young People in Care

In the following sections, various factors that may lead to exclusion and marginalization for young people in care will be considered.

Coming into care

Care and protection orders are granted when courts have found that the young people concerned need the state community services department to have greater authority over and responsibility for them. As such, particular arrangements, including guardianship, custody and supervision orders, are made for these young people where there are serious concerns for their well-being (AIHW, 2005).

Experiences in the home environment have long been regarded as important in developing a sense of well-being in children and young people. Also, there is ample evidence to suggest that their environment plays a significant part in the process of young people forming their identities. If the development of emotional regulation, attention and memory is controlled by brain structures that peak at 16 years of age (Horwath, 2007), then negotiating questions of identity and development during the adolescent years is clearly particularly significant.

This significance takes on particular poignancy when young people are marginalized through no fault of their own. Young people who have been placed on care and protection orders have most often experienced neglect or abuse. Common reasons for young people moving into out-of-home care include problems in the family home, such as violence, drug and alcohol abuse, criminal behaviour and mental health problems. Additionally, there is a growing recognition that young people often face a combination of factors prior to entering care (Bruun and Hynan, 2006).

Understanding the link between early family experiences, development and behaviour is vital to working with young people in care. An Australian longitudinal study of over 10,000 families and children found that 'family and parenting characteristics "matter" for children's development, with parenting practices having a particularly prominent role', which is likely to persist over time (AIFS, 2006). Further, the well-being of a child or young person is related to criminal activity later in life (AIHW, 2007).

This strongly suggests that a primary concern for human services workers must be to action early intervention and prevention strategies that focus on the well-being of young people from an early age to avoid the possibility of negative consequences occurring later in their lives.

Being in care

Because most young people are in care as a result of abuse or neglect, many bring various emotional, social and behavioural issues with them. These can include aggression, substance abuse, mental health problems, including depression or anxiety, and low levels of educational achievement (AIHW, 2005).

The transition into the care environment can be a confusing time for young people already on the margins. Sadly, some do not fully understand the reasons for their being put into care and, as a result, may believe that it is their own fault (Community Affairs References Committee, 2005). Thus, the transition can be traumatic and confusing, leaving young people feeling vulnerable and uncertain (Tilbury et al., 2007).

The increasing numbers of children and young people in care mean that there is ever-growing pressure on systems that are already under siege in many ways. It is not uncommon to see newspaper headlines relating a tragedy befalling a young person who was known to 'the system', but not placed in care. In such cases, workers are often blamed for not adequately protecting the young person from harm. As a result, government departments charged with the statutory care of young people often find it difficult to retain workers, with rural and remote areas often experiencing extended periods of time between workers leaving and new ones joining. There is also a dwindling pool of foster carers to draw from, which increases pressure on the system, too.

For many young people, there is not just one transition into the care system, but multiple transitions as they move from one placement to another (CC&YP&CG, 2006). One can only imagine the effects of experiencing multiple family situations on such young people.

Multiple placements mean forming new relationships with strangers, perhaps every few months. It requires getting used to new daily routines, sharing new bathrooms and bedrooms, potentially attending different schools and making new friends, eating different foods, getting to know new doctors and dentists.

Attachment theory is based on the understanding that young people develop strategies to enable them to cope with and manage the environment in which they live (Howe et al., 2000). Children learn these coping mechanisms from the early home environment and adapt the strategies as they grow. Young people who have experienced positive parenting and care and are securely attached will develop constructive traits, such as trust and the ability to form positive relationships (Tilbury et al., 2007). If, however, those early experiences have been disrupted through abuse or neglect, such as is the case with most young people coming into care, they may have developed avoidant, ambivalent or disorganized attachment styles and patterns of behaviour (Howe et al., 2000; Tilbury et al., 2007), which hinder their adjustment to the new care environment. If, added to this, they have to move from one placement to another, it may mean a string of challenging new relationships that end all too abruptly in trauma.

Some young people suffer further abuse while under the care of those charged with their protection. Documentation of such abuse ranges from historical accounts to issues uncovered in recent times and so cannot be dismissed as a problem that relates only to government and charitable institutions in past decades (Community Affairs References Committee, 2005).

To address the problem of abuse occurring while young people are in the care of those charged with their protection, new processes and standards must be developed. In this regard, human services workers have a part to play in changing the environment in which such abusive practices can (re)occur. From a critical theory perspective, an important step in achieving such change lies in critiquing the discourses in which the processes and systems designated to protect society's most vulnerable can, in turn, abuse and neglect them. To do this, it is important to understand power and oppressive practices.

From an anti-oppressive perspective, power is an inevitable consequence of social relations, potentially leading to both oppressive and productive practices (Fook, 2002). Where power is exercised over young people in the form of abusive or neglectful actions, they become acts of oppression, in as much as they affect and shape their life chances (Thompson et al., Mullender and Ward, 1993, cited in Thompson, 1997).

Leaving care

When young people in out-of-home care reach the age of 18, they then, generally, are no longer under the care and protection of the state. At a time when the trend is to delay partnering and having children and many young people are staying at home longer than in the past, those in out-of-home care often move into independent living between the ages of 16 and 18 (Cashmore and Paxman, 2006). Research has shown that many of them do not feel adequately prepared for this final transition to independent living. Outcomes on a range of measures, such as education, occupation, well-being, social support, relationships, finances, housing and homelessness and mental health, are regarded as generally poorer for young people who had experienced out-of-home care in many parts of the world than those who had not (Cashmore and Paxman, 2006).

Research also shows that young people have a range of concerns when leaving care. These include feeling nervous and unprepared for leaving, being unable to find accommodation and having to rely on shelters and temporary accommodation, a lack of independent living skills, not being heard by their caseworkers and vulnerability to drug dealers (Low, 2006). Sometimes the challenges seem very simple, as 'Carissa' tells us (CREATE Foundation, 2008):

> When you move from foster care there can be a lot of questions you want to ask but you might think some of the questions are too stupid to ask. It could be as simple as how to boil an egg – you have to find out somehow!

Not all young people struggle to make the transition, however, as some have completed independent living skills workshops and for some others, their foster carers continue to provide care and support privately after their   eighteenth birthday (CREATE Foundation, 2008; Low, 2006). The latter situation underlies the importance of the relationship for both young people and their carers as they forge new ways of being 'family' after the care officially ends.

Human Services Workers and Kids in Care

What can we learn from this overview of out-of-home care?

From an anti-oppressive perspective, an important first step involves understanding the concepts of power and oppression, as they may be constituted within everyday professional practices on various levels. There are various things that research informs us will improve the outcomes for one of the most vulnerable groups in our society – our young people.

First, there needs to be a 'whole-of-the-population' or public health approach, as is often championed at child protection conferences around the world. This means ensuring that there is a universal provision of support and services for families in order to reverse current trends and reduce the numbers of young people coming into care. Placing the onus on already stressed and under-resourced families and tertiary services, such as out-of-home care, provides a temporary fix at best. Viewing this issue as being owned by society rather than the individual family is a first step.

To turn such situations around, services need to be provided at the local level. A good example is the extensive maternal and child health system in the Australian state of Victoria, which sees 98 per cent of all families with a baby (Scott, 2007). Scott advocates a European-style local and holistic primary care responsibility for children at risk of abuse and neglect that incorporates education, health and social services (Scott, 2007), rather than the often disjointed, segregated and reactive service system that exists in many places. Other whole-population approaches include parenting programmes that utilize primary care services, such as those mentioned above, rather than remedial approaches.

At the service system level, there can be an integrated delivery of services rather than silos. Funding arrangements reflecting the complex and multiple issues that young people and families experience can replace those shaped by artificial organizational structures. Examples of excellent cooperative and integrated options for delivering services that do exist have an efficacious, embedded nature, reflecting the fact that they are home-grown solutions to local and regional issues and privilege expertise in the workers, young people and families.

Inclusive practices, such as those outlined above, can operate at a systemic level (embedded in guidelines and manuals for statutory care), as well as in the individual work undertaken by human services workers. As an individual human services worker, you can think about the concept of expertise. You will have expertise in a variety of areas, such as practice theory, communication, networking and more. Understanding the power dynamic in each and every interaction with young people and their families is key. Listening to the voices of young people is also part of the changed thinking required to better practice in this arena.

Research has demonstrated the importance of listening to young people (see, for example, Cashmore et al., 2006; McLeod, 2007) and yet it would appear that a gap exists between knowledge and action. To listen to the voices of young people, families and carers is to appreciate their uniqueness in each situation, their unique lived experiences. The human services worker is not the expert here: each young person, their families and/or carers, are the ones who *know* about their lives.

Sharing power in child protection is a vexed issue, however, as power is an inescapable aspect of this work. We therefore need to act with the awareness that power relations are always involved (Healy, 2000), understanding that, from time to time, decisions must be made for the safety of young people. Engaging in a constructive conversation with sometimes disaffected young people is not always easy (McLeod, 2007). In a context of ethically honouring their right to self-knowledge and autonomy as far as is possible, human services workers may negotiate relationships with them that reflect the partnership/power dynamic by means of open communication, honesty and a genuine interest in the experiences of those young people.

Every year in the UK, an estimated 100,000 children and young people run away from home or care, with one in six ending up on the streets. They run away for various reasons, but, when they do, it usually means that something in their life isn't going right. Furthermore, those young people face the particular range of risks that come from having to find alternative places to stay and the means to survive.

The UK government's Young Runaways Action Plan sets out what local agencies need to do to give these vulnerable young people the help that they need and demonstrates a commitment to supporting improvements in services for young runaways.

Drawing on evidence and recommendations from key delivery partners and practitioners, the action plan will make sure that, wherever possible, young people get the help they need to sort out issues in their lives *before* they run away. In recognition of the fact that some young people will still run away, it will also ensure there are services that can go into action quickly to support these young people and keep them safe.

Concluding Remarks

This chapter has provided an overview of some of the issues faced by young people in out of home care. It has drawn attention to the fact that there are growing numbers of young people being taken into care, the intense problems inherent in the present intervention systems and the potential for change.

Human services workers can operate at structural, family and individual levels to challenge dominant discourses about young people and work for change in policies and programmes that deal with what is arguably Western society's most pressing issue in current times.

Resources

Further reading

D'Cruz, H. and Stagnitti, K. (2008) 'Reconstructing child welfare through participatory and child-centred professional practice: a conceptual approach', *Child and Family Social Work*, 13:156–65.

London, Z. and Halfpenny, N. (2006) 'Transitioning from (and with) care: the next steps', *Children Australia*, 31 (3): 42–6.

Tilbury, C., Osmond, J., Wilson, S. and Clark, J. (2007) *Good Practice in Child Protection*. Frenchs Forest, NSW: Pearson Education.

Websites

Association of Children's Welfare Agencies www.acwa.asn.au
This site has information sheets available to assist workers when working with young people and their families, from early intervention and prevention through to support provided when young people are in out-of-home care.

DCSF http://publications.dcsf.gov.uk/default.aspx?PageFunction=productdetails& PageMode=publications&ProductId=RUNAWAYS08
The Young Runaways Action Plan is available from the DCSF's website.

Department of Human Services, Victoria, Australia, Children, Youth & Families Division www.cyf.vic.gov.au/every-child-every-chance
Every Child Every Chance is the Victorian government's initiative to work towards every child having a full and productive life, regardless of family circumstances and background. The Factsheets available on the website (click on 'keeping informed') provide an excellent overview of a range of protective and out-of-home care issues for workers. The Best Interests Series also provides useful resources, including the 'Child development and trauma guide'.

National Council for Voluntary Youth Services (NCVYS) www.ncvys.org.uk
The NCVYS is a registered charity and membership organization. Its aims are to raise the profile of youth work, share good practice and influence policy development.

KEY POINTS

- 'At risk' conditions precipitating authorities to put young people into care include their suffering abuse, involvement in antisocial behaviour, abuse of drugs and/or alcohol and criminal behaviour.
- Transition into care and multiple placements may result in young people being marginalized and traumatized.
- Young people are vulnerable and may experience anxiety when they make the transition to living independently out of care.
- It is important for workers to listen to young people and have an understanding of the power dynamics that may impact them.

QUESTIONS FOR DISCUSSION

1. How do your values and attitudes affect your work with young people?
2. What is the link between the way we think about young people in care, the language we use with and about those with whom we work and the success of our practice?

References

Australian Institute of Family Studies (AIPS) (2006) *Growing up in Australia: The longitudinal study of Australian children: 2005–06 annual report*. Melbourne: AIFS.

Australian Institute of Health and Welfare (AIHW) (2005) *A Picture of Australia's Children*. Canberra: AIHW.

AIHW (2007) *Australia's Welfare 2007*. Canberra: AIHW.

Ainsworth, F. (2003) 'Unfounded assumptions and the abandonment of "at risk" youth', *Children Australia*, 28 (1): 24–8.

Bruun, A.H.C. and Hynan, C. (2006) 'Where to from here?: Guiding for mental health for young people with complex needs', *Youth Studies Australia*, 25 (1):19–26.

Cashmore, J., Higgins, D., Bromfield, L. and Scott, D. (2006) 'Recent Australian child protection and out-of-home care research: what's been done – and what needs to be done?', *Children Australia*, 31 (2): 4–11.

Cashmore, J. and Paxman, M. (2006) 'Wards leaving care: follow-up five years on', *Children Australia*, 31 (3): 18–25.

Commission for Children and Young People and Child Guardian (CC&YP&CG) (2006) *Child Guardian Views of Children and Young People in Care Queensland 2006*. Queensland: CC&YP&CG.

Community Affairs References Committee (2005) *Protecting Vulnerable Children: A national challenge: Second report on the inquiry into children in institutional or out-of-home care*. Canberra: Commonwealth of Australia.

CREATE Foundation (2008) 'A guide for young people leaving care', available only online at: www.createyourfuture.org.au/home/home.do;jsessionid=407AEBBEESBB9F7291A 4302BAE5690CA

Elkington, J., van Beurder, E., Zask, A., Dight, R. and Johnson, W. (2006) 'RRISK: a sustainable intersectoral partnership', *Youth Studies Australia*, 25 (2):17–24.

Fook, J. (2002) *Social Work: Critical theory and practice*. London: Sage.

Gibson, J. (2008) 'Elders to get a say on fate of children', *Sydney Morning Herald*, 21–23 March.

Horwath, J. (2007) *Child Neglect: Identification and assessment*. Houndmills: Palgrave Macmillan.

Howe, D., Dooley, T. and Hinings, D. (2000) 'Assessment and decision-making in a case of child neglect and abuse using an attached perspective', *Child and Family Social work*, 5 (2): 143–55.

Low, S. (2006) 'Supporting positive leaving care and transition experience: a report on the FACE to FACE 4th National Forum – the superhero's journey', *Children Australia*, 31 (3): 55–8.

McLeod, A. (2007) 'Whose agenda?: Issues of power and relationship when listening to looked after young people', *Child and Family Social Work*, 12: 278–86.

Scott, D. (2007) 'Children need protection from the grassroots up', *Brisbane Times* 18 December. Also available online at: www.brisbanetimes.com.au/articles/2007/12/17/ 1197740178867.html?page=2

Thompson, N. (1997) *Anti-discriminatory Practice*. London: Macmillan.

Tilbury, C., Osmond, J., Wilson, S. and Clark, J. (2007) *Good Practice in Child Protection*. Frenchs Forest: Pearson Education.

Vassallo, S., Smart, D., Sanson, A. and Dussuyer, I. (2004) 'At risk but not antisocial: changes from childhood to adolescence', *Family Matters*, 68: 13–21.

Part IX

Summary

Summary and Concluding Remarks

Kathryn Geldard

You, the reader, will have gained some overall impressions from reading this book. Similarly, as editor, I am very familiar with the contents of each chapter and, when I think about the various contributions made by the authors, who have many different perspectives and varied experience, I recognize some very clear themes and messages that are common to all the chapters.

First, in providing practical interventions for young people at risk, it is essential that we join with them collaboratively, using interventions that suit them. In doing this, we must seek to establish relationships with the young people who engage with us that are respectful of both the young people themselves and the stories they tell us. As discussed in many places in this book, this relationship is a critical factor in enabling successful outcomes to be achieved.

Second, it has become very clear to me that there is no one best way to deal with a specific challenge facing a young person. What is important is to provide interventions that enable a creative, collaborative relationship between practitioners and young people to develop and be maintained.

The concept of positive youth development promoted in this text, posits that all young people have strengths. This suggests that increases in well-being are possible for all young people by aligning their strengths with the assets present in their social and physical environment (Silbereisen and Lerner, 2007). This notion provides a landscape for the solutions and interventions presented in this book.

Third, I have been reminded that we practitioners, like the young people we seek to help, are not an homogeneous group. We, too, are all individuals, with our own personalities, beliefs, attitudes, behaviours and specialized skills. The way that I practise is likely to be different from the way that you practise in some important respects, because I am me and you are you. What is important, is that, as practitioners, we offer ourselves in the working relationship in a way that enables young people to trust us, recognize our individuality and, thus, feel free to further explore themselves.

I would like you to know that I have found editing this book an extremely exciting and creative experience because the work entailed has enabled me to get in touch with ideas, philosophies and ways of practising of a variety of different expert practitioners. My hope is that you will also have found this book exciting to read and a source of inspiration for your work or, if you are a student, for your preparation for a future career.

Finally, if you the reader gain as much satisfaction as I have from working with young people and find this book a useful reference, then I will be delighted.

Kathryn Geldard

Reference

Silbereisen, R.K. and Lerner, R.M. (eds) (2007) *Approaches to Positive Youth Development*. London: Sage.

Index

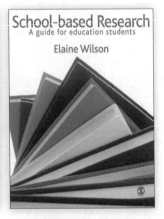

Research Methods Books
from SAGE

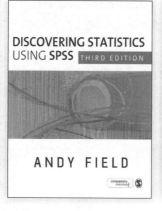
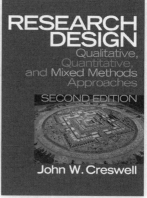

Supporting researchers for more than forty years

Research methods have always been at the core of SAGE's publishing. Sara Miller McCune founded SAGE in 1965 and soon after, she published SAGE's first methods book, *Public Policy Evaluation*. A few years later, she launched the Quantitative Applications in the Social Sciences series – affectionately known as the 'little green books'.

Always at the forefront of developing and supporting new approaches in methods, SAGE published early groundbreaking texts and journals in the fields of qualitative methods and evaluation.

Today, more than forty years and two million little green books later, SAGE continues to push the boundaries with a growing list of more than 1,200 research methods books, journals, and reference works across the social, behavioural, and health sciences.

From qualitative, quantitative and mixed methods to evaluation, SAGE is the essential resource for academics and practitioners looking for the latest in methods by leading scholars.

www.sagepublications.com